Also by Andrew Soltis

The Inner Game of Chess
Karl Marx Plays Chess

PAWN
STRUCTURE
CHESS

PAWN STRUCTURE CHESS

ANDREW SOLTIS

DAVID McKAY
COMPANY, INC.

All rights reserved under International and Pan-American
Copyright Conventions. Published in the United States by
David McKay Company, Inc., a subsidiary of
Random House, Inc., New York, and simultaneously in
Canada by Random House of Canada Limited, Toronto.

ISBN: 0-8129-2529-7

Designed by Michael Mendelsohn

Manufactured in the United States of America on
acid-free paper

24689753

First Edition

CONTENTS

INTRODUCTION:
THE SOUL OF WHAT GAME?

CHESS IS NOT EASY. IT SEEMED EASY, AFTER I FIRST LEARNED THE moves. But like all beginners, I quickly found out there was an awful lot to learn, a lot I didn't know. In fact, there were libraries full of books—chess books—and each book was filled with pearls of wisdom that, it seemed, would take me a lifetime to master.

And the most mysterious bit of wisdom was one quotation that seemed to be fobbed off by chess authors in virtually every book. "As Andre Philidor, once said," the authors would write, "the pawns are the soul of the game."

Great, I'd say to myself each time I came across this gem of insight. A Frenchman who's been dead for two hundred years is telling me I shouldn't be worried about losing my queen or allowing my king to be mated. I should be worried about pawns.

In fact, it wasn't until I was nearly a master that I found out what Philidor was getting at. The pawns are the most permanent features of a position: Between the end of the opening and the beginning of the endgame, they change relatively little. As a result, the pawns' *structure* becomes the terrain of a battlefield. The stronger center offers the high ground that every general desires. The absence of pawns creates open files and diagonals—the valleys and ridges that deliver access routes into the hands of the attacking army.

I also came to understand that studying pawns is no dismal science. Philidor himself explained why they enable you to be brilliant in carrying out middlegame plans: Pawns "alone create attack and defense," he wrote. In fact, many if not most great sacrificial battles seem to spring naturally out of favorable pawn structures.

For example, Kuzmin–Groszpeter, Kusadasi 1990:

1 e4 c5   2 Nf3 d6   3 d4 cxd4   4 Nxd4 Nf6   5 Nc3 a6   6 Be2 e5   7 Nb3 Be7   8 0-0 0-0   9 Kh1 b5 10 Nd5! Nxd5   11 Qxd5 Ra7   12 Be3 Be6   13 Qd1 Rd7   14 a4 b4   15 f4! Qc7?   16 f5! Bc4   17 Bxc4 Qxc4

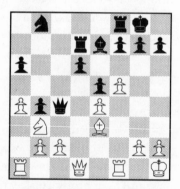

Position after 17 . . . Qxc4

At first glance we notice that Black is attacking an e-pawn which is difficult to defend comfortably (18 Qf3 Qxc2). Then we might appreciate that White has a clear positional advantage thanks to the pawn structure: The d5-hole gives

White an excellent outpost and the f5-pawn gives him the basis for kingside attack.

But protecting e4 through normal means will vaporize those advantages (18 Qd3? Qxd3   19 cxd3 Rc8 or   18 Nd2 Qc6 and   19 . . . d5). Moreover, White understands that whatever advantage the structure offers him will be wiped out once Black activates his poorly placed pieces (. . . Rc7 and . . . Nd7-f6).

Putting it all together, White concludes his advantage is fleeting and he must use it immediately regardless of material consequences. And so he finds:

18	f6!	Bxf6
19	Rxf6!	gxf6
20	Qg4+	

The attractive 20 Bh6, threatening 21 Qg4+ and mates, would allow 20 . . . Qxe4!.

20	. . .	Kh8
21	Qh4	Qe6

Black cannot allow 22 Qxf6+ and 23 Bh6, with mate to follow on g7. But now . . .

22	Nd4!!	Qe7

After 22 . . . exd4 23 Bxd4 Black cannot defend against Bxf6+ (e.g., 23 . . . Kg7 24 Qg5+).

23	Nf5	Qe6
24	Rf1	d5

A last, desperate attempt to get his pieces into defensive (. . . Rd6, . . . Nd7) action.

25	Ng7!	Qe7

Or 25 ... Kxg7 26 Bh6+ Kh8 27 Bxf8, threatening 28 Qh6.

Position after 25 ... Qe7

| 26 | Bc5! | Qxc5 |
| 27 | Nh5 | Resigns |

There is no adequate defense to Qxf6+-g7mate or Nxf6/Qxh7 mate. For example, 27 ... Rd6 28 Nxf6 Rxf6 29 Qxf6+ Kg8 30 Rf3 and Rg3+.

This is a book about how to recognize different pawn structures and how to play the middlegame in a manner appropriate to each structure. As we'll see, the positional plan or sacrificial attack that works well in one structure may prove disastrous against another.

There is a natural tendency to change pawn structures through advances and captures, and it's a tendency that has to be resisted. One of the differences between a master and an amateur is the experience that tells the master when he holds a superior pawn structure which should not be altered.

This was underlined by the second game of the 1990 world championship match between Garry Kasparov and Anatoly Karpov. It began with an opening that had been considered to be fairly well balanced:

1 e4 e5   2 Nf3 Nc6   3 Bb5 a6   4 Ba4 Nf6   5 0-0
Be7   6 Re1 b5   7 Bb3 d6   8 c3 0-0   9 h3 Bb7
10 d4 Re8   11 Nbd2 Bf8   12 a4 h6   13 Bc2 exd4
14 cxd4 Nb4   15 Bb1 bxa4   16 Rxa4 a5   17 Ra3
Ra6   18 Nh2 g6

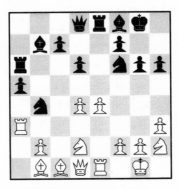

Position after 18 . . . g6

This, and similar positions, had been occurring in Karpov's games for years, and he had consistently shown a masterful skill at obtaining counterplay for Black against targets such as White's e-pawn. Previously, 19 Ng4, 19 e5 and 19 f4 had been tried and found wanting.

What, the dozens of grandmasters at the New York match press room wondered, had Kasparov found in his preparations?

The answer was a remarkably modest one-square advance—*19 f3!!*. Knowing smiles suddenly broke out in the press room as the GMs realized what now appeared obvious:

White has ensured that his superior center will remain un-changed until *he* wants to change it.

Black's counterplay vanished, and there was little to be done about the slow but inevitable marshaling of White's pieces into a decisive kingside attack—*19 . . . Qd7   20 Nc4 Qb5   21 Rc3   Bc8   22 Be3   c6   23 Qc1   Kh7   24 Ng4! Ng8   25 Bxh6!*.

Black resigned soon after *25 . . . Bxh6   26 Nxh6 Nxh6 27 Nxd6 Qb6   28 Nxe8 Qxd4+   29 Kh1   Qd8   30 Rd1! Qxe8   31 Qg5 Ra7   32 Rd8*.

The important thing to remember here is that a pawn struc-ture is not an isolated feature of a position but an intrinsic part of it. You can't claim to have a good pawn structure but a bad game. It is the arrangement of pawns that determines whether you will have good piece play—whether your rooks will have files and your bishops have diagonals.

An illustration of this was Romanishin–Mueller, Altensteig 1992, which began *1 e4 e6   2 d4 d5   3 e5 c5   4 c3 Nc6 5 Nf3 Qb6   6 a3 c4!   7 Be2 Na5   8 Nbd2 Bd7   9 0-0 h6 10 a4 0-0-0   11 Ne1*.

Position after 11 Ne1

Black's fine sixth move goes a long way towards crippling the enemy queenside pawn because any advance of the b-pawn can be answered by . . . cxb3. That leaves White with a backward c3 pawn exposed to attack along a half-open c-file.

But what if White doesn't try to open the queenside? What if he decides, as his last move indicates, to work on the kingside, with f2-f4-f5? Black needs a plan of his own. The best chance would be 11 . . . f6!—even though it would expose his own weak e-pawn to attack along a half-open file after exf6.

Instead, Black played *11 . . . f5?* This is a structurally sound move: Black's kingside is now solid and he need no longer fear f2-f4-f5. But it is dynamically bad because it leaves him without kingside play of his own.

Black compounded this error with a second one: After *12 b4!* he captured en passant. Again, this is positionally desirable, but strategically awful. After *12 . . . cxb3?   13 Nd3 Kb8   14 Ba3! Bxa3   15 Rxa3 Rc8   16 Qa1! Ne7   17 Rb1,* it was clear that White would dominate the only area of the board that was open.

Black never had a second to take aim at c3 and he succumbed swiftly: *17 . . . Qc7   18 Nc5 Ka8   19 Ndxb3 Nec6   20 Bb5 Nxb3   21 Raxb3 Rb8   22 Bxc6! Bxc6   23 Nxe6 Qe7   24 Nc5 f4   25 f3 g5   26 a5 Rh7   27 Rb6! Rc8   28 a6!* (based on *28 . . .* axb6 29 axb7+) *bxa6   29 Qxa6 Qe8   30 Rb7! Bxb7   31 Rxb7* Resigns

Changing the Scenery

When a pawn structure does change, it forces the players to reconsider their previous line of thought. Or at least it should.

Too often, a player will regard a change, particularly when it involves wing pawns, as trivial and ignorable. And he ends

up paying a heavy price. There are a number of games in which
the outcome was decided by move 15, even though play continued for another 20 moves.

Case in point, Spraggett–Dominguez, Badalona 1991:

1 c4 g6   2 Nc3 Bg7   3 d4 Nf6   4 e4 d6   5 Nf3 0-0
6 Be2 e5   7 0-0 Nc6   8 d5 Ne7   9 Ne1 Nd7
10 Nd3 f5   11 Bd2 Nf6   12 f3 f4   13 g4 h5? 14 g5!
Nh7   15 h4

Position after 15 h4

Black has made one serious error and is about to make another. The first slip was his failure to keep the kingside open
with 13 . . . fxg3!, after which he has enough maneuvering
space to mount serious counterplay against the enemy king
(14 hxg3 h6   15 c5 g5 and 16 . . . Ng6).

An indication of how serious that error of omission was is
this: Black's position is so critical in the diagram that he should
offer two pieces (15 . . . Nxg5!   16 hxg5 Nf5!) to avoid get-

ting positionally squished. White should then avoid the possible mating attack (17 exf5 Qxg5+ 18 Kh1 Qh4+) in favor of 17 Rf2! and Rg2 with balanced play.

Black never appreciated how urgent the matter was until it
was too late. After 15 . . . Kh8? 16 Rf2! Ng8 17 Rg2 Rf7
18 c5! his lack of operating space on the kingside—and
White's virtually complete freedom on the queenside—was
beginning to crystallize.

In short, White was left with five of the board's eight ranks,
leaving only three to Black. Guess what? Five beats three.

The game ended at move 36 but the outcome was already
pretty much determined: 18 . . . Bf8 19 cxd6 cxd6
20 Be1 Be7 21 Rc1 Rg7 22 Kh1 a6 23 Bf2 Bd7
24 Na4 b5 25 Nb6 Ra7 26 Nxd7 Qxd7 27 Nb4 Qb7
28 Bf1 Nf8 29 Bg1 Nd7 30 Rgc2 Nc5 31 Nc6 Ra8
32 Bh3 Bf8 33 Bxc5 dxc5 34 Nxe5 Bd6 35 Nc6 Ne7
36 e5! Resigns

That pawn center, as we'll see in Chapter 4, is one of the
more popular forms of pawn chains. Simply put, you can't play
1 d4 well if you don't understand it. There are other structures
that naturally evolve out of particular openings, such as the
Caro-Kann, French, Sicilian, and Slav Defenses. You may
have to live for forty moves with the pawn decisions you made
as early as the third.

There are also quieter openings that delay major decisions
about the center. Then the task facing the players is much
more difficult. Instead of finding the appropriate middlegame
plan that suits the center, they have to decide what type of
center they really want. For example, 1 c4 c5 2 Nc3 Nc6
3 g3 g6 4 Bg2 Bg7 5 e3 d6 6 Nge2 Nf6 7 0-0 0-0
8 d3 Bd7 9 h3 a6 10 b3 Rb8 11 Bb2 b5 12 Qd2 Nb4.

Position after 12 . . . Nb4

In this position, from Agdestein–Kasparov, Tilburg 1991, White has a relatively free hand in choosing a middlegame plan. A good one would be to leave the center unchanged while attacking on the kingside (13 Rad1, 14 f4, 15 g4 and 16 Ng3). Instead, play continued:

13 Rfd1   Re8
14 e4?

White wants to play Nd5 but prefers to recapture with an e-pawn, thereby opening the e-file. The alternative, 14 Nd5 Nfxd5 15 cxd5 Bxb2 16 Qxb2, allows Black to seize the initiative with 16 . . . c4!.

14 . . .   Nc6
15 Nd5?

Missing his best chance for opening lines with 15 cxb5 axb5 16 d4!

15 . . .   e5!

This locks the center so that Black can begin a queenside attack with . . . Nd4 and . . . bxc4. White now begins to panic in search of a favorable structure.

16	Kh2	h5
17	f4?!	

Black's last move was directed to make this advance risky because . . . h4 will now cripple White on the dark squares of the kingside.

17	. . .	bxc4
18	dxc4	Nxd5!

Position after 18 . . . Nxd5

A well-timed exchange in the center. White now appreciates how ugly 19 cxd5 Nd4 can become—20 fxe5 Nxe2 21 Qxe2 Bb5 22 Qf2 Bxe5 with advantage to Black (23 . . . h4!).

19	Qxd5?	Nd4
20	Nxd4	cxd4
21	Qxd6	

The only move consistent with his 19th.

21	...	h4!
22	g4	Bf8

Here 23 Qd5 is essential—although Black may then exploit the key b8-h2 diagonal with 23 ... Qc7! 24 fxe5? Rxe5 25 Qxd4 Rxe4+.

23	Qxa6?	Re6
24	Qa7	Ra8

Resigns

Because the queen is trapped after 25 Qb7 Bc6.

This book explores several of the more important pawn structures, each with its own set of priorities, targets, and weaknesses, and appropriate middlegame plans. The differences are often subtle and the one-square advance of a single pawn will often demand a change in your way of thinking about the future course of the game. But mastering those subtleties will pay off in your results.

As I said, chess is not easy.

PAWN
STRUCTURE
CHESS

1

THE CARO-SLAV FAMILY

By a family we mean a group of closely related pawn structures that share the same features or derive from a common opening. In the Caro-Slav family only one player has a center pawn on the fourth rank and it is on d4. This player's opponent has exchanged off his own d-pawn for either an e-pawn (the Caro formation) or a c-pawn (the Slav formation). These are the only center pawn exchanges made.

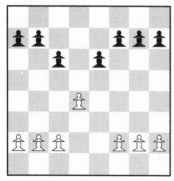

The Caro formation

The Slav formation

Besides the facial resemblance the two structures also share a basic solidity and conservativeness. It is hard for White to break open the center without taking risks. The middlegame is often slow-paced. But White still has a basic advantage in his d-pawn. It confers upon him greater center control, better outposts for his pieces, and the opportunity for a major break (d4-d5). His opponent must try to overcome the cramped quarters the pawn structure forces on him with his own breaks (. . . c5 or . . . e5).

The Caro Formation

This popular structure is by no means limited to the Caro-Kann Defense (1 e4 c6   2 d4 d5   3 Nc3 dxe4   4 Nxe4). It includes positions that arise out of the French Defense when Black gives up the center (e.g., 1 e4 e6   2 d4 d5   3 Nc3 Nf6   4 Bg5 dxe4), out of the Center Counter Defense (1 e4 d5 2 exd5 Qxd5 or 2 . . . Nf6 and 3 . . . Nxd5), and in various forms the Queen's Gambit Declined and Catalan Opening when White plays e4 and Black responds . . . dxe4.

In these examples it is Black who "gives up" the center. But it may be White who precipitates this formation as in Karpov–Campos-Lopez, San Antonio 1972, which went 1 e4 Nf6   2 e5 Nd5   3 d4 d6   4 Nf3 g6   5 Bc4 c6   6 0-0 Bg7   7 exd6 Qxd6. Or the exchange of pawns can take places on other squares: e.g., Alekhine–Euwe, world championship match 1937. 1 Nf3 d5   2 c4 d4   3 e3 Nc6   4 exd4 Nxd4   5 Nxd4 Qxd4   6 Nc3 Nf6   7 d3 c6   8 Be3 Qd7 9 d4 = Caro formation.

The qualities of the formation, rather than how it is reached, are our main concerns. Looking back at the Caro formation diagram we can readily see that White has excellent outpost squares at e5 and c5. The e5 outpost is especially significant since Black would have to weaken his kingside and center severely with . . . f7-f6 to keep the outpost square clear of pieces. (The consequences of this can be seen in *Supplemental Game #1* at the end of the chapter.)

Black also has outposts at d5 and f5, but they are farther from the enemy and it is easier to dislodge pieces from the d4 outpost of Black than the e5 outpost of White. This is because White frequently finds c2-c4, the dislodging move, to be part of his middlegame plan.

The Penalty of Passivity

The primary lesson of this formation is that Black's natural inferiority is fatal unless he can compete actively in the center. A wait-and-see policy may work in a few games because of exceptional reasons of tactics, but in general it is a bankrupt strategy.

A model game to illustrate this is Lasker–Capablanca, Moscow 1935, a classic battle of titans. It began:

1 e4 e6   2 d4 d5   3 Nc3 Bb4   4 Ne2 dxe4   5 a3 Be7   6 Nxe4 Nf6   7 N2c3 Nbd7?   8 Bf4! Nxe4   9 Nxe4 Nf6   10 Bd3 0-0   11 Nxf6+ Bxf6   12 c3 Qd5

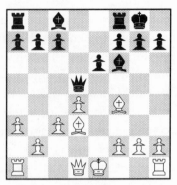

Position after 12 ... Qd5

In a few pages we'll see why Black must begin to think of either . . . c5 or . . . e5 as early as his seventh move. Here, for example, Black can liberate himself with 7 . . . Nc6! (e.g., 8 Be3 Nxe4 9 Nxe4 e5 10 dxe5 Qxd1+ with equality or 10 d5 Nd4! 11 Bxd4 Qxd5 with advantage).

With White's eighth move he made . . . e5 difficult to enforce. But now Black threatens 13 . . . c5 as well as 13 . . . Qxg2.

13   Qe2!

This powerful move shows how the prevention of Black's liquidating break (. . . c5) is more important than castling to safety or protecting one's pawns. On 13 . . . c5 White wins a clean pawn with 14 Be4! (e.g., 14 . . . Qb3 15 Bd6).

Black can play 13 . . . Qxg2, but White then retains a strong initiative after 14 Be4 Qh3 whether he plays a gambit (15 0-0-0) or regains his material (15 Bxc7). In either case Black's pawns in the center are inferior to White's and his pieces should therefore also be inferior.

13	...	c6
14	0-0	Re8
15	Rad1	Bd7
16	Rfe1	

Position after 16 Rfe1

With . . . e5 and . . . c5 prevented, White's powerful centralization gives him a free hand in the middlegame. The simplest and least risky plan is a kingside attack. White could even have begun it with 16 Be5! (instead of 16 Rfe1) with the ideas of using his bishops against the kingside and of trapping the Black queen in the center with b2-b4 followed by c3-c4. (Note that 16 Be5 Bxe5 loses a pawn to 17 Bxh7+! Kxh7 18 dxe5 and 19 Rxd7.)

White reaches the next diagrammed position by first weakening and then attacking the enemy kingside. Black had no discernible counterplay once his central activity was neutralized. The game continued: *16 . . . Qa5   17 Qc2 g6*   (or 17 *. . . h6 18 Qe2! followed by 19 Qe4) 18 Be5 Bg7   19 h4! Qd8   20 h5 Qg5   21 Bxg7 Kxg7   22 Re5 Qe7   23 Rde1 Rg8   24 Qc1! Rad8 25 R1e3 Bc8   26 Rh3.*

Position after 26 Rh3

White's pieces dominate the center and kingside. With the e5 outpost as a jumping-off point, White's heavy pieces are ready for the final mating attack. He threatens 27 hxg6 and 28 Qh6+. Neither 26...Kh8   27 Qh6 Rg7   28 hxg6 fxg6   29   Bxg6! nor 26 ... f6   27 hxg6 hxg6   28 Qh6+ Kf7   29 Rg3! (29 ... fxe5?   30 Bxg6+ Rxg6   31 Qxg6+ mates) is a defense.

Black played 26 . . . Kf8 but succumbed to 27 Qh6+ Rg7 28 hxg6 hxg6   29 Bxg6!. Since he could not capture the bishop because of 30 Qh8+ and 31 Rf3+, Black had to surrender his queen after 29 . . . Qf6 30 Rg5! Ke7 31 Rf3! White won easily.

White's d4-d5 Plan

An even more aggressive strategy for White is to prepare d4-d5 by way of c2-c4. This contains great rewards for White if he is better developed. It can, however, contain great risks if his d-pawn, stripped of the protection of its neighbor, comes under fire along the open d-file.

An ideal example of the d4-d5 strategy's paying off is Spassky–O'Kelly, San Juan 1969:

```
1 e4    e6    2 d4    d5    3 Nc3    dxe4?!    4 Nxe4    Bd7
5 Nf3   Bc6   6 Bd3   Bxe4  7 Bxe4   c6        8 0-0     Nf6
9 Bd3   Nbd7  10 c4   Bd6   11 b3    0-0       12 Bb2    Qc7
13 Qc2  Rfe8  14 Rfe1 Bf8   15 Radl  g6
```

Position after 15 . . . g6

In contrast to the Lasker–Capablanca game, here Black has a very solid kingside. White turns his attention to d4-d5, an idea that can be realized only after several moves of preparation and can be successful only after even more preparation. Note White's steps of redevelopment. Redevelopment is the maneuvering of already developed pieces to squares that better promote the chosen plan.

Step I. He repositions his king bishop so that it doesn't block the d-file and promotes d4-d5: *16 Bf1 Bg7   17 g3! Rad8 18 Bg2.*

Step II. He places his rooks so that they gain the utmost mobility from d4-d5: *18 . . . Nh5   19 Re2! Rc8   20 h4 Rcd8 21 Rde1.*

Step III. He adds the queen to the exploitation of the open lines that will result from d4-d5: *21 . . . Nhf6   22 Qc1! h5 23 Bh3 Nf8   24 Qa1 Ng4   25 Bc3 Nh6   26 Qb2.*

After continued passive play (26 . . . Nh7, for example) Black might have prevented d4-d5 or required extensive preparation by White (such as Re4 followed by Ne5-d3-f4). White could have turned to another strategy such as c4-c5 followed by Ne5-c4-d6. White has the options. Black played *26 . . . Nf5?*

Position after 26 . . . Nf5?

White was now permitted to play d4-d5 as part of a positional pawn sacrifice. White obtained a strong passed c-pawn, and this eventually tied up Black's pieces so badly that a frontal attack on the Black king won easily. (The game continued *27 Bxf5! gxf5   28 d5! Bxc3   29 Qxc3 cxd5   30 Nd4 Qd7   31 c5! Nh7   32 b4 a6   33 a4 Rc8   34 b5 axb5   35 axb5 Rf8 36 c6 bxc6   37 bxc6 Qd8   38 Rc1 Nf6   39 c7! Qd7 40 Qe3! Ne4   41 f3 e5?   42 fxe4 f4   43 gxf4 exd4   44 Rg2+ Resigns.*) See also *Supplemental Game #2.*

The important lesson here is that d4-d5 did not simply happen. It was the result of planning and preparation. And it should be compared with White's mindless play in the following game: Rellstab–Böök, Kemeri 1937:

1 e4 e6   2 d4 d5   3 Nc3 Bb4   4 Ne2 dxe4   5 a3
Be7   6 Nxe4 Nc6   7 Be3 Nf6   8 Qd3 b6   9 0-0-0
Bb7   10 Nxf6+? Bxf6   11 Rg1? Qd7   12 g4? g6
13 Bg2 0-0-0   14 f4 h5!   15   g5 Bg7   16   Bf2 Ne7!
17 Bxb7+ Kxb7   18 Kb1 Qc6   19 c4? Rd7   20 b4 a6
21 Nc3 Rhd8   22 b5 axb5   23 Nxb5 Nf5   24 Kb2
Qc5!   25 Kb3 Nxd4+   26 Bxd4 Bxd4   27 Rg2 c6
28 Qf3 Bg7   29 Rxd7+ Rxd7   30 Rc2 Qf5   31 Nc3
Rd3   32 Qf1 b5   33 c5 Qd5+   34   Kb2 Rxc3 White
resigns.

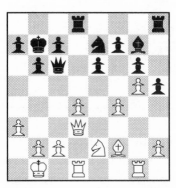

Position after 18 . . . Qc6

White had an optimistic position after nine moves but suddenly decided upon a grossly weakening kingside attack against an enemy king that castled to safety on the opposite wing. Then, when White should have battened down the hatches with 19 c3 he destroyed the support of his center with 19 c4?. Black needed only to pile up on the enemy d-pawn, which White had voluntarily stripped of pawn defense.

* * *

The problems of White's d-pawn become amplified with the exchange of minor pieces. It is surprising how often this position is misplayed by masters. Below are two positions from games played in international tournaments a few weeks apart in 1968.

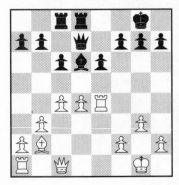 

Black stands slightly better in both positions because he can prevent d4-d5 and also attack the weak d-pawn. In the first diagram Black continued *1 . . . Be7!*, signaling the assault on the d-pawn. White should immediately have foreseen the dangers and played 2 Bc3 and 3 Qb2, but he fumbled about with *2 Qc2? Bf6 3 Bc3 Qe7 4 a4? Rd7! 5 Rae1 Rcd8 6 Qb2 g6.*

White then had no chance to reposition his rooks at d2 and d1, where they would be optimally effective in defense (e.g., 7 Rd1 Qf8! 8 Re2 Qg7 9 Red2 c5! winning a pawn through pins). So White tried a desperation attack and was quickly lost: *7 h4 Qe8 8 h5 Rd6 9 hxg6 hxg6 10 Kg2 Qd7 11 Rh1 Bxd4 12 Rxd4 Rxd4 13 Qd2! f6! 14 Qh6 Qg7!*.

The position in the second diagram is only slightly better for White than the previous example, but Black tried to hurry the natural pileup against the d-pawn. Instead of 1 . . . Rcd8 (2 Qf4 Kh8 and . . . c5 or 2 Ree4 g6 and 3 . . . Bg7) Black played *1 . . . h5?*.

While this helped demolish the d-pawn it also permitted White to develop a vicious kingside attack. The kingside pawns are also part of the structure. The game continued *2 Rf4 Qd8 3 Qxh5 c5 4 Qf3 cxd4 5 Bd2* and, with some further bad play by Black, White won: *5 . . . b5 6 Rg4! bxc4 7 bxc4 Rxc4 8 h5 Rc2 9 Bh6 Rc3 10 Qf4 Kf8?* (10 . . . Kh8!) *11 Bxg7+! Bxg7 12 h6 Bf6 13 h7 Bg7 14 Qh6! Bxh6 15 h8Q+ Ke7 16 Qxh6 Qa5 17 Qh4+ f6 18 Rg7+ Kd6 19 Qxd4+ Qd5 20 Rxd7+* Resigns.

Black's . . . c5

This is Black's most natural source of counterplay and is easier to engineer than . . . e5. The reason is simple: Black has much greater control of c5—and White less of it—than of the e5 square. But . . . c5 has pluses *and* minuses.

Chief among the pluses is the freedom given to Black's minor pieces. The move . . . c5 opens up a good long diagonal for

Black's queen bishop. If after . . . c5xd4 White recaptures on d4 with a piece, then Black has obtained the use of c5 and e5 for minor pieces, especially knights. If White can recapture with a pawn (e.g., c2-c3/ . . . c5xd4/c3xd4) then Black can blockade the newly created isolated d-pawn with a knight on d4.

A simple illustration on the penetrating power of Black's pieces after . . . c5 is Gligoric–Smyslov, Moscow 1963:

1 e4 c6	2 d4 d5	3 Nc3 dxe4	4 Nxe4 Nd7	5 Nf3

1 e4 c6   2 d4 d5   3 Nc3 dxe4   4 Nxe4 Nd7   5 Nf3
Ngf6   6 Nxf6+ Nxf6   7 Bc4 Bf5   8 Ne5 e6   9 0-0
Be7   10 Bb3 a5   11 c4? 0-0   12 Bf4

Position after 12 Bf4

"Distrust a pawn move," Emanuel Lasker warned. "Examine carefully its balance sheet." Here White has overrated the values of c2-c4 and minimized the dangers. White's d-pawn is not truly weak, but the *square* it stands on is. After *12 . . . c5!* White can no longer maintain d4 square as a personal possession; he must compete with Black for its control. Had he not moved his c-pawn before he could now play c3.

White could not play 13 d5 (because of 13 ... exd5 14 cxd5 Be4), nor could he try the retreating 13 Be3 (13 ... cxd4 14 Bxd4 a4). He chose *13 dxc5 Bxc5 14 Qe2* since this permits him to contest the d4 square with Rad1 and it avoids an ending in which Black's minor pieces, already superior to White's, would run over the board.

Black's thematic reply was *14 ... Qd4!* *15 Bg3 a4*, a series that wins a pawn after 16 Bd1 a3! or 16 Rad1 Qe4! or (White's choice) *16 Bc2 Qxb2*. Black won a long ending. His pieces simply leaped into action after ... c5. (For similar instances see *Supplemental Games #3–4*).

When White has not played c2-c4 he can, as we mentioned, support his d4 at the cost of an isolated d-pawn. A fuller discussion of the Isolani appears in Chapter 7, but for the time being a useful illustration is Yefseyev–Flohr, Odessa 1949:

1 e4 c6 2 d4 d5 3 Nc3 dxe4 4 Nxe4 Nd7 5 Nf3 Ngf6 6 Ng3 e6 7 Bd3 Be7 8 0-0 0-0 9 Qe2 c5! 10 c3?! b6 11 Ne5 Bb7 12 f4

Position after 12 f4

The forthright plan for White was 10 Rd1 cxd4 11 Nxd4 Nc5 12 Bc4, which would have given him the benefit of increased activity for his minor pieces and rook. Instead, he tried to maintain a semiclosed center so that his plan of f4-f5 would give him an uncontested kingside attack. Black must act quickly because f4-f5 *is* dangerous. He did so with *12 . . . cxd4! 13 cxd4 Nxe5! 14 dxe5 Ng4!*.

Position after 14 . . . Ng4!

Suddenly the center is cleared away, and Black's minor pieces, abetted by the queen, are about to take over. Black threatens 15 . . . Bc5+ 16 Kh1 Qh4 or 16 . . . Nxh2. White gets a poor game after either 15 Qxg4 Qxd3 or 15 Ne4 Qd4+ 16 Kh1 Rad8 (17 Bc2 Bxe4 18 Bxe4 Qxe4! 19 Qxe4 Nf2+ 20 Rxf2 Rd1+ mates).

Therefore White accepted the pawn offer with *15 Bxh7+ Kxh7 16 Qxg4* but could not resist the swarm of Black pieces after *16 . . . Qd4+ 17 Kh1 Rac8 18 Nh5* (or 18 Qe2 Qc4 followed by an eventual . . . Rc2) *g6 19 Qh3* (hoping for a perpetual check after 19 . . . gxh5 20 Qxh5+) *Rh8! 20 Nf6+ Kg7 21 Qe3 Rc2!!*

This beautiful game concluded with continued offers of the Black queen (22 Qxd4 Rxg2 or 22 Rg1 Qd1! 23 Ne4 Bxe4 24 Qxe4 Qh5 would mate): *22 Qg3 Qd3! 23 Qxd3 Rxg2 24 Ng4 Rgxh2+* White resigns.

White's Anti- . . . c5 Strategies: dxc5

Of White's options after . . . c5, the most commonly chosen is readily to trade pawns with dxc5. White may obtain the use of the newly opened d-file and a long diagonal from a1 to h8. White gets d4 for a minor piece, ideally a knight, and obtains a semipassed c-pawn. The first player can build a position of domination in the center very quickly; e.g., Steinitz–Marco, Nuremberg 1896:

1 d4 d5 2 c4 e6 3 Nc3 c6 4 e4 dxe4 5 Nxe4 Nf6? 6 Nxf6+ Qxf6 7 Nf3 Bb4+ 8 Bd2 Bxd2+ 9 Qxd2 Nd7 10 0-0-0! 0-0 11 Qe3! c5 12 dxc5 Qf5 13 Bd3 Qxc5 14 Rhe1

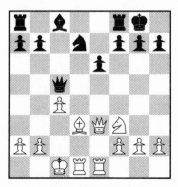

Position after 14 Rhe1

Black could have eased his development early on with 5 . . . Bb4+ (6 Bd2 Qxd4 or 6 Nc3 c5!), but he assumed that the exchanges of minor pieces would reduce White's spatial advantage. They don't. In fact, exchanges have hurt Black because he is now weak on black squares. Black eventually played the liberating . . . c5 at his 11th move. But is he free?

Certainly not. In the ending that would follow 14 . . . Qxe3+ 15 Rxe3 Black is in trouble after 15 . . . Nf6 16 Ne5 (since 16 . . . Bd7 17 Nxd7 Nxd7 18 Bxh7+ costs a pawn) or after 15 . . . Nc5 16 Bc2 a5 (to stop b4) 17 Ng5 h6 18 Ne4.

Black stayed in the middlegame with *14 . . . Qc7*, but after *15 Ne5! Re8 16 Kb1* his difficulties persisted. Had Black then developed his knight to f6 he would have invited a ready-made kingside attack with g4-g5. Black put the knight at f8, and after *16 . . . Nf8 17 c5!* White secured d6 for his own knight. White's maneuver strongly countered Black's intention of . . . f6 and e5 and there followed *17 . . . f6 18 Nc4 e5 19 Nd6 Re7 20 f4 Bd7*. The free hand White enjoyed in the center was easily converted into a kingside attack. White managed a mating finish in a dozen moves: *21 f5! Bc6 22 Bc4+ Kh8 23 g4! b6 24 g5 fxg5* (else 25 gxf6 gxf6 26 Rg1 Rg7 27 Rxg7 and 28 Rg1) *25 Qxg5 h6 26 Qh5 bxc5 27 Nf7+ Kh7 28 Ng5+ Kh8 29 f6 gxf6 30 Qxh6+ Nh7 31 Nxh7 Rxh7 32 Qxf6+ Rg7 33 Rxe5* Resigns. (See also *Supplemental Game #5* to illustrate the use of the long diagonal, the d4 square, and the c4-c5 idea.)

A long-term advantage of d4xc5 is the queenside majority of pawns that White obtains. This is a frequent factor of the Caro formation. The possibility of two opposing pawn majorities—one on White's queenside and one on Black's kingside—exists as soon as Black trades his d-pawn for White's e-pawn. Later, if the White d-pawn is exchanged for the Black c-pawn it becomes clear that White has three queenside pawns to Black's two. This majority can create a passed pawn, a key factor, perhaps even a decisive one, in an endgame. It is not always a factor in the middlegame. But when Black seeks exchanges to reduce a White initiative the existence of majorities increases in importance.

A basic illustration of this is a 1955 game, Teschner–Golombek:

1 e4 c6 2 d4 d5 3 Nc3 dxe4 4 Nxe4 Bf5 5 Ng3
Bg6 6 h4 h6 7 Nf3 Nd7 8 Bd3 Bxd3 9 Qxd3
Qc7 10 Bd2 Ngf6 11 0-0-0 e6 12 c4 0-0-0 13
Bc3 Bd6 14 Ne4 Nxe4? 15 Qxe4 Nf6 16 Qe2
Rhe8 17 Rhe1 c5 18 dxc5! Bxc5 19 Ne5 Rxd1+
20 Rxd1 Rd8 21 Rxd8+ Kxd8

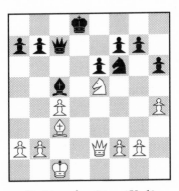

Position after 21 . . . Kxd8

For the record, Black could have equalized with 14 . . . Bf4+
15 Kb1 Ne5! 16 Nxe5 Bxe5 17 Qe3 Nxe4 (18 dxe5
Nxc3+ 19 Qxc3 Rxd1+ 20 Rxd1 Rd8 trades down to

nothingness and 20 Qxe4 Bf6, as we know, favors Black because of the weak d-pawn). But in the diagram White has a solid advantage because of his superior minor pieces. The queenside majority is so far a silent majority.

After 22 g4! White took aim at the Black g-pawn. After Black's knight dropped back, 22 . . . Ne8, White's pieces took up stronger positions buttressed by pawns: 23 g5 hxg5   24 hxg5 Bd6   25 Nf3   g6   26 b4!   Be7   27 Kb2   Nd6   28 c5   Nf5 29 Qe4   Ke8   30 Qe5!   Qxe5   31 Bxe5   a5   32 a3   axb4 33 axb4   Bd8   34 Kb3   Ne7   35 Nd2!   Nd5   36 Ne4   Be7.

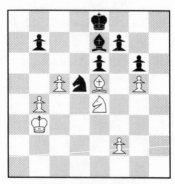

Position after 36 . . . Be7

Note that White has what we call a "bad" bishop, one blocked by its own pawns. But the pawns also confine Black's pieces and they pose the threat of b4-b5 and c5-c6. This was threatened after 37 Bf6! since the king-and-pawn ending after 37 . . . Nxf6   38 Nxf6+ Bxf6   39 gxf6 is hopeless for Black. Black played yet another retreat, 37 . . . Bf8, and was soon pinned to his first rank: 38 Kc4 Kd7 39 b5 Kc8   40 Nd2 Kd7   41 Nf3 Be7   42 Ne5+ Ke8

43 Bxe7 Kxe7   44 Ng4 Nf4   45 Nf6 Kd8   46 b6 (now
c5-c6 is a winning idea) *e5   47 Ne4 Kd7   48 Nd6 Nh3
49 Nxb7 Nxg5   50 Kd5* Resigns. The threat of creating a
passed pawn from the queenside majority was decisive in the
last 25 moves.

To counterbalance one majority there has to be another—
if pawns are equal. White's majority is effective in the ending,
but, not surprisingly, the more centralized Black majority on
the kingside often makes itself felt in the middlegame. This is
illustrated by Maroczy–Charousek, Nuremberg 1896:

**1 d4 d5   2 c4 e6   3 Nc3 c6   4 e4 dxe4   5 Nxe4
Nf6   6 Nc3 Be7   7 Nf3 0-0   8 Bd3 c5!   9 0-0 cxd4
10 Nxd4 Nbd7   11 Nf3 Qa5   12 Bd2? Ne5   13 Ne4
Nxf3+   14 Qxf3 Qc7   15 Bc3 Nxe4!   16 Qxe4**

Position after 16 Qxe4

White's bishops look murderous, but this is exactly when
the blocking effect of enemy pawns is most useful. Black acti-
vated his majority with *16 . . . f5!   17 Qe2 Bd6!   18 h3 e5*,
and he has already usurped the initiative.

White managed to equalize by forcing the exchange of part of the kingside majority—*19 b4 e4 20 Bc2 b6 21 f3!*—but Black could have improved over Charousek's *21 . . . exf3?* which led to a level game. The correct method was *21 . . . Bb7 22 fxe4 Rae8* after which Black's kingside majority has been converted into a domination of the center.

White's Anti . . . c5 Strategies: d4-d5

There are two cases when White can effectively meet . . . c5 with d4-d5!. The first occurs when Black has taken inadequate precautions and allows White to maintain a powerful pawn on d5, an even stronger one than he had at d4. This comes about most frequently when Black fails to play . . . e6 before . . . c5. This is shown by Benko–Hoffmann, New York 1968:

1 Nf3 g6   2 e4 Bg7   3 d4 c6   4 Nc3 d5   5 h3 dxe4
6 Nxe4 Nd7   7 Bd3 Ngf6   8 Nxf6+ Nxf6   9 0-0 0-0
10 Re1 Re8   11 c4 Qc7   12 Be3 Nd7?   13 Qd2

Position after 13 Qd2

Black's last move was a preparation for a positional blunder, *13 . . . c5??*, which permitted *14 d5!*. For the rest of the game Black pieces are inhibited by the White d-pawn. Black's e-pawn remains backward and a target attack on the e-file. Or, after . . . e5, White will be granted a protected passed d-pawn. Either way, White benefits.

The inhibiting effect of the d-pawn permitted White to go straight for mate: *14 . . . Nb6   15 Bh6 Qd6   16 Bxg7 Kxg7   17 Ng5! Qc7   18 Re4*. After 18 . . . h6 White would win the fastest (*19 Nxf7! Kxf7   20 Qxh6* and mates), but after *18 . . . Bd7* his huge advantage was sufficient to score positionally after *19 Nf3 e5   20 Rael f6   21 R4e3 g5   22 Qc2 Re7   23 Nd2! Be8   24 Ne4*.

(For contrast see *Supplemental Game #6* in which d4-d5 is met by . . . exd5 and the occupation of White's d5 with a piece. Black equalizes because, in this instance, he has a d4 to occupy.)

The second situation in which d4-d5 commonly occurs is when Black has taken precautions against it but White insists on playing d4-d5 as a pawn sacrifice. This is similar to Spassky's d4-d5 of a few pages ago—White rips open diagonals and central files for his presumably superior pieces. A spectacular example of this, which ironically developed out of one of the most conservative of openings, is Geller–Ciric, Oberhausen 1961:

> 1 d4 d5   2 c4 e6   3 Nf3 Nf6   4 g3 Be7   5 Bg2 0-0
> 6 0-0   c6   7 b3   Nbd7   8 Bb2   b6   9 Qc2   Bb7
> 10 Nbd2 Rc8   11 Rad1 Qc7   12 e4! dxe4   13 Nxe4
> Nxe4   14 Qxe4 c5

Position after 14 ... c5

With 15 *d5!* White unleashes the dynamism of his rooks and bishops at the temporary expense of a pawn. It is temporary because after *15 . . . Nf6   16 Qc2 exd5   17 Be5! Qd8   18 Ng5 g6* (Bxf6 was threatened)   *19 h4* Black is caught in two pins, one on the d-file, the other on the long white diagonal.

Position after 19 h4

After the simplification *19 . . . Nh5   20 Bxd5 Bxd5 21 Rxd5* the sacrifice has been proven temporary and White now has powerful control of the open d-file. White improved his position with *21 . . . Qe8   22 Re1 Qc6   23 Bb2 Rfe8* and then unleashed a farsighted combination: *24 Nxh7! Bxh4* (not 24 . . . Kxh7   25 Rxh5+) *25 Red1!* (the combination fails after 25 Rxe8+ Rxe8   26 gxh4 Re1+   27 Kh2 Qc7+) *25 . . . Qe6   26 Qc3! f6   27 Qd3 Qg4   28 Rg5!!* (now 28 . . . Bxg5   29 Qxg6+ Ng7   30 Nxf6+ Bxf6   31 Qxg4 wins) *28 . . . Qe4   29 Nxf6+   Nxf6   30 gxh4   Red8   31 Qxd8+ Rxd8   32 Rxd8+ Kf7   33 Bxf6 Kxf6   34 Rd6+ Kf7   35 Rdxg6 Qxh4   36 Rg7+* and White won.

Preventing . . . c5 with c4-c5

A third option for White, besides exploiting the d4xc5 exchange and the d5 advance, is to prevent . . . c5 *mechanically* by putting a White pawn on the square that Black wants for *his* pawn.

This advance has a thoroughly muddled "balance sheet" (to use Lasker's term): it cedes d5 to Black pieces, it makes White's d-pawn a backward, permanent target, and it permits Black to open lines with . . . b6. But occasionally the advantages of stopping . . . c5 and of further confining Black outweigh the minuses. A model example of this is Pillsbury–Winawer, Budapest 1896:

1 d4 d5   2 c4 e6   3 Nc3 c6   4 e3 Nf6   5 Nf3 Nbd7
6 Bd3 Bd6   7 0-0 0-0   8 e4 dxe4   9 Nxe4 Nxe4
10 Bxe4

Position after 10 Bxe4

10 ...   Nf6?!

This takes away a piece from control of c5. Why not 10 ...
c5? At the turn of the century it was believed that 11 Bc2 Qc7
12 Qd3 was strong enough to deter 10 ... c5 because of lines
such as 12 ... Nf6 13 Bg5! and 12 ... g6 13 Bh6   Re8 14
Rad1 with considerable pressure. But later it was discovered
that 12 ... f5!, activating Black's h7 was sufficient for equality
despite the temporary backwardness of Black's e-pawn.

11   Bc2   h6

Now the direct 11 ... c5 runs into 12 Bg5! (threatening
13 Qd3 and 14 Bxf6) cxd4   13 Qxd4 Be7   14 Qh4! h6
15 Bxh6 gxh6   16 Qxh6 and 17 Ng5, which would be overwhelming.

12   Be3   Re8?

Here 12 . . . Qc7 and 13 . . . c5 are called for. White could
have recognized the inevitability of . . . c5 by playing 12 Qe2
(instead of his 12 Be3) followed by Bd2-c3. Then . . . c5 would
give him a bishop pair that would cut a wide swath through
the Black kingside.

13   Qd3   Qc7

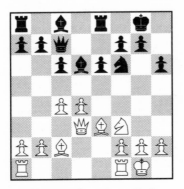

Position after 13 . . . Qc7

14   c5!   Bf8
15   Ne5!

Because of Black's delay in promoting . . . c5 White can stop
it once and for all. White has an iron grip on the center now,
and this is quickly converted into attack. Black's only counterplay is a slow-moving assault on the White d-pawn and the
line-opening . . . b6 (which would be met by b4).

It is not surprising that White won quickly. He threatens
16 Ng4 and a mate on h7. Perhaps Black's best is 15 . . . g6

16 Qd2 Kh7, but then 17 Bf4 Qd8 (or 17 ... Nd5? 18 Nxg6) 18 Nc4 followed by the occupation of d6 favors White greatly.

Winawer panicked by trying to achieve with tactics what he should have tried to do with astute pawn play: *15 ... Bxc5 16 Bxh6 Bxd4* (or 16 ... gxh6 17 Qg3+ followed by a knight check that wins Q) *17 Qxd4 gxh6 18 Qf4* (again threatening Qg3+) *Nd5 19 Qxh6 f6* (mate follows 19 ... Qx e5 20 Bh7+ Kh8 21 Bg6+) *20 f4! Re7 21 Ng6 Re-* signs. (For another illustration see *Supplemental Game #7*.)

Black's ... e5 Strategy

If Black has a choice between ... c5 and his other liberating move, ... e5, there is good reason to prefer the latter. The first pawn break emphasizes White's queenside majority; the second neutralizes it. The first break helps free Black's pawn-bound queen bishop, the second immediately gives it air.

But ... e5 is harder to achieve because of the way the two sides normally develop. White usually has a knight on f3 and a rook or queen on the e-file to stop ... e5. He develops no piece that guards c5 easily (except Be3, which blocks the e-file). Black's king bishop is usually developed at e7 where it observes his c5 and not his e5.

The choice becomes clear out of this opening:

1 d4 d5   2 c4 e6   3 Nc3 Nf6   4 Bg5 Nbd7   5 Nf3 c6   6 e4 dxe4   7 Nxe4 Be7   8 Nc3

Position after 8 Nc3

Black can try for either pawn break. On 8 . . . c5?! White can take over the heartland of the center with 9 Qc2 cxd4 10 Nxd4. (For example, in Lilienthal–J. Bolbochan; Stockholm 1937, White had a comfortable edge after 10 . . . h6 11 Bh4 0-0 12 Be2 a6 13 0-0 Qb6 14 Rad1 Re8 15 Bg3 Nf8 16 Na4! Qa5 17 c5!, and a won game after 17 . . . Nd5 18 Nb6! Nxb6 19 Nb3 Qa4 20 cxb6 Bf6 21 Bf3 e5 22 Rfe1 Qb5 23 Qc5!.)

From the diagram, however, Black can make a better try for equality with 8 . . . 0-0 9 Qc2 e5! followed by an idea based on the tactics of 10 dxe5 Ng4 11 Bf4 Bc5 12 Ne4 Bb4+ or 10 Nxe5 Nxe5 11 dxe5 Nd7 12 Bxe7 Qxe7 13 f4 f6. White acquiesces to the break with 10 0-0-0 exd4 11 Nxd4 Qa5 12 Be3 Nc5. Black has good chances.

Equality isn't all that . . . e5 may confer on Black, and White is therefore justified in taking a few steps to restrain . . . e5. This is especially worthwhile when Black has gone out of his way to play . . . e5 at the expense of making . . . c5 an impossible option. A drastic illustration of this is Bronstein–Nei, U.S.S.R. team championship 1962:

1 e4 e6   2 d4 d5   3 Nc3 Nf6   4 Bg5 dxe4   5 Nxe4
Be7   6 Bxf6 Bxf6   7 c3 Bd7   8 Bd3 Bc6   9 Qe2
Qd5?

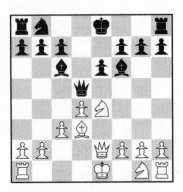

Position after 9 . . . Qd5?

Clearly Black has abandoned hope of . . . c5. He doesn't fear 10 Nxf6+ gxf6 because that would exchange a strong piece for his king bishop, which bites on granite at d4. The exchange of pieces would also open up Black's useful g-file and give him pawn control of his e5.

White put . . . e5 out of the range of possibility with 10 f4!. This means that Black is dangerously passive and vulnerable to a quick attack. His pieces appear active, but this condition cannot continue for long in a position with an interior structure. The game continued: 10 . . . Bh4+   11 g3 Be7 12 Nf3 Nd7   13 Rf1! (preparing to move the knight from e4) 0-0?   14 h4! b5   15 Neg5! (now 15 . . . Nf6 is sharply met by   16 Ne5 Be8   17 f5)   15 . . . h6   16 Bh7+ Kh8

17 Be4 Qd6   18 Ne5! (decisive since 18 ... hxg5 allows mate in two) *Nxe5   19 fxe5 Qd7   20 Nxf7+ Kg8   21 Bg6 Resigns* (in face of 22 Qc2 and 23 Bh7 mate).

Another effective method of stopping ... e5 is the mechanical way with Ne5. If Black captures the outpost knight he can find himself reduced to his first two ranks, conceding White the other six. See *Supplemental Game #8*.

Supplemental Games

(1) Passive play by Black and . . . f6. Spassky–Donner, Leiden 1970: 1 e4 e6   2 d4 d5   3 Nc3 Nf6   4 Bg5 dxe4 5 Nxe4 Be7   6 Bxf6 Bxf6   7 Nf3 Bd7   8 Qd2 Bc6 9 Nxf6+ Qxf6? (9 . . . gxf6 gives Black pawn control of his e5 at less cost than he subsequently pays)   10 Ne5! 0-0   11 0-0-0 Rd8   12 Qe3 Be8   13 g3 Nd7   14 Bg2 c6   15 f4 Qe7   16 h4! f6?   17 Nf3 Bh5   18 Bh3 Bxf3   19 Qxf3 Nf8   20 Rhe1 Qf7   21 Bf1! (the main target is Black's e-pawn, weakened by . . . f6) Rd6   22 Bc4 Rad8   23 f5! Rxd4 24 fxe6 Rxd1+   25 Rxd1 Rxd1+   26 Qxd1 Resigns (in face of 26 . . . Qe7   27 Qd8! Qxd8   28 e7+).

(2) Passive play by Black renders d4-d5! devastating. Tal–Putjudruwa, Latvia 1955: 1 e4 c6   2 Nc3 d5   3 Nf3 Bg4   4 h3 Bxf3   5 Qxf3 e6   6 d4 Nf6   7 Bd3 dxe4 8 Nxe4   Nxe4 9 Qxe4 Nd7   10 c3 Nf6   11 Qe2 Qc7 12 Bd2 Bd6   13 c4 h5?? (Totally out of character for the position; 13 . . . c5 is met by 14 d5, but 13 . . . 0-0 and 14 . . . c5 is OK.)   14 0-0 Bf4   15 Bc3 Rd8   16 Rad1 Kf8 (castling is out of the question after . . . h5)   17 Rfe1 h4   18 Bc2 Rh6   19 Rd3 Qb8   20 Rf3 Nh5   21 Qe4 Qc7   22 d5! exd5   23 cxd5   cxd5   24 Bb4+   Bd6   25 Qxd5   Nf6

(25 . . . Bxb4 26 Rxf7+! mates) 26 Qe5 Qxc2
27 Bxd6+ Kg8 28 Be7 Rd1 29 Rxd1 Qxd1+ 30 Kh2
Qa4 31 Rf4 Qc6 32 Qb8+ Kh7 33 Bxf6 gxf6
34 Rg4 Rg6 35 Rxh4+ Rh6 36 Rxh6+ Kxh6
37 Qh8+ Kg6 38 Qg8+ Kf5 39 Qxf7 Qd6+ 40 g3
Qd2 41 g4+ Resigns (because the f-pawn falls with check).

(3) Black's . . . c5 liberates his pieces. Roizman–Sokolsky,
Byelorussia 1961: 1 d4 Nf6 2 c4 e6 3 Nc3 Bb4 4 e3 d5
5 a3 Be7 6 Nf3 0-0 7 Bd3 b6 8 e4 dxe4 9 Nxe4
Nbd7 10 0-0 Bb7 11 Qe2 c5! 12 Rd1? cxd4
13 Nxd4 Ne5! (Black has a material edge after 14 Nxf6+
Bxf6 15 Nxe6 fxe6 16 Bxh7+ Kxh7 17 Rxd8 Raxd8)
14 Bc2 Nxe4 15 Bxe4 Bxe4 16 Qxe4 Nxc4 (White's attack is some compensation) 17 Bf4 Qd5 18 Qe2 Na5
19 Be5 Bf6!? 20 Bxf6 gxf6 21 b4 Nc4 22 Nb3 Qc6
23 Qg4+ Kh8 24 Rac1 Rac8 25 Rd4? b5 26 Na5 Qa6
27 Nxc4 Rxc4 28 Rcxc4 bxc4 29 Qf3 e5 30 Rh4 Rg8
31 Qc3 Qa4 32 g3 Qd1+ 33 Kg2 Rg4 34 Rxg4 Qxg4
35 Qf3 Qd4! 36 Qxf6+ Kg8 37 Qg5+ Kf8 38 Qh6+
Ke7 39 Qg5+ Ke6 40 Qc1 c3 41 Kf1 Qd3+ 42 Ke1
Kd5 43 Qd1 Kc4 White resigns. The passed pawn wins.

**(4) Black's . . . c5 allows him to keep pawn control of his
d5. He attacks on the kingside.** Napier–Teichmann, Cam-
bridge Springs 1904: 1 d4 d5 2 c4 e6 3 Nc3 Nf6 4 Bg5
Nbd7 5 Nf3 c6 6 e4 dxe4 7 Nxe4 Bb4+! 8 Bd2 Be7!
9 Bd3 c5! 10 Bc3 b6 11 0-0 Bb7 12 Qe2 0-0
13 Rad1 Qc7 14 dxc5 bxc5 15 Ng3 Rfd8 16 Rfe1
Qc6 17 Qe3 Nf8 18 h4 (an illogical attack that is neatly
repulsed) h6 19 h5 N8h7 20 Bf1 Qa4 21 Rxd8+ Rxd8
22 Ne5 Ng5 23 Bd3 Bd6! 24 f4 Bxe5 25 Qxe5 Nh3+!

26 gxh3 Rxd3   27 Qb8+ Kh7 28 Qxb7 Rxg3+
29 Kh2 Nxh5 (threatening 30 . . . Qc2+ and 31 . . . Rxh3+)
30 Qe4+ Rg6 31 Rg1 f5 32 Qe2 Rxg1 33 Kxg1 Nxf4
34 Qe5 Qd1+ 35 Kh2 Qc2+ 36 Kg3 Qg2+ 37 Kxf4
Qf2 mate.

(5) To shorten White's strong diagonal a1-h7, Black weakens his kingside further. Trifunovic–Djantar, Kragujevac
1959: 1 d4 Nf6 2 c4 c6 3 Nc3 d5 4 Nf3 e6 5 e3
Nbd7 6 Qc2 Be7 7 b3 b6 8 Bd3 Bb7 9 0-0 0-0
10 Bb2 Rc8 11 e4 dxe4 12 Nxe4 Nxe4 13 Bxe4 Nf6
14 Bd3 Qc7 15 Rae1 h6 (safer is . . . g6) 16 Qe2! Rfe8
17 Bb1 Nd7 18 Qc2 Nf8 19 Re3 c5 20 Ne5 cxd4
21 Bxd4 Rcd8 22 Bc3 Bc5 23 Rg3 Bd4 24 Re1 Bxc3
25 Qxc3 f6 (to counter 26 Ng4!) 26 Ng4 Kf7 27 Qe3
Re7 28 Nxh6+! gxh6 29 Qxh6 e5   30 Bf5 Ke8
31 Rg8 Rf7 32 Bg6 Qe7 33 Bxf7+ Qxf7 34 Rg7 Resigns.

(6) White plays d4-d5 after . . . c5 but Black contests the center well. Udovcic–Ragozin, Leningrad 1934: 1 d4 Nf6
2 c4 e6 3 Nc3 d5 4 Bg5 Nbd7 5 Nf3 c6 6 e3 Qa5
7 Bxf6 Nxf6 8 Bd3 Be7 9 0-0 0-0 10 e4 dxe4
11 Nxe4 Rd8 12 Qe2 Bd7 13 Rfd1 Be8 14 a3 Rac8
15 Rd2 g6 16 Rad1 Qc7 17 Bc2 Nxe4 18 Bxe4 c5!
19 d5 (to avoid the exchanges along the d-file that could lead
to a superior endgame for Black because of his two bishops)
exd5 20 Bxd5 Bf6 21 Rd3 b5! 22 b3 a6 23 Qe3 Kg7
24 Ng5! Rd7 25 Ne4 Re7 26 Qd2 Be5 27 g3 Bd4
(Black's bishop is at least equal to White's knight) 28 Kg2
Bc6 29 Nc3 Rce8 30 Rf3 Bd7! 31 h3 Qc8 32 g4 f5
33 Rd3 Qc7 34 Bf3 fxg4 35 hxg4 Rf7 36 Nd5 Qe5

37 Rh1 g5   38 Rfl h5!   39 gxh5 g4 40 Bd1? (better was 40 Bxg4 Bxg4   41 Rg3 Kh8   42 Rxg4 Rg8)   40 ... Rh8 41 Rg3 Qxh5 White resigns.

(7) Slow pressure against White's c4-c5 plan. Pillsbury–Tchigorin, Vienna 1898: 1 d4 d5   2 c4 e6   3 Nc3 c6   4 Nf3 Nd7   5 e4 dxe4   6 Nxe4 Ngf6   7 Bd3 Nxe4   8 Bxe4 Bb4+   9 Bd2   Bxd2+?   10 Qxd2   0-0   11 0-0   Qf6 12 Rfe1 Rd8   13 Rad1 Nf8   14 c5 Bd7   15 Ne5 Be8 (A good square for the bishop. Black readies a counterattack with ... Ng6 and doubling rooks on the d-file before ... b6.) 16 Re3 Ng6   17 Bxg6 hxg6   18 Nc4 Rd5!   19 Nd6 b6 20 b4   Rd8   21 Rd3 Qe7   22 Qe3   Qc7   23 f4   Qd7 24 Rf1 Qc7   25 Rf3 a5! (necessary counterplay since White otherwise wins by doubling on the h-file)   26 Nc4 bxc5 27 bxc5 Rb8   28 Nb6 Rdd8   29 Ra3 Rxb6!   30 cxb6 Qxb6   31 Rf1 Rxd4   32 Rxa5 c5   33 Ra8 Kf8   34 Qh3 Ke7   35 Qh4+   f6   36 Qh8   Rd8   37 Qxg7+?   Bf7 38 Rxd8 c4+!   39 Kh1   Qxd8   40 Rbl   c3   41 f5   c2! 42 Rg1 Qd1!   43 fxg6 Qxg1+   44 Kxgl clQ+   45 Kf2 Qc2+, and Black won after 46 ... Qxg6.

(8) White's Ne5 stifles ... e5 and leads to a domination of the board. Maroczy–Mieses, Vienna 1908: 1 e4 d5   2 exd5 Qxd5 3 Nc3 Qa5   4 d4 Nf6   5 Bd2 c6   6 Bc4 Bf5 7 Nf3 Qc7   8 0-0 e6   9 Ne2 Bd6   10 Ng3 Bg6   11 Re1 Nbd7   12 c3 Rd8   13 Qe2 0-0   14 Rad1 Bf4   15 Ne5! Bxd2   16 Rxd2 Nxe5   17 dxe5 Rxd2   18 Qxd2 Rd8 19 Qe3 (if Black could play ... c5 and maneuver his knight to c6 he might equalize)   19 ... Nd7?!   (19 ... Nd5!)   20 h4! h6   21 h5 Bh7   22 Rd1 Nb6   23 Rxd8+ Qxd8   24 Be2 a6   25 c4 Nc8   26 a3 Ne7   27 Qa7! Qc7   28 b4 Nc8

29 Qd4 Kf8   30 Bf3 Ke8   31 Be4 Bxe4   32 Nxe4 Qd7
33 Nd6+! Nxd6   34 exd6 f6 (White only needs room for the
penetration of his Q now)   35 f4 b5   36 c5 Kd8   37 g4
Qf7   38 Qe4 Kd7   39 Qe2 Qg8   40 Qa2!! (threatening to
win with either a3-a4 or f4- f5) g6   41 hxg6 Qe8 (or 41 . . .
Qxg6   42 Qxe6+! Kxe6   43 f5+)   42 f5 Resigns.

THE SLAV
FORMATION

THERE ARE AS MANY ROADS TO THE SLAV FORMATION AS TO THE Caro. There is, first of all, the Slav Defense to the Queen's Gambit and its relatives (Queen's Gambit Accepted, Queen's Gambit Declined, Catalan, Gruenfeld Defense). The Colle System illustates the formation in reverse after 1 d4 d5 2 Nf3 Nf6 3 e3 e6 4 Bd3 c5 5 c3 Be7 6 0-0 Nc6 7 Nbd2 Qc7 8 dxc5 and 9 e4, an example of what we'll call Tchigorin's plan.

The only difference between Caro and Slav is the substitution in the latter of White's e-pawn for his c-pawn. This difference eliminates some Caro features (White's queenside majority), alters plans (often making . . . e5 preferable to . . . c5 as Black's means of liberation), but leaves the solidity of the position pretty much alone.

As in the Caro, passivity can be fatal to Black. The explosive nature of d4-d5 is exemplified by Rubinstein–Schlechter, Berlin 1918:

1 d4 d5   2 Nf3 Nf6   3 c4 c6   4 Nc3 dxc4   5 e3
Bg4   6 Bxc4 e6   7 0-0 Nbd7   8 h3 Bxf3   9 Qxf3
Be7   10 Rd1 0-0?   11 e4 Re8   12 Bf4 Nf8

Position after 12 . . . Nf8

13 d5!

Black's position is solid enough to withstand anything but
a d5 break. Because of the pawn structure, White's pieces are
aggressive and Black's are passive. With the defensive line of
pawns stripped away White's superiority will be overwhelming.

| 13 | . . . | exd5 |
| 14 | exd5 | Qb6? |

If the center is completely opened Black loses at least
a pawn (14 . . . cxd5   15 Nxd5 Nxd5   16 Bxd5 Qb6
17 Bxb7   Rad8   18 Bd5   Qxb2?   19 Bxf7+!   Kxf7
20 Be5+).

15	d6	**Bd8**
16	g4!	**Ne6**

There is no defense against White's threat of 17 g5.

17   d7!

And White won swiftly after *17 . . . Re7   18 Bd6 Rxd7 19 Bxe6 fxe6   20 g5.* (Also see *Supplemental Game #1* at the end of this chapter.)

With a few exceptions Black's counterplay comes from . . . e5 or . . . c5, just as in the Caro. One of the exceptions is the attack on White's center (after e2-e4) by way of . . . f5. Although this idea has had many failures, its most spectacular success is worth mentioning.

Pillsbury–Tchigorin, St. Petersburg 1895–96: *1 d4 d5 2 c4 Nc6   3 Nf3 Bg4   4 cxd5 Bxf3   5 dxc6 Bxc6   6 Nc3 e6   7 e4 Bb4   8 f3 f5!?*

Position after 8 . . . f5!?

Black's last move was condemned—for good reason—by the Classical masters. Black has opened up his kingside and made his e-pawn backward. But White must find a way of ex-

ploiting this. The correct plan, 9 Bc4 fxe4 10 0-0!, was discovered to be an effective gambit—half a century later.

In the original game White played a move even more antipositional than 8 . . . f5: 9 e5??. This advance shields Black's
weaknesses and stresses the vulnerability of White's own center and his white squares. The speed with which Black took
iron control of the white squares was remarkable: 9 . . . Ne7
10 a3 Ba5 11 Bc4 Bd5! 12 Qa4+ c6 13 Bd3 Qb6!
14 Bc2 Qa6! 15 Bd1 Bc4! after which White was already
lost. He couldn't hold his d-pawn after 16 f4 0-0-0 17 Be3
Nd5 18 Bd2 Nb6 and lasted 20 moves more before his king
was mated at g2.

Tchigorin's . . . e5 Plan

The same player who handled Black in the last illustration de-
vised the most popular method of liberating Black's game. On
several occasions Mikhail Tchigorin held the Black pieces after 1 d4 d5 2 c4 e6 3 Nc3 c6 4 e3 Nf6 5 Bd3 Nbd7
6 Nf3 Bd6 7 0-0 0-0 8 e4.

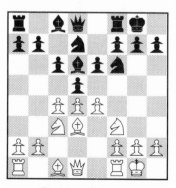

Position after 8 e4

With 8 . . . dxe4 we have the Caro formation with its usual problems, but Tchigorin found that Black could equalize much more easily with 8 . . . dxc4! 9 Bxc4 e5!. Although other masters had experimented with Black's plan, it was Tchigorin, the first great Russian player, who showed that Black could compete with White's pieces by using the black squares after . . . e5. If Black can play . . . exd4 he will use e5 and f4 as outposts for his minor pieces. If White keeps the center closed with d4-d5, Black can maneuver his pieces for kingside attack with . . . Bg4 and . . . Nf8-g6-f4.

In Janowski–Tchigorin, Budapest 1896, White closed the center with 10 Bg5 Qe7 11 d5, and Black missed the correct followup (11 . . . Rd8 followed by . . . Nf8-g6) when he continued 11 . . . Nb6 12 Bb3 Bg4 13 h3 Bh5 14 dxc6 bxc6.

Position after 14 . . . bxc6

Black correctly permitted the isolation of his c-pawn because he knew that 11 . . . cxd5 12 exd5 or 12 Bxd5 favors White because of his better control of open lines in the center. In the diagram it is clear that Black will be the first to profit from the d-file and that it will be several moves before White can think of attacking the c-pawn. Black intends . . . Rfd8 followed by moving his queen knight to d4 via f8 and e6.

White took the bull by the horns and played *15 g4! Bg6 16 Nh4 Kh8   17 Nf5 Bxf5* but then turned over the initiative with *18 gxf5?.* Had he captured with his e-pawn White could use the e4 square well; however, after the bad recapture he was on the defensive in the center and on the kingside: *18 . . . h6   19 Bh4 Rad8   20 Qe2 g5!   21 Bg3 Rg8 22 Kg2 Rg7   23 Rad1 h5   24 Rh1 h4   25 Bh2 Rdg8 26 Kf1 Bc5   27 Nb1 g4   28 hxg4 Nxg4   29 Bg1 Qg5 30 Qf3 Bd4   31 Nc3 c5!   32 Ke2 c4   33 Bc2 Qh6 34 Nb5 Nxf2!   35 Bxf2 Bxf2,* and White resigned shortly because of *36 Kxf2 Rg3!* or *36 Qxf2 Rg2.*

Three years later at London in 1899, with the position after *8 e4,* Maroczy (as White) played *8 . . . dxc4   9 Bxc4 e5 10 Bg5 Qe7   11 Kh1 Rd8   12 Qc2 h6* against Tchigorin and kept the center fluid. If White now retreats his bishop to h4 he invites strong play on black squares after *13 Bh4 exd4! 14 Nxd4 Nb6   15 Bd3 Bxh2!.* So, there followed *13 Bxf6 Qxf6   14 dxe5 Bxe5!.*

Position after 14 . . . Bxe5!

Black has excellent control of the kingside now. Note that 14 . . . Bxe5 is better than a capture with the queen knight because White would be able to mobilize his kingside majority after 14 . . . Nxe5   15 Nxe5 Bxe5   16 f4! (e.g., 16 . . . Bxf4 17 g3 Rd2   18 Qxd2 Bxd2   19 Rxf6 gxf6   20 Rd1 or 16 . . . Bxc3   17 e5!).

But now in the diagram White cannot play 15 Nxe5 Nxe5 without risking disaster after 16 Bb3 Nf3!   17 Rad1 Bh3! or 16 Be2 Qf4!   17 g3 Qf6   18 f4 Ng4. As it turned out White eventually did mobilize his pawns, but by then Black had too much command of the center to be stopped. The game ended with   15 Rad1 Re8   16 Be2 Bc7!   17 Ne1 Ne5 18 f4 Ng4   19 Bxg4 Bxg4   20 Rd3 Rad8   21 Qf2 Rxd3 22 Nxd3 Rd8   23 Qg3 Be6   24 e5 Qf5   25 Nc5 Bxe5 26 Nxe6 fxe6   27 Qe3 Bxc3   28 bxc3 b6   29 h3 Rd3 30 Qe2 Rxc3   31 Qa6 Qd5   32 Kg1 Rc2   33 Rf3 Qd1+ White resigns.

Consequences of the . . . exd4 Exchange

An important point of Tchigorin's plan is that . . . e5 is most effective *after* White has played e2-e4. This insures that White will not be able to keep a pawn on his d4 or retain control of the square with other pawns. This may also mean that White's e-pawn, the anchor of his center, will become a target. Or it could become a battering ram.

When the pawn is strong it can be used dynamically with its brother, the f-pawn. Then e4-e5 drives Black's pieces away

from the kingside and prepares a disruptive f4-f5. This is shown
by Taimanov–Matulovic, Majorca 1971:

**1 d4 d5   2 c4 dxc4   3 Nf3 Nf6   4 e3 Bg4   5 Bxc4
e6   6 Nc3 Nbd7   7 h3 Bh5   8 0-0 Bd6   9 e4 e5**

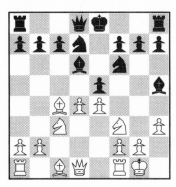

Position after 9 . . . e5

White can proceed patiently with Be3, but the immediate
liquidation gives him a slight initiative because he has one
more pawn in the center than Black after *10 dxe5 Nxe5
11 Be2*. Black eagerly traded pieces with *11 . . . Bxf3
12 Bxf3 Nxf3+?!   13 Qxf3 Qe7   14 Bf4 Be5?*, making a
common misjudgment about the strength of White's mobile
kingside majority.

The bankruptcy of this attitude was shown by *15 Bxe5!
Qxe5   16 Qe3!*, which prepares a forceful f2-f4. True, Black
has his queenside majority, but it is inactive and therefore irrelevant to the middlegame. There followed *16 . . . 0-0
17 f4 Qe7   18 e5!*.

Position after 18 e5!

Black is in bad shape: e.g., 18 ... Nd7   19 Rad1 c6
20 Ne4 and Nd6. The game quickly proceeded into an ending in which Black was lost: *18 ... c6   19 Rfe1 Rfe8
20 Qf3 Qc5+   21 Qf2 Qxf2+   22 Kxf2 Nd5   23 Nxd5
cxd5   24 Red1   Red8   25 Rac1   Rd7   26 Ke3   Rad8
27 Kd4 Kf8   28 f5* and White won in 14 more moves.

On the other hand, White can keep his e-pawn protected
and on e4 so that it restricts Black's pieces and permits the first
player to dominate the d-file. In the diagram below White has
no pawns in the center, but he is ready to secure his rightful
share of center squares (Simagin–Kotov, Moscow 1944).

White continued *1 Qd4!* encouraging a favorable ending (*1 ... Qxd4 2 Rxd4 Re8 3 Rad1* followed by e2-e4 and f2-f4). Black could have contested the center with *1 ... Qa5* and *2 ... Be6* so that he could play *3 ... Rfd8*, but his *1 ... Qh5? 2 f3 Bh3?* permitted White to achieve a most favorable form of Slav family with *3 e4 Bxg2 4 Kxg2 Rfe8 5 Rd2*.

Again Black's queenside majority was insignificant, whereas the *threat* of e4-e5 and f3-f4 in coordination with White's control of the d-file was enough to turn the course of the game to the first player's favor. White took command after *5 ... Qa5 6 Rad1 Re7 7 Qc4 Rae8 8 Rd6 Qb6 9 b4! Re6 10 R6d4 R6e7 11 Na4 Qc7 12 Nc5 Qc8 13 R1d2 Nh7 14 h4 Nf8 15 Rd6*.

Position after 15 Rd6

White's structural advantages have given him tremendous pressure, and he has a choice of ways to proceed; e.g., a2-a4 and b4-b5 to isolate a queenside pawn target or g4-g5 to mate. Most important, as long as White maintains pressure he does not fear exchanges. This became apparent after 15 . . . Ne6 16 Nxe6 Rxe6 17 Rxe6 Rxe6, which permitted White to glide into a won endgame: 18 Qd4 Qf8   19 f4! Re8   20 e5! Qe7   21 a3 a6   22 h5 Qe6   23 Qd7.

This is won because White can create a passed pawn from his majority much more easily than Black can from his. This exceptionally well handled game concluded with 23 . . . Re7 24 Qxe6 fxe6   25 Kf3 Rc7   26 Ke4 Kf7   27 Rd6 Ke7 28 f5 exf5+   29 Kxf5 c5   30 bxc5 Rxc5   31 Rb6 Rc7 32 g4   Kf7   33 a4   Ke7   34 a5!   Kf7   35 Ke4!   Ke7 36 Kd5 Rd7+   37 Rd6! Rc7   38 e6 Ke8   39 Rb6 Ke7 40 Rb1! Ke8   41 Rb4! (gaining a zugzwang position after 41 . . . Ke7   42 Rb6) Rc1   42 Rxb7 Rd1+   43   Ke5 Re1+ 44 Kf5 Rf1+   45 Kg6 Rf4   46 g5 Rg4   47 Kxg7 Rxg5+ 48 Kf6 Resigns.

The lesson therefore is that Black must retain pressure against the weaknesses of the White center. He may pound against the e-pawn or may occupy the weakened black squares. This requires a sharp tactical eye, as Alekhine demonstrated with Black in the following example:

Davidson–Alekhine, Semmering 1926: 1 d4 d5 2 c4 c6 3 Nf3 Nf6 4 e3 e6 5 Nc3 Nbd7 6 Qc2 Bd6 7 Bd3 0-0 8 0-0 Qe7 9 e4 dxc4! 10 Bxc4 e5 11 Rd1 exd4 12 Nxd4 Nb6 13 Bf1.

Position after 13 Bf1

13 ...   Rd8!

Black begins his middlegame work with a tactical threat of 14 ... Bxh2+! 15 Kxh2 Rxd4 16 Rxd4 Qe5+. If White covers h2 with 14 g3 Black can find other methods of keeping White busy (14 ... Bg4 15 f3? Bc5 or 15 Nde2 Bf3). White can't hide from the tactics with 14 Bg5 Bxh2+ 15 Kxh2 Ng4+ or 14 f3 Nh5 15 g3 Bc5 16 Be3 f5.

14 h3   Bc7!

This revives the threat of 15 ... Rxd4 16 Rxd4 Qe5. Note that both sides have active pieces and that White doesn't have the license to play f2-f4 (15 f4 Nh5 16 e5 f6! prematurely opens the position).

	15 Be3	Re8!

After this move White's e-pawn is under constant pressure and he is not given a fair chance for f2-f4. The game continued 16 Bd3 Nh5 17 Nce2 g6 18 Re1 Nd7, after which 19 f4 would have invited 19 ... Ndf6 20 e5 Nd5 21 Bd2 Bb6 and excellent play for Black. As it went, Black continued to use his superior pieces with 19 Nf3 Bb6 20 Bg5 Qc5 (so that 21 Qxc5 Nxc5 22 Nc1 f6 23 Bd2 Nxd3 and ... Ng3 favors Black, Alekhine said) 21 Nc3 Ne5.

The result of all this was a mating attack that flowed naturally from Black's use of the black squares where White was weakest. White resigned shortly after 22 Nxe5 Qxe5 23 Be3 Bc7 24 Ne2 Qh2+ 25 Kf1 Bxh3! 26 gxh3 Qxh3+ 27 Kg1 Bh2+ 28 Kh1 Nf4 29 Nxf4 Bxf4+ 30 Kg1 Bh2+ 31 Kh1 Qf3+! 32 Kxh2 Re5 33 Qc5 Rxc5 34 Bxc5 Qh5+ and 35 ... Qxc5.

White Plays d4-d5 After ... e5

If White is not willing to acquiesce in the exchange of his d-pawn for Black's e-pawn, he will push his d-pawn. That leaves Black three prospects. Alexander Alekhine, commenting on a world championship game, explained them succinctly:

(1) to exchange at d5, thus leaving this square free for the opponent's pieces; (2) to play . . . c5 after which White would have a strong passed pawn; (3) to allow the exchange at c6; which obviously weakens his pawn position.

These three options illustrate the different values of pawn strength and piece play in evaluating a position. The first option, cxd5, is the least interesting. It will lead to a symmetrical pawn structure if White recaptures on d5 with a minor piece. But while Black's pawns are strong, his pieces are most likely to be inferior to White's in ability.

The second option leads to blocked play, and this tends to favor White provided that Black cannot mobilize his own pawn majorities on the two wings. The third option gives Black a weak c-pawn, but it takes d5 away from White's pieces and this is very annoying to the first player. Black gets the best mobility for his pieces out of the third option but at the cost of weak pawns.

The second option—the blocked center—is difficult to handle with Black, as the following game shows:

Gligoric–Gheorghiu, Tel Aviv 1966:

1 d4 Nf6	2 c4 g6	3 Nc3 d5	4 Nf3 Bg7	5 Bf4 c6
6 e3 0-0	7 Rc1 dxc4?	8 Bxc4 Bg4	9 h3 Bxf3	
10 Qxf3 Nbd7	11 0-0 e6	12 Rfd1 Qe7	13 Bg5!	
h6	14 Bh4 Rad8	15 e4 e5	16 d5 Nb6	17 Bb3

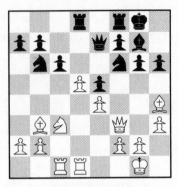

Position after 17 Bb3

White's threat of e4-e5 virtually forced 15 . . . e5. Black has the trilemma Alekhine described. With 17 . . . cxd5 Black could ease his game, but the result would be a simplified position in which White's pieces would remain superior for many moves (after 18 Bxf6! Bxf6 19 Nxd5 Nxd5 20 Bxd5 or just 19 Bxd5).

Black went the blockade route with *17 . . . g5 18 Bg3 c5 19 h4 Nc8* intending . . . Nd6. This would have worked out better with 19. . . Ne8 and . . . Nd6 because of the tactical problems that followed *20 hxg5 hxg5 21 Qe3 Nh5 22 d6!*.

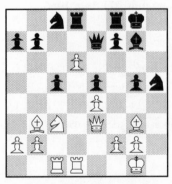

Position after 22 d6!

Here White obtains d5 for his pieces through a pawn sacrifice. After 22 ... Nxd6   23 Nd5 Qe6   24 Qxg5 Black's
position is in ruins because of the threats such as 25 Ne7+.
Black preferred 22 ... Rxd6   23 Nd5 Qd8 preserving his
g-pawn, but this lost the c-pawn and resulted in a positionally
lost game after 24 Rxc5 Nb6   25 Qf3 Nf4   26 Bxf4 gxf4
27 Qg4! Kh8   28 Rd3. The game ended with a swarm of
White pieces: 28 ... Rg6   29 Qf5 Nxd5   30 Rh3+ Rh6
31 Rxd5 Qb6   32 Rdd3 Rd8   33 Rxh6+ Bxh6   34 Qxe5+
Kg8   35 Qe7 Rf8   36 Rd6 Qa5   37 Rxh6. For a more
sophisticated destruction of the blockade see *Supplemental
Game #2.*

The most challenging middlegames arise when Black ignores
d4-d5 and permits Alekhine's third option, dxc6. That the
pawn is weak is obvious. That it can be exploited depends on
what the players do. While it remains on the board it tends to
give Black greater control of the center (two pawns in the center to White's one).

Black's kingside attack often becomes vital. The center is
semiclosed, and a wing attack grows in strength because of the
lack of center counterplay. One of the major trumps held by
Black is his f5 outpost. For example:

Kan–Romanovsky, Moscow 1945:

1 Nf3 d5   2 d4 Nf6   3 c4 e6   4 Nc3 c6   5 e3 Nbd7
6 Bd3   Bd6   7 0-0   0-0   8 e4   dxc4   9 Bxc4   e5
10 Bg5 Qe7   11 d5? Rd8!   12 Qe2 h6   13 Bh4 Nf8!
14 Rad1 Ng6   15 Bg3

Position after 15 Bg3

| 15 | ... | Nh5! |

This strong and thematic move gives Black a bridgehead to the kingside on f4. White cannot stop ... Nf4 and ... Bg4. He can play dxc6 immediately, but this doesn't stop the kingside attack and it doesn't permit White to win the c-pawn for many moves.

16	Qc2	Bg4
17	dxc6	bxc6
18	Ne2?!	

White can keep his kingside uncorrupted with 18 Be2, but then Black's knight would remain permanently on f4. The winner of the game gave 18 Be2 Nhf4 19 Bxf4 Nxf4 20 Kh1 (intending Ng1) Bc7 21 Ng1 Bd7 22 Na4 Ne6 or 20 ... Nxe2 21 Qxe2 Bc5 as examples of ways Black's energetic play could continue.

| 18 | ... | Bxf3 |
| 19 | gxf3 | Nf6! |

With this Black prepares to weaken White's kingside black squares further with ... h5-h4. The next series of moves was consistent: *20 Qc1 Nh7   21 Rd3 h5   22 h3 Ng5   23 Kg2 h4   24 Bh2 Qf6   25 Rfd1 Kh7   26 Qe3 Bc7   27 Rxd8 Rxd8   28 Rxd8 Qxd8!* (not 28 . . . Bxd8   29 f4! regaining control of f4) *29 Qxa7? Bb6   30 Qa3.*

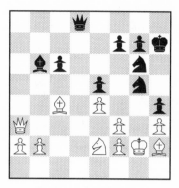

Position after 30 Qa3

Black finished off by completing his exploitation of the kingside black squares: *30 . . . Qd7!   31 Ng1 Qd2   32 Ne2 Qe1!* and now *33 Bg1 Nxh3!   34 Kxh3 Qf1+   35 Kh2* (or 35 Kg4 Qg2+   36 Kh5 Nf4+   37 Nxf4 g6+) *35 . . . Bxf2 36 f4 Nxf4   37 Qf3 Bg3+* White resigns.

A good illustration of White's strategy can be found at the end of the chapter as *Supplemental Game #3*.

Stopping . . . e5

When Black has made inaccurate moves that delay . . . e5 White has good reason to stop the break altogether with e4-e5 or f2-f4. This requires great caution because after either of these moves Black has the potential to strike back effectively with . . . c5.

If Black delays in moving . . . c5 he is likely to be crushed;
e.g., Pillsbury–Burn, Hastings 1895:

1 d4 d5   2 c4 e6   3 Nc3 Nf6   4 Bg5 Be7   5 e3 0-0
6 Nf3 b6   7 Rc1 Bb7   8 cxd5 Nxd5   9 Bxe7 Qxe7
10 Nxd5 Bxd5   11 Bd3 Rc8   12 e4 Bb7   13 0-0
Nd7   14 Qe2   a6?   15 Rc3   c6?   16 Rfc1   b5
17 Qe3 Rc7   18 Qf4 Rac8

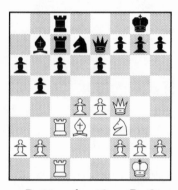

Position after 18 . . . Rac8

Black's play has been methodical but too slow. He could
have played . . . e5 or . . . c5 earlier, but he wanted to stop
White from exploiting queenside holes with Ba6. Now he is
ready for . . . c5. But his negligence encourages 19 e5! with a
threat of the ancient Bxh7+ sacrifice.

Black should now decide to take precautions with 19 . . . h6,
although White would retain his advantage with Nd2-e4-d6.
But Black remained consistent and this was fatal: 19 . . . c5?
20 Bxh7+! Kxh7   21 Ng5+ Kg8   22 Rh3 Qe8   23 Qh4 Kf8
24 Nh7+ Kg8   25 Nf6+ and won in a few moves.

A remarkable illustration of the f2-f4 plan is
Taimanov–Novak, Harrachov 1966:

1 d4 Nf6   2 c4 e6   3 Nc3 Bb4   4 e3 Nc6   5 Ne2
d5   6 a3 Bf8?!   7 Ng1!? dxc4   8 Bxc4 Bd6

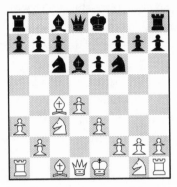

Position after 8 . . . Bd6

After the bizarre retreats in the opening Black is ready
for . . . e5. Although he has a piece instead of a pawn on c6,
the . . . e5 break is still indicated. The reason White developed his king knight backward to g1 instead of forward to f4
was 9 f4!!, a move that assured him of a mighty pawn center.
Black had no chance for . . . e5, and it would take several
moves to play . . . c5 (e.g., 9 . . . Na5   10 Ba2 c5?   11 dxc5
and b4).

Black proceeded routinely with 9 . . . 0-0   10 Nf3 b6
11 e4 Be7   12 e5 Nd5   13 Nxd5 exd5   14 Bd3, and he
was soon lost after 14 . . . Bg4   15 Be3 Qd7   16 Rc1 Na5?
17 h3 Bf5 (or 17 . . . Bh5   18 g4 or 17 . . . Bxf3   18 Qxf3
c6   19 f5) 18 Bxf5 Qxf5   19 Rxc7.

See *Supplemental Game #4* for Black's . . . c5 in its best light.
After White plays e4-e5 and Black undermines the center
with . . . c5 and cxd4, White's e-pawn is weak.

Black's . . . c5 Break

Although . . . e5 is Black's most interesting stroke in the Slav formation, he can also attack the center with his c-pawn. In the Queen's Gambit Accepted and several Slav Defense variations the move . . . c5 is part of an overall queenside advance that includes . . . b5.

After . . . c5 the pawn structure can resolve itself into symmetry (with dxc5, for example) or into an isolated d-pawn game (after Black plays . . . cxd4 and White recaptures on d4 with his pawn on e3). But there are two special cases to be considered here.

The first is d4-d5 by White, a move that seeks to exploit White's superiority in the center before Black's queenside majority becomes a factor. Here Black can again establish a center blockade with . . . e5 after d4-d5, or he can capture d5 and try to minimize the effect of the open center. This is the case in the Queen's Gambit Accepted after *1 d4 d5 2 c4 dxc4 3 Nf3 Nf6 4 e3 e6 5 Bxc4 c5 6 0-0 a6 7 Nc3 b5 8 Bb3 Bb7 9 Qe2 Nbd7 10 Rd1 Qb8*

Position after 10 . . . Qb8

Black put his queen on b8 so that it wouldn't be embarrassed by an opened center (as it would, for example, on c7 following ... cxd4 or dxc5). A game Boleslavsky–Dzhindzhikhashvili, U.S.S.R. 1967, continued from the diagram *11 d5! exd5 12 Nxd5 Nxd5 13 Bxd5 Bxd5 14 Rxd5 Qb7 15 e4.* Black has problems completing his development after *15 . . . Be7 16 Bg5!* because *16 . . . Bxg5* would be met by *17 Rad1! Nb6 18 Rxg5* with dominating rooks for White.

In the game Black tried *16 . . . Nb6* first. White played *17 Rad1!* anyway with the idea of *17 . . . Nxd5 18 exd5* threatening d5-d6 (e.g., *18 . . . f6 19 d6 fxg5 20 Re1 Rd8 21 Qe6! Rd7 22 Nxg5* winning). Black refused the offer with the lame *17 . . . h6* and lost to a pretty series of hammerblows: *18 Bxe7 Nxd5 19 Bxc5 Ne7 20 Ne5 Rc8 (20 . . . Rd8 21 Rxd8+ and 22 Nxf7+) 21 Rd7 Rc7 22 Rd8+!! Kxd8 23 Nxf7+ Kd7 24 Qg4+ Kc6 (or 24 . . . Ke8 25 Nd6+) 25 Qe6+,* and Black resigned in face of *25 . . . Kxc5 26 Qd6+* and mates. (See also *Supplemental Game #5*).

The second interesting feature of ... c5 is an option of Black's: he can advance his c-pawn to the fourth rank, establishing a queenside majority. This is very double edged because White can use his two strong center pawns as battering rams with d4-d5 or e4-e5.

This frequently comes up in another variation of the Queen's Gambit Accepted:

**1 d4 d5   2 c4 dxc4   3 Nf3 Nf6   4 e3 e6   5 Bxc4 c5
6 0-0 a6   7 Qe2   Nc6   8 Rd1   b5   9 Bb3   c4!?
10 Bc2 Nb4!**

Position after 10 . . . Nb4!

Black has less to fear than normally after 10 . . . Nb4 because he will play . . . Nxc2 and . . . Bb7 to control e4. For example, after *11 e4 Nxc2 12 Qxc2 Bb7 13 d5* he can play *13 . . . Qc7!* (better than 13 . . . exd5 14 Nc3 Be7 15 e5!, which gives White a strong initiative after 15 . . . Nd7 16 Nxd5 0-0 17 Qf5). There is no great danger to Black after 14 dxe6 fxe6 (15 Nd4 Kf7) because White's good attacking piece, his king bishop, has been exchanged and the center will remain semiclosed, and if White permits a closed blockade with 14 a4 e5!, Black will quickly take over the black squares, such as c5.

An illustration of the advantage of Black's queenside majority and of the weakness of White's center is Evans–Bisguier, U.S. Open 1950: *14 Bg5 Nd7 15 dxe6 fxe6 16 a4 Bb4 17 axb5 axb5 18 Rxa8+ Bxa8 19 Nc3 Bxc3!*

Position after 19 . . . Bxc3!

Black would have a solid edge after 20 bxc3 0-0 and . . .
Nc5-d3. Black's weak e-pawn is unexploitable, but White's e-
pawn and his queenside can be under continuous attack.
White chose apparently aggressive moves, *20 Qxc3 0-0
21 Be7 Re8   22 Bd6 Qc6   23 e5*, but after *23 . . . Nc5
24 Qe3 Nd3   25 b3 Qe4!* Black had a clearly superior
endgame. This proved to be sufficient after *26 Qxe4 Bxe4
27 Nd4 c3   28 f3 Bg6   29 Ra1 Rc8   30 Kf1 h5   31 Ne2
c2   32 Nc1   Kh7!   33 Ke2   Ra8!   34 Rxa8   Nxc1+
35 Ke3 Nd3!   36 Ba3 b4   37 Bb2 Nxb2.*

White Plays e2-e3, Not e2-e4

The basic Slav formation we've concentrated on so far has
White's two center pawns at d4 and e4. Frequently, however,

e2-e4 is delayed. When White has played e2-e3 and Black has continued . . . e5, the square e4 can become a battleground upon which the fate of the middlegame is decided. If Black succeeds in advancing his pawn to e4 he can obtain an attacking wedge directed at the White kingside (as explained further in Chapter 5); on the other hand, the Black pawn at e4 can become a target. A demonstration of an effective . . . e4 is Dus-Chotimirsky–Fahrni, Karlsbad 1911:

> 1 d4 d5   2 c4 c6   3 Nc3 Nf6   4 Nf3 e6   5 e3 Nbd7
> 6 Be2   Bd6   7 0-0   0-0   8 Qc2   dxc4   9 Bxc4   e5
> 10 Rd1 Qe7

Position after 10 . . . Qe7

After 11 e4 exd4   12 Nxd4 Nb6 we have play along the lines of the Alekhine game mentioned a few pages ago. If White doesn't want to play e3-e4 he should do something about the threat of 11 . . . e4   12 Ng5 Bxh2+.

White's choice was *11 h3!?*, and there followed *11 . . . e4 12 Ng5 Nb6   13 Bb3 Bf5*. Black has excellent piece play, the use of d5 for minor pieces, and a dangerous threat (. . . h6) which forces the following exchange: *14 f3 Rae8   15 Ngxe4 Nxe4   16 Nxe4 Bxe4   17 Qxe4 Qxe4   18 fxe4 Rxe4.*

White suddenly has two pawns alone in the center, but they can become targets. He should continue 19 Bc2 Re7 20 e4, liberating his queen bishop at the cost of permitting Black to use his slight initiative with a subsequent . . . c5. However, White tried *19 Rf1* and had inadequate compensation for a pawn after *19 . . . c5!   20 Bd2 cxd4   21 exd4 Rxd4   22 Bc3 Rf4.* Black eventually won.

The battle for e4 becomes clearer in the following example: Maroczy–Romih, San Remo 1930:

1 d4 d5   2 Nf3 Nf6   3 c4 c6   4 e3 e6   5 Nc3 Bb4 6 Bd3 0-0   7 Qc2 Nbd7   8 0-0 Qe7   9 Bd2 dxc4 10 Bxc4 Bd6   11 Bd3

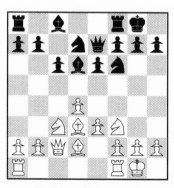

Position after 11 Bd3

Here 11 . . . c5 is out of character since White would be the first to benefit from the opening of queenside lines (e.g.,

12 Rac1 b6   13 Ne4 or 12 . . . cxd4 13 exd4 Nb6   14 Nb5. Black played the natural 11 . . . e5   12 h3 Re8.

But White's 13 Ng5! stopped the immediate . . . e4. Black could open up the e-file with 13 . . . exd4   14 exd4 but would have to cede control of it after 15 Rfe1. It is in Black's interest to keep the center closed until he has completed development; so he challenged White for control of e4 with 13 . . . h6   14 Nge4 Bc7   15 Rae1 Nxe4   16 Nxe4 Nf6.

Black still didn't have time for . . . e4, however. If he had played 16 . . . f5 his f-pawn would become very weak after 17 Ng3. This skirmish for control of e4 has been won by White who now converted the structure into a more familiar one with 17 Nxf6+ Qxf6   18 Bc3! Qh4   19 dxe5 Bxe5   20 Bxe5 Rxe5   21 . . . f4!. The rest of the game was the familiar story of the mobile White kingside: 21 . . . Re8   22 Kh2 Bd7   23 Qc3 Rad8   24 e4 Bc8   25 Re3 Qe7   26 e5 Qd7   27 Rd1 Qe7   28 Rde1 Qh4   29 Rf1 Qe7   30 Bb1! Rd5   31 Qc2 g6   32 Rg3 Kf8   33 Qe2 Qb4   34 Bxg6! fxg6   35 Rxg6 Ke7   36 Qh5 Kd8   37 Qxh6 Qxb2   38 e6 Rh8   39 e7+! Ke8   40 Re1! Rd2   41 Qh5 Rxg2+   42 Rxg2+ Rxh5   43 Rxb2 Rxh3+   44 Kg1 Rh7   45 Rh2 Rg7+   46 Kf2 Rg8   47 Rh6 Kf7   48 e8Q+ Rxe8   49 Rh7+ Resigns. (See also *Supplemental Game #6*).

Supplemental Games

(1)White breaks with d4-d5 in the center when Black plays passively. Botvinnik–Tsvetkov, Moscow 1947: 1 c4 Nf6 2 d4 e6   3 g3 d5   4 Bg2 Be7   5 Nf3 0-0   6 0-0 dxc4 7 Qc2 Nbd7   8 Nbd2 Nb6 (Black should strive for . . . c5) 9 Nxc4 Nxc4   10 Qxc4 Rb8   11 Bf4 Nd5   12 Bd2 Bd7

13 Ne5 Be8 14 Rac1 c6 15 Rfd1 f6 16 Nd3 Bf7
17 Qc2! Bd6 18 e4 Nc7 19 Be3 (White begins a diver-
sionary attack on the queenside that will make a subsequent
e4-e5 or d4-d5 decisive) 19 ... Qe8 20 a4 a6 21 Qc3!
Bg6 22 Qa5 (threatening e4-e5) Rf7 23 Nf4! Rd7
24 Nxg6 Qxg6 25 Qb6 (threatening 26 e5 Bf8 27 Bxc6)
25 ... Qh5 26 Qb3! (and finally with two threats, d4-d5
and Rxc6) Rdd8 27 d5 exd5 28 Ba7 Rbc8 29 Qxb7 f5
30 exd5 Resigns.

**(2) White plays d4-d5 and Black puts pawns at e5 and c5.
White breaks the blockade.** Polugaevsky–Biyiasas, Petropolis 1973: 1 d4 Nf6 2 c4 e6 3 Nf3 d5 4 Nc3 c6 5 e3
Nbd7 6 Bd3 dxc4 7 Bxc4 b5 8 Bd3 a6 9 e4 c5
10 d5 e5 11 b3 Bd6 12 0-0 0-0 13 Re1! Rb8
14 Bf1! Re8 15 a4! b4? (For better or worse, Black should
sacrifice a pawn with 15 ... c4 16 axb5 axb5 17 bxc4 b4
and later ... Nc5. Now White can occupy c4 and destroy the
blockade at d6.) 16 Nb1 Nb6 17 Nbd2 Re7 18 Bb2
Ne8 19 Rc1 f6 20 a5 Na8 21 Nc4 Rc7 22 Nfd2 Bd7
23 f4! Qe7 24 fxe5 fxe5 25 Nxd6 Nxd6 26 Nc4 Nxc4
27 Bxc4, and Black resigned because 27 ... Qd6, to stop 28
d6, would walk into 28 Bxe5 Qxe5 29 d6+.

**(3) White weakens Black's pawns with d5xc6 and wins one
of them in the ending.** Petrov– Stahlberg, Kemeri 1937: 1 d4
d5 2 c4 c6 3 Nc3 Nf6 4 Nf3 e6 5 Bg5 h6 6 Bxf6
Qxf6 7 Qb3 dxc4 8 Qxc4 Nd7 9 e4 e5 10 d5 Nb6
11 Qb3 Bc5 12 Be2 0-0 13 0-0 Bg4 14 Rac1 Rfd8
15 Nd1! (now he is ready to play 16 dxc6 and 17 Ne3 with
a strong queenside attack) Bxf3 16 Qxf3! Qxf3 17 Bxf3

Nd7   18 dxc6 bxc6   19 Bg4 Bb6   20 Rxc6 Nf6   21 Bf3
Rd2 (Black has substantial compensation)   22 a4! Rad8
23 b4 R8d4   24 Rc8+ Kh7   25 a5 Bd8   26 Ne3! Rxb4
27 Nd5 Rxd5? (27 ... Bxa5   28 Nxb4 Bxb4   29 Rc7 a5
30 Rxf7 a4 holds out better chances)   28 exd5 Bxa5
29 Rd1 Rb2   30 Kf1 Bb6   31 Be2 Ne4   32 Rc6! (so that
White wins after 32 ... Bxf2 33 Bd3 or 32 ... Nxf2
33 Rxb6)   32 ... Bd4   33 d6 Nf6   34 Rc7 Rb6
35 Rxd4! exd4   36 Bd3+ g6   37 Rxf7+ Resigns.

(4) White's e5 is refuted by Black's . . . c5. Taimanov–Geller,
Leningrad 1963: 1 d4 d5   2 c4 dxc4   3 Nf3 Nf6   4 Qa4+
c6   5 Qxc4 Bf5   6 g3 Nbd7   7 Bg2 e6   8 0-0 Be7
9 Qb3 Qb6   10 Nbd2 0-0   11 Re1 Rfd8   12 Qa4 a5
13 e4 Bg6   14 a3? Qa7! (preparing a general pawn advance
on the queenside, the side of the board where Black's pieces
are superior)   15 e5? Nd5   16 Ne4 c5! (now the e-pawn is
the target)   17 Bg5 cxd4   18 Bxe7 Nxe7   19 Qxd4 Qxd4
20 Nxd4 Nxe5   21 Nc5 Nd3   22 Nxd3 Bxd3   23 Bxb7
Rab8   24 Nc6   Nxc6   25 Bxc6 Rxb2   26 Re5   Bb1!
27 Rxa5 Rd1+   28 Kg2 g6   29 Bf3 Rdd2   30 Kg1 Ba2
31 Rf1 Bc4   32 Rc1 Rxf2   33 Be4 Bd5   34 Bxd5 exd5
35 Rd1 Rg2+   36 Kf1 Rbf2+   37 Ke1 Ra2   38 Kf1 Rxh2
White resigns.

(5) White answers . . . c5 with a strong d4-d5. Alekhine–H.
Steiner, Bradley Beach 1929: 1 d4 d5   2 c4 dxc4   3 Nf3
Nf6   4 e3   e6   5 Bxc4 c5   6 0-0 a6   7 Qe2 Nbd7?
8 Nc3 Qc7   9 d5! (this obtains a lasting initiative because
9 . . . e5 can be met by 10 Ng5 Bd6   11 a4 Nb6   12 Nge4
with strong play) 9 . . . exd5   10 Bxd5! (better to have a
knight than a bishop on d5 after an exchange of pieces) Bd6

11 e4 0-0   12 Bg5 Ng4?   13 h3 Nge5   14 Nh4! (White's attack with his f-pawn decides) Nb6   15 f4 Nc6   16 f5! Ne5   17 Qh5 Re8   18 Rf4 Be7   19 f6 Bf8   20 fxg7 Bxg7   21 Raf1   Be6   22 Nf5   Bxd5   23 Nxg7!   Ng6 24 Nxe8 Rxe8   25 Nxd5 Resigns.

(6) White wins the battle for e4 and mobilizes his majority. Smyslov–Hort, Leipzig 1960: 1 d4 d5   2 c4 e6   3 Nf3 Nf6 4 Bg5 Be7   5 e3 Nbd7   6 Nc3 0-0   7 Rc1 c6   8 Qc2 Re8   9 a3 dxc4?! (better is 9 . . . a6 preparing for a later . . . dxc4   and   . . .   b5)   10 Bxc4 Nd5   11 Bxe7   Qxe7 12 Ne4 h6? (Loses time. Better is 12 . . . N5f6 to contest e4.) 13 0-0   b6   14 Ba2   Bb7   15 Bb1   N5f6   16 Ng3   g6 17 e4 e5   18 Qd2! Qf8   19 dxe5! Nxe5   20 Nxe5 Rxe5 21 f4   Re7   22 e5   Rd8   23 Qc3   Nd5   24 Qb3   h5 25 Ne4 Qh6   26 Rcd1 Rf8   27 Nd6 Kh7   28 f5 Ba6 29 Rfe1 Nf4   30 Qf3 Rd8   31 Nxf7! Rxd1   32 Rxd1 Be2   33 fxg6+   Nxg6   34 Nxh6 Bxf3   35 gxf3 Kxh6 36 Rd6 Resigns.

THE OPEN
SICILIAN-ENGLISH

IT IS HARDLY A SECRET TODAY THAT THE ENGLISH OPENING AND its brother, the Sicilian Defense, are enormously popular with both masters and amateurs. In 1993, for example, 467 games were played at the Biel interzonal tournament leading to the world championship. More than a quarter of the games (118) began with either 1c4 or 1 e4 c5.

"It is no exaggeration to say that Black's middlegame plan is clear from the very first move of the Sicilian Defense," Harry Golombek once wrote. Once the center is open (after 1 e4 c5 2 Nf3 d6 3 d4 cxd4 or 1 c4 e5 2 Nc3 Nf6 3 g3 d5 4 cxd5 Nxd5, for instance) one side has an e-pawn on the fourth rank, a half-open d-file, and a slight initiative in the center. His opponent has a half-open c-file and a potentially broader center. If Black survives the middlegame he is often better placed for the ending. Bent Larsen has even suggested that d2-d4 by White in a Sicilian is a positional error—giving up a center pawn for one less useful.

A. THE SCHEVENINGEN FORMATION

Of the major structures of the open English or Sicilian games, by far the most common is one in which Black (the one who plays . . . c5) posts his central pawns at e6 and d6. This eases his development and, unlike the structures in succeeding pages, denies White free control of e5 and d5.

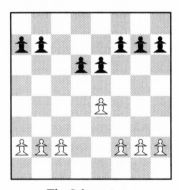

The Scheveningen

The complex middlegames that arise out of the popular Najdorf variation, the sharp Richter-Rauzer and Sozin systems, the solid Scheveningen variation, and other Sicilian subsections are built upon a few thematic ideas. White's fundamental pawn-based plans are e4-e5 (the attacking break), f4-f5 (the strategic fight for d5), and g4-g5 (the kingside pawn storm). Black's options include . . . b5-b4 (queenside counterplay and indirect attack on White's e-pawn), . . . d5 (center counterplay), and . . . e5 (a blockading thrust).

Each of these ideas can be good or bad depending on other circumstances—and this is why the Sicilian-English positions are so difficult to play. Timing is much more important than in the structurally solid Caro-Slav formation. One bad move in the Caro-Slav by Black can delay his liberation for many moves; but one bad move in a Sicilian can be immediately fatal—for either player.

The basic theme of the Sicilian Defense is that White obtains an initiative and an advantage in space in exchange for a central pawn (. . . cxd4). Black has excellent chances for counterplay along the c-file and on the queenside generally. Black may also have superior chances in the ending because of his majority of pawns in the center. White can force the tempo of the game but must be aware of his limitations.

One of the earliest Scheveningen formations—having taken place 60 years before the Dutch tournament from which we get the name of the structure—was Hannah–Anderssen, London 1862:

1 e4 c5   2 Nf3 e6   3 d4 cxd4   4 Nxd4 Nf6   5 Bd3?
Nc6   6 Be3 d5!   7 Nd2 Bd6   8 0-0 0-0   9 f4?

Position after 9 f4?

Black's majority of pawns in the center already gives him the initiative, and within a few moves he can claim a decisive position: *9 . . . Bc5 10 c3 e5! 11 Nc2* (11 fxe5 Nxe5 12 Bc2 Neg4 13 Bg5 Qb6) *11 . . . Bxe3+ 12 Nxe3 Qb6 13 Qe1 Ng4 14 Rf3 exf4* and wins a piece.

This indicates another feature of the Scheveningen. White frequently advances his f-pawn two squares to make his center work for him (with e4-e5 or f4-f5). But that advance undermines pawn support for his e-pawn and it weakens the diagonal that leads to g1, a square usually reserved for White's king.

Before examining specific plans we should take note of a common positional error that increases Black's central majority. There are occasions when it pays White to exchange a minor piece on c6. In these instances, Black has not played . . . d6 yet, and thus White can play e4-e5 effectively. For example, 1 e4 c5 2 Nf3 Nc6 3 d4 cxd4 4 Nxd4 e6 5 Nc3 a6 6 Nxc6 bxc6 7 e5! favors White slightly because Black will almost surely play . . . d6 and accept a weak queenside after exd6. But this is not the case *after* . . . d6 as the following diagram shows.

Spielmann–Euwe, Bad Kissingen 1928: *1 e4 c5 2 Nf3 Nc6 3 d4 cxd4 4 Nxd4 Nf6 5 Nc3 d6 6 Be2 e6 7 0-0 Be7 8 Be3 0-0 9 Qd2 a6*

Position after 9 . . . a6

White chose a discredited plan, the exploitation of Black's minor weaknesses on the queenside: *10 Nxc6? bxc6   11 Rfd1 Qc7   12 f3* and now *12 . . . d5!*. Black obtains an easy game with . . . Bb7, . . . Rd8, and . . . e5, whereas White's queenside attack runs out of steam. Black had a dynamic game after *13 exd5 cxd5   14 Qe1 Rb8   15 Rab1 Bd6   16 g3 Bb7   17 Bf2 e5 18 Rd2 d4   19 Nd1 Ng4!* because of his tremendous center.

White's Options: e4-e5

The most disruptive break White can achieve is e4-e5. This is double edged because it may lead to a weak e-pawn if White loses the initiative, but the opening of lines and the forced retreat of Black's knight from f6 are usually worth the risk. A model example of White's domination after e4-e5 is Parma–Larsen, Teesside 1972:

1 e4 e6   2 d4 c5   3 Nf3 cxd4   4 Nxd4 Nf6   5 Nc3 d6   6 Be2 Nc6   7 Be3 Bd7   8 0-0 a6   9 a4 Be7 10 f4 0-0   11 Nb3 Na5

Position after 11 . . . Na5

White has stopped Black's most natural source of counter-play, . . . b5-b4, and threatened 12 a5, which would have weakened Black's control of black squares. Black stopped this but now permits *12 e5!*; e.g., *12 . . . dxe5 13 fxe5 Ne8 14 Nxa5 Qxa5 15 Qxd7* or *12 . . . Nxb3 13 exf6* winning material.

Black had to retreat with *12 . . . Ne8 13 Nxa5 Qxa5 14 Qd2 Qc7* (to avoid *15 b4 Qxb4 16 Nd5! Qxd2 17 Nxe7+*) *15 Bd4*.

Position after 15 Bd4

This is a dangerous position for Black because White can exploit the d-file if it is opened and because 15 . . . d5, closing the position, would leave Black without any counterplay against a kingside attack (e.g., 16 Qe3 Rc8 17 Bd3 Bc5 18 Ne2 and 19 Rf3). Although it is very risky to open up the side of the board on which your opponent has greater strength, the best idea here is probably 15 . . . f6.

Black played *15 . . . dxe5 16 fxe5 Bc5*, and after *17 Ne4! Bxd4+ 18 Qxd4 Bc6 19 Rad1* White had an overwhelming game and went on to convert his advantage into a win-

ning endgame with *19 . . . Qa5   20 Nc5! Qc7   21 a5 g6*
(*21 . . . Qxa5   22 Nxe6 fxe6   23 Rxf8+* leads to a killing
attack along the f-file) *22 b4 Ng7   23 Qd6 Qxd6   24 exd6.*

Black need not play . . . d5 or . . . dxe5 after e4-e5, but he
then faces the prospect of a thorough liquidation of the center
after f4-f5. See *Supplemental Game #1* at the end of this section.

The most obvious problems for White after e4-e5 are the
isolation of his e-pawn (see *Supplemental Game #2*) and the
opening of lines that lead to his own king rather than to
Black's. The latter theme is graphically shown by Zinn–Monti,
Budva 1963:

**1 e4 c5   2 Nf3 d6   3 d4 cxd4   4 Nxd4 Nf6   5 Nc3
a6   6 Bc4 e6   7 0-0 Be7   8 Bb3 0-0   9 Be3 Nc6
10 f4 Bd7   11 Kh1 Nxd4   12 Bxd4 Bc6   13 Qe2
Qc7**

Position after 13 . . . Qc7

White would be wise to play 14 f5 so that he can later occupy d5 square after . . . e5 or . . . exf5. White's *14 e5?* was fur-

ther mishandled after *14 . . . Nd7   15 Rae1 dxe5   16 fxe5 Nc5* by *17 Bxc5?*, a move designed to leave White free to attack Black's castled position with his rooks and queen.

But White has a king too, and he discovered how vulnerable it was—and how secure Black's was—after *17 . . . Bxc5 18 Rf4 Rad8   19 Rh4 Rd4   20 Rh3 Rfd8   21 Qh5 Rd2!!.*

Position after 21 . . . Rd2!!

White's attack is based on heavy pieces, and they have succeeded in crippling h7; but Black's counterattack, based on bishops that sweep the board, is more dangerous, Black's king can escape check; White's cannot.

The White attack died in three moves, *22 Qxh7+ Kf8 23 Qh8+ Ke7   24 Qh4+ Ke8*, and Black took over: *25 Ne4 Qxe5 26 Nxd2 Rxd2! 27 Rf3   Bxf3   28 gxf3 Rxh2+ 29 Qxh2 Qxe1+*. Black won another pawn and traded queens into a simple endgame. Black's spectacular bishops, which could have administered the final mate after *27 Rxe5 Bxg2*, enjoyed their freedom only after f2-f4 and e4-e5.

White's Options: f4-f5

The strategic objective of f4-f5 is to eradicate Black's pawn control of d5. If White can force . . . e5, for example, and use his minor pieces to restrain . . . d5, he will have time to pursue a kingside attack with g4-g5. Once the strategic task is accomplished, timing can be slowed since Black's counterplay is minimal.

This is the lesson of Hennings–McCurdy, Harrachov 1967:

1 e4 c5   2 Nf3 d6   3 d4 cxd4   4 Nxd4 Nf6   5 Nc3
a6   6 Bc4   e6   7 Bb3   Be7   8 f4   0-0   9 f5   e5
10 Nde2 Nbd7   11 Ng3 b5   12 Bg5! Bb7   13 Bxf6!
Nxf6   14 Nh5! Nxh5   15 Qxh5   Rc8   16 Qe2 Qb6
17 0-0-0 Rc5   18 Nd5 Bxd5   19 Bxd5 Rfc8   20 c3

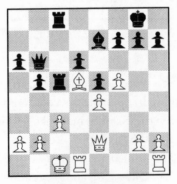

Position after 20 c3

White has a positionally won game because Black has no counterplay with which to interrupt a well-coordinated kingside 'attack. Note White's moves 12–14, the series that resolved the position into one in which White has an all-seeing bishop on d5 and Black has a passive one on e7. It doesn't matter much where White's king is placed, kingside or queenside, since White can keep all files closed except the ones he wants opened. If Black plays . . . b4, White locks the position with c3-c4.

The game proceeded *20 . . . R5c7   21 h4! a5   22 Kb1 a4 23 a3! Bf8   24 g4 Kh8   25 g5 f6* (otherwise White plays f5-f6 h4-h5, and Rhf1) 26 *Rhg1 Be7   27 Rg3 Rf8   28 Rdg1 Qb8   29 Qd2 Bd8   30 Ka1 Qa7   31 Be6 Qb6   32 Rd1 Be7   33 Rd3 Qc6.* White could shift his pieces back and forth for another dozen moves without fear of interruption, but he found the decisive plan, Qh5 and Bg6. The game ended prettily after *34 Qe2! Qb6   35 Qh5 Qb8   36 Bf7! fxg5 37 Bg6! h6   38 hxg5 Bxg5   39 Qxg5!* because Black is mated following 39 . . . hxg5   40 Rh1+ and 41 Rdh3.

The opposite side of this coin is shown by *Supplemental Game #3* in which the backwardness of White's e-pawn after f4-f5 is turned to Black's advantage.

White's Options: g4-g5

When White pushes up his most protective kingside pawn he takes the greatest risks. Siegbert Tarrasch, the great German master of the turn-of-the-century tournaments, often called g4-g5 the "harikari move." This advance is often misunderstood. A beginning player sometimes mistakes g4-g5 for a desperate bid for attack. If White mates quickly, he believes, the idea is a success; otherwise it is a failure.

But g4-g5 is also a strategic device. It removes Black's king knight from the square (f6) that most effectively permits it to attack White's center and to liberate Black's game (with . . . d5). Black will have to think twice about . . . e5 after g4-g5 because then the squares d5 and f5 will be available to White's attacking pieces.

To appreciate this, examine the following (Smyslov–Hort, Petropolis 1973). It was expertly handled by a mature grandmaster not known for his gambling attacks. The game began with *1 e4 c5   2 Nf3 e6   3 d4 cxd4   4 Nxd4 Nf6   5 Nc3 d6   6 Be2 Be7   7 0-0 a6   8 f4 0-0   9 Be3 Qc7   10 a4! b6   11 Bf3 Bb7   12 Qe1 Nbd7?!   13 Bf2 Rac8*.

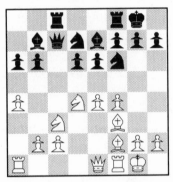

Position after 13 . . . Rac8

Two special features of the position make g2-g4 attractive. Black's queenside has been stilled by a2-a4, and he has chosen to develop his queen knight at d7. The trouble with the latter is that it denies the d7 square as a retreat for the other knight. Thus, when White played *14 g4!* Black's pieces became confused: *14 . . . Nc5   15 g5 Nfd7   16 Rd1*. White is already threatening to win a piece with 17 b4 Nb3   18 Nde2.

This set the pace for further retreats, which permitted White to take his time in developing an attack: *16 . . . Nb8*

17 Be3 Nc6   18 Qg3 Rfe8   19 Bg2 Bf8   20 Rf2 Qd7. In the final stage White played *21 Nf3!* intending to maneuver this piece to g4 where it would threaten e5, f6, and h6.

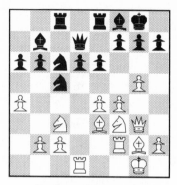

Position after 21 Nf3!

Black made one more error, *21 . . . Nb4*, and the White attack was unstoppable: *22 Ne5! Qc7   23 Ng4 Nd7   24 Bd4!* (threatening 25 Nh6+!) *e5   25 fxe5 Nxe5   26 Rdf1 Re7   27 Bxe5 dxe5   28 Nf6+ Kh8   29 Nxh7! Re6* (29 . . . Kxh7 30 g6+ Kg8   31 gxf7+ or 30 . . . fxg6   31 Rxf8) *30 Rxf7 Bc5+   31 Kh1 Re7   32 Rf8+* and Black resigned.

Black's Queenside Counterplay

Although many players regard the Sicilian Defense as a 20th-century weapon, the opening gained a brief period of popularity in the middle of the last century. But in those days the positions remained closed. White did not exchange his d-pawn for Black's c-pawn—or make any pawn exchanges—in the first dozen moves. Instead, White's army of pawns swept forward on the kingside while Black's pawns, like von Moltke's troops in August 1914, expanded on the right hand (see Chapter 10).

In the open Sicilian-English formations the pawn storm is occasionally seen on White's kingside (g4-g5) but is a regular feature of Black's queenside. The queenside play should belong to Black simply because of his use of the half-open c-file and because White is more concerned with his e-pawn. It is because of Black's superiority on the queenside that White usually turns to attack. Passivity is death, as the following game (Wotulo–Larsen, Manila 1973) shows.

White made a crucial error very early, *1 e4 c5   2 Nf3 e6 3 d4 cxd4   4 Nxd4 Nf6   5 Nc3 d6   6 Be2 a6   7 Be3 Qc7 8 0-0?* and found that he had to defend his e-pawn in the most restricting manner: *8. . . b5!   9 a3 Bb7   10 f3 Be7 11 Qe1 Nbd7   12 Qg3 0-0   13 Rad1 Kh8   14 Kh1 Rac8 15 Nb3.*

Position after 15 Nb3

Without f3-f4 White cannot engineer any of the middlegame plans mentioned earlier in this chapter. The course of the game turns to Black's queenside initiative, and Black began with *15 . . . Ba8!* He intends to bring a knight to c4 and, if it is captured, to recapture with the b-pawn so that he can use the b-file that he has just cleared. White couldn't stop this idea, but he shouldn't have encouraged it with *16 Rd2? Ne5   17 Qf2 Rb8   18 Nd1 Nc4!*.

After *19 Rd3* Black's queenside attack has reached a limit. It is difficult for him to attack any of the White weaknesses on that side of the board without more maneuvering. But the effect of the attack so far has driven White's pieces into an uncoordinated muddle, which is why *19 . . . d5!* is so strong. In the diagram below the extension of Black's queenside empire is obvious.

Position after 19 . . . d5!

In the remainder of the game White's pieces continued to be denied good squares, and Black took his time to mount a kingside attack: *20 exd5 Nxd5   21 Bc1 Ne5   22 Rd2 Bd6   23 c3   Rbd8   24 Rc2 Rd7   25 Qg1   h6   26 Nf2   f5   27 Bd1   Re7   28 Re1   Nc4   29 Nd3   e5   30 Nb4   a5   31 Nxd5 Bxd5   32 Rce2 Rdf7   33 Qf2 Rf6   34 Qh4 Qc6*

35 Qh3   a4   36 Na1   e4   37 f4   Bc5   38 Nc2   Qb6
39 Nb4 Bb7   40 Qg3 Rg6   41 Qh4 Rg4   42 Qh5 Qd8
43 Rd2 Nxd2   44 Bxg4 Bxb4 and White resigned.

Two specific points about . . . b5 should be noted. First, like every pawn move, it has its minuses. It can be attacked by a2-a4 with the result that Black must concede control of his c4 to enemy pieces. The most famous example of . . . b5 being repulsed is *Supplemental Game #4* at the end of this section.

Secondly, while White can delay or stop . . . b5 with a2-a4, this move also creates problems. By advancing his a-pawn White weakens b4, a square well occupied by a bishop or knight. It also makes . . . Ne5-c4 a more dangerous source of Black counterplay.

Black's Central Play: . . . d5

The natural antidote to any overly aggressive ambition by White is the dynamic advance of Black's d-pawn. The advance is also dangerous when White has played passively, as in the Larsen game just mentioned. But it should be remembered that . . . d5 is basically a *counteridea*. (The Larsen game is an exception since White played that opening very passively.) Black must weigh . . . d5 very carefully. When it is unprovoked, . . . d5 can lead to a warped middlegame.

An early example of this lesson was Tchigorin–Paulsen, Berlin 1881, which led to the position below after a normal opening:

1 e4   c5   2 Nf3   Nc6   3 d4   cxd4   4 Nxd4   Qb6
5 Nb3 Nf6   6 Nc3 e6   7 a3 Be7   8 Be2 0-0   9 0-0
a6   10 Qd3 Qc7   11 f4 d6   12 Qg3 Bd7   13 Be3

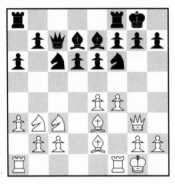

Position after 13 Be3

Black's position calls for—actually it screams for—queenside counterplay with 13 . . . b5 followed by putting rooks at c8 and either d8 or b8. Black, however, followed what appeared to be a logical idea: *13 . . . Rad8? 14 Nd2 d5?* The . . . d5 idea worked in many games in which White had attacked violently, Black may have reasoned. Therefore, the move may be good *before* White launches his attack.

However, . . . d5 actually creates an attack for White. After *15 e5!* Black's best defensive piece on the kingside, his king knight, is pushed back. White has the use of d4 for minor attacking pieces, and he has a closed center that will permit him plenty of time for a slow buildup.

This is exactly what happened: *15 . . . Ne8 16 Nf3 f5 17 Qf2 Qb8 18 Bb6 Rc8 19 Bd3 Nc7 20 Ne2! Na8 21 Be3 Na5 22 b3 b5 23 h4! Nb7 24 b4! Qc7 25 Ned4 Nd8 26 g4! fxg4 27 Ng5 Bxg5 28 hxg5 g6 29 Kg2 Rb8 30 Rh1 Rf7 31 Rh6 Rg7 32 Rah1 Nf7 33 R6h4 Rf8 34 Qg3 Nd8 35 Qxg4 Nb6 36 Rxh7! Rxh7 37 Rxh7 Rf7 (37 . . . Kxh7 38 Qh5+) 38 Rh6 Nc4 39 Rxg6+ Kf8 40 Bf2 Bc8 41 Qh4 Ke7 42 Rg8 Kd7 43 g6 Re7 44 Qxe7+!* and Black resigned.

When Black is provoked, . . . d5 can be very potent. A good rule of thumb for a player with White is to consider whether Black can answer g2-g4 effectively with . . . d5. If Black can't, then g2-g4 is likely to bring White an advantage.

This is shown by Baturinsky–Panov, Moscow 1936, when White underestimates the power of the Black pieces that are shielded from him in the center.

1 e4 c5   2 Nf3 e6   3 d4 cxd4   4 Nxd4 Nf6   5 Nc3
d6   6 Be2 a6   7 a4 Be7   8 0-0 Nc6   9 Kh1 Bd7
10 b3 Qc7   11 Bb2 0-0   12 f4 Rfd8   13 Bf3 Rac8

Position after 13 . . . Rac8

The center is only semiclosed and the heavy strength of Black's pieces only temporarily blocked. White's *14 g4?* was a denial of this. The attack cannot succeed if Black can activate his pieces, which Black did with *14 . . . d5!*.

White's problems are illustrated by 15 e5, which, unlike the Tchigorin–Paulsen game, could now be answered by 15 . . . Ne4! e.g., 16 Nxe4 dxe4   17 Bxe4 Nxd4   18 Bxd4 Bc6 with a virulent counterattack. Note that without g2-g4 this counterstroke could simply be answered by 19 Bxc6.

In the Russian game White accepted the pawn sacrifice in a different manner: *15 exd5 Nxd4! 16 Qxd4 Bc5 17 Qc4 (17 Qd3 Qxf4 or 17 Qd2? Bb4) 17 . . . exd5 18 Nxd5 Nxd5 19 Bxd5 Bc6!*

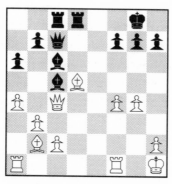

Position after 19 . . . Bc6!

This position is even worse for White than the one arising from 15 e5 Ne4. Black threatens the king along the long diagonal that was opened by g2-g4. White cannot play the natural 20 Rad1 because of 20 . . . Rxd5! 21 Rxd5 Rd8 22 Rd1 Rxd5 23 Rxd5 Qd6!!

White fell back on *20 Bf3*, but then *20 . . . Qd7!* led to an ending in which Black's centralized rooks were decisive: *21 Qc3 (21 h3 Bxf3+ 22 Rxf3 Ba3!) 21 . . . Qxg4 22 Bxc6 Rxc6* (threatening . . . Bd4 and . . . Rg6) *23 Qf3 Qxf3+ 24 Rxf3 Rd2 25 Rd3! Rd6! 26 Rc3 R6d5 27 Re1 f6 28 Re8+ Kf7 29 Rb8 Re2 30 Rxb7+ Ke6 31 Rd3 Rxd3 32 cxd3 Rxb2* White resigns.

Black's . . . e5

This is a relatively new discovery in the Scheveningen formation and is less frequently seen than other attempts at counterplay. But when Black plays . . . e5, usually after exchanging off the White knight on d4 so that the enemy can't respond Nf5, Black achieves several ends: he stops e4-e5; he acquires a share of the center for himself; he turns White's king bishop into an inferior piece whose horizons are limited by his own e-pawn; and he may threaten . . . exf4 thus freeing e5 for a minor piece.

Although the structure after . . . e5 is properly studied under the Boleslavsky Hole formation, one example of the transition from the Scheveningen is appropriate here. It is Mazzoni– Gligoric, Monte Carlo 1967:

1 e4 c5   2 Nf3 d6   3 d4 cxd4   4 Nxd4 Nf6   5 Nc3
e6   6 Be2 Be7   7 0-0 0-0   8 Be3 Nc6   9 f4 Bd7
10 Kh1 a6   11 Bf3 Qc7   12 Qe1 Rac8

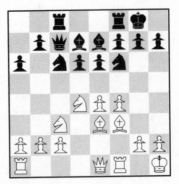

Position after 12 . . . Rac8

Black's last move carries a minor threat. If he had played 12 ... Nxd4 13 Bxd4 e5 immediately, White would have 14 fxe5 dxe5 15 Qg3!, pinning the Black pawn to his queen. Because of the threat White should try 13 Qg3 or 13 Nb3. His routine *13 Rd1?* walked into *13 ... Nxd4! 14 Bxd4 e5 15 fxe5* (15 Be3 Bc6 16 Qg3 is better) *15 ... dxe5 16 Be3 Be6.*

Position after 16 ... Be6

The difference between the diagrams is clear. White's attack is over before it began. Black has plenty of room for counterattack on the queenside. Black's minor pieces are all excellent, but White's bishop on f3 serves the function of a pawn only.

Black handled the next series of moves expertly: *17 Qg3 Kh8 18 Be2 b5 19 Bd3 Rfd8 20 a3 Qb8 21 Ne2 Nd7! 22 Ng1 Nc5.* To keep his pawns healthy White parted with his best minor piece, *23 Bxc5,* and soon found himself in an endgame in which his e-pawn and queenside pawns were under continual assault: *23 ... Rxc5 24 Nf3 Bf6 25 Ng5*

*Bxg5   26 Qxg5 Re8   27 Rd2 Qc7   28 Rfd1 h6   29 Qh4
Qe7!   30 Qxe7 Rxe7   31 Be2 Kh7   32 Kg1 a5.* The end
came quickly: *33 c3 Rb7   34 Rd6 Bb3   35 R1d2 b4!
36 cxb4 axb4   37 Ra6 bxa3   38 bxa3 Bc2   39 Bf3 Rc4
40 Re2 Rb1+   41 Kf2 Bd3!   42 Rd2 Bxe4   43 Ra7 Bxf3*
and White resigned.

Supplemental Games

(1) White plays e4-e5 and f4-f5 to open the kingside.
Shamkovich–Damjanovic, Sochi 1967:   1 e4 c5   2 Nf3 e6
3 Nc3 Nc6   4 d4 cxd4   5 Nxd4 a6   6 Be2 Qc7   7 0-0
Nf6   8 Kh1 Be7   9 f4 d6   10 Be3 0-0   11 Qe1 Bd7
12 Qg3 Kh8 (The freeing idea of . . . e5 can be accomplished
with 12 . . . Nxd4   13 Bxd4 Bc6   14 Bd3 e5!   15 fxe5
Nh5 followed by 16 . . . dxe5.)   13 a3 Rac8   14 Bd3 b5
15 Rae1 Qb8   16 e5! Ng8? (During the 1940s Miguel
Najdorf popularized the . . . Kh8 and . . . Ng8 motif in answer
to e4-e5, but the defensive device fell out of favor because of
the subsequent f4-f5.)   17 Nxc6   Bxc6   18 Bd4!   b4
19 f5!! (This sweeps away the protective pawns. On 19 . . .
exf5 White wins with 20 Rxf5 bxc3 21 exd6 Bf6
22 Qh3 h6 23 Rxf6.)   19 . . .   bxc3 20 f6 Bxf6
21 exf6 g6   22 Bxg6! e5 (22 . . . fxg6   23 f7+ e5
24 Rxe5!)   23 Rxe5 Bxg2+ (23 . . . dxe5   24 Be4)
24 Kxg2 dxe5   25 Be4 Nxf6   26 Bxe5 Resigns.

**(2) White's e4-e5 creates a weak e-pawn and insufficient at-
tacking chances.** Jimenez–Lein, Cienfuegos 1972: 1 e4 c5
2 Nf3 Nc6   3 d4 cxd4   4 Nxd4 Nf6   5 Nc3 d6   6 Bc4
e6   7 Be3 Be7   8 Bb3 0-0   9 0-0 Bd7   10 f4 Nxd4
11 Bxd4 Bc6   12 Qd3 b5!   13 e5 dxe5   14 fxe5 Nd7

15 Ne4 Bxe4!   16 Qxe4 Nc5 (Black has equalized piece play. White should try 17 Qe3 and preserve his slight superiority in the center.)   17 Bxc5?? Bxc5+   18 Kh1 Qd4! (From now on White's e-pawn is a constant target in the ending that Black forces.)   19 Rae1 Qxe4   20 Rxe4 Rad8 21 Re2   b4!   22 Bc4   Bd4!   23 b3   g6   24 g3   Bc3 25 Kg2   Kg7   26 Rf3   Rd1   27 Rd3   Rd8   28 Kf3   h5 29 h4 Kh6   30 Rxd8 Rxd8   31 Bd3 Rd5   32 Kf4 Ra5 33 Re4 Rxa2   34 g4 hxg4   35 Kxg4 Ra1   36 Kf3 Rd1 37 Rf4 Kg7   38 Rg4 Rh1   39 Kg2 Re1   40 h5 Rxe5! 41 hxg6 f5   42 Rg5 Bd2   43 Rg3 Bf4   44 Rh3 Kxg6 45 Rh8 Be3   White resigns.

(3) Black answers f4-f5 . . . e5 but later wins control of d5 to free his game with . . . d5. Bena–Pavlov, Bucharest 1969: 1 e4 c5   2 Nf3 Nc6   3 d4 cxd4   4 Nxd4 Nf6   5 Nc3 d6 6 Bc4 e6   7 0-0 a6   8 Be3 Qc7   9 Bb3 Na5   10 f4 b5! 11 f5 e5! (Black can leave the center fluid with 11 . . . Nxb3 but then 12 cxb3! gives White an excellent game, e.g.   12 . . . Be7   13 Rc1 Qd7   14 Qf3 Bb7   15 Qh3 or 14 . . . 0-0 15 e5   Bb7   16 exf6! Bxf3   17 fxe7 Qxe7   18 Rxf3) 12 Nde2 Bb7   13 Ng3 (On 13 Nd5 Black gets a fine game with 13 . . . Nxd5   14 Bxd5 Nc4!   15 Qc1 Bxd5   16 exd5 Rc8   or   15 Bc1   Bxd5   16 Qxd5 Rc8)   13 . . . Nc4 14 Bxc4 Qxc4   15 Qf3 h5!   16 h4 d5!   17 Nxd5 Nxd5 18 b3 Qc6   19 exd5 Qxd5   20 Qe2 Be7 (Black has a strong   advantage.)   21 Rad1   Qc6   22 Rd2   Rd8!   23 Rxd8+ Kxd8   24 Bg5 Bxg5   25 hxg5 h4   26 Rd1+ Kc8 27 Nf1 h3   28 Ne3 Qb6   29 Qf2 hxg2 White resigns.

(4) Black's premature . . . b5 is repulsed by a2-a4. Smyslov–Kottnauer, Groningen 1946;   1 e4 c5   2 Nf3 d6

3 d4 cxd4 4 Nxd4 Nf6 5 Nc3 a6 6 Be2 e6 7 0-0 b5?
8 Bf3! (Usually this is a clumsy move when it is played before
f2-f4 but here Black is upset by the e4-e5 threat, e.g. 8 . . .
Bb7 9 e5!.) 8 . . . Ra7 9 Qe2 Rc7 10 Rd1 Nbd7
11 a4! bxa4 (Black's queenside also becomes vulnerable after
11 . . . b4 12 Na2 a5 13 Nb5 and a subsequent c2-c3.)
12 Nxa4 Bb7 13 e5! Nxe5 14 Bxb7 Rxb7 15 Qxa6
Qb8 16 Nc6 Nxc6 17 Qxc6+ Nd7 18 Nc5! (A beautiful combination which forces acceptance of the sacrifice
since 18 . . . Rc7 allows 19 Nxd7 Rxd7 20 Ra8.) 18 . . .
dxc5 19 Bf4! Bd6 20 Bxd6 Rb6 21 Qxd7+ Resigns.

B. THE DRAGON FORMATION

The Dragon

If Black's pawn formation in the center and on the kingside in
the diagram doesn't look dragonlike to you, it's not surprising.
The name comes from a constellation, not a monster. One of
the pre-Revolution Russian masters, F. Y. Dus-Chotimirsky, re-
called in his memoirs that in 1901 he was studying astronomy
in Kiev. One day it struck him that the pawns at d6, e7, f7, g6,

and h7 resembled the pattern of Draco the Dragon in the northern sky. The name stuck.

The Dragon formation is among the most popular systems in competitive chess. It appears in both a highly aggressive variation of the Sicilian Defense and in the most natural variations of the open games of the English Opening. Both systems can be reached in different ways. For example, 1 e4 c5 2 Nf3 Nc6 3 d4 cxd4 4 Nxd4 g6 and . . . d6; or 1 e4 c5 2 Nf3 d6 3 d4 cxd4 4 Nxd4 Nf6 5 Nc3 g6; or even 1 Nf3 c5 2 e4 g6 3 d4, etc.

What distinguishes all members of the family is Black's kingside fianchetto. (We'll call him Black for simplicity. In the English Opening, it is of course White who has the Dragon formation.) The bishop at g7 is directed across a center that has been loosened by d2-d4 and . . . cxd4. The queenside is under pressure by that bishop. It is not surprising that Black quickly mounts an attack in the Dragon because of the use of the c-file and his king bishop.

White has three basic ideas: the attack with f2-f4 and kingside castling, the attack with f2-f3 and queenside castling, and the positional plan of occupying d5 with a minor piece.

White's f2-f4 Attack

Unlike the Scheveningen, the Dragon has little to fear from e4-e5. After White's e-pawn advances to the fifth rank and becomes isolated by . . . dxe5 and fxe5, it is subject to capture by the Black king bishop and other pieces. In most cases, the pawn is simply too weak on e5 to be advanced.

More solid, although not without drawbacks, is f4-f5. Take the following diagram (reached by 1 e4 c5 2 Nf3 d6 3 d4 cxd4 4 Nxd4 Nf6 5 Nc3 g6 6 Be3 Bg7 7 Be2 Nc6

8 0-0 0-0 9 Qd2 Ng4 10 Bxg4 Bxg4 11 f4 Be6?
12 Rad1 Qa5) as an example.

Position after 12 ... Qa5

In a game between two lesser-known masters (Rodl–Herman, Bad Pyrmont 1949), White played *13 f5!*. The advance is both an attack—threatening to open up part of the f-file—and a positional idea, winning control of d5 for a White knight. Here it has the further benefit of being accomplished with a gain of time since fxe6 is threatened. Tactically it is based on 13 ... Nxd4 14 Bxd4 Bxd4+ 15 Qxd4 gxf5 16 exf5 Bxf5 17 Nd5!, a variation that leaves White with a winning game because of the Nxe7 mate and Rxf5 threats.

The game continued *13 . . . Bd7 14 Qf2*, and White prepared for Qh4 and Nd5. Black regained control of d5 with a general liquidation of material, but that had the effect of drawing attention to his weakened kingside: *14 ... Nxd4 15 Bxd4 Bxd4 16 Qxd4 Bc6 17 f6!*. With a weak d-pawn and a vulnerable king, Black lasted only 11 more moves: *17 ... Rae8 18 b4 Qg5 19 b5! Bxb5 20 h4 Qh5*

*21 fxe7 Rxe7 22 Nd5 Qe5 23 Nxe7+ Qxe7 24 Rf6!
Rc8 25 Rxd6 Qxh4 26 Qe5 a6 27 g3!*

The move f4-f5 is more familiar as part of an overall king-side advance as shown by *Supplemental Game #1* and the following diagram. With f4-f5 and g4-g5 White secures open lines and control of d5. The latter consideration is important only if he has a *knight* to occupy the center square.

1 e4 c5   2 Nf3 d6   3 d4 cxd4   4 Nxd4 Nf6   5 Nc3
g6   6 Be2 Bg7   7 Be3 Nc6   8 0-0 0-0   9 Nb3 Be6
10 f4 Na5   11 f5 Bc4!   12 Nxa5 Bxe2   13 Qxe2
Qxa5   14 g4

Position after 14 g4

Black has succeeded in exchanging some dangerous material but he has a problem here. White has an immediate threat of g4-g5 and Nd5. Once that is accomplished the knight can be driven back only by . . . e6, a very weakening move.

This example highlights Black's ideas in f4-f5 positions. He can stop his knight from being driven off with 14 . . . h6, but this insures the opening of another file after 15 Kh1! Rac8

16 g5 or 15 . . . g5   16 h4. Another idea is 14 . . . d5, attacking in the center as in the Scheveningen, but here it is inappropriate because of   15 e5 Nd7   16 Bd4 followed by Rad1 or Rae1. Black then has problems in the center as well as on the kingside.

A third idea is to occupy e5, the square that White conceded when he played f4-f5. But again there are problems here because a White knight on d5 is more valuable than a Black knight on e5. For instance, 14 . . . Nd7   15 Nd5 Rfe8   16 g5 and now if 16 . . . e6 White makes a strong pawn sacrifice with 17 Ne7+! Rxe7   18 f6 Ree8   19 fxg7 Kxg7   20 Rad1.

The elimination process boils down to two ideas, one logical, one dramatic. Black can occupy e5 immediately with a more useful piece, 14 . . . Qe5!, and on 15 Qf3 d5! should equalize (16 exd5 Nxg4! or 16 Nxd5 Nxd5   17 exd5 Qxb2) because White has more kingside weaknesses in the simplified position than Black.

Finally, the theoretically best move is 14 . . . Rac8! with the idea of meeting 15 g5 with 15 . . . Rxc3!!. This radical solution to the problem of Nd5 works well because of the overexposed White kingside after 16 bxc3 Nxe4 or 16 gxf6 Rxe3   17 Qxe3 Bxf6. Although slightly ahead in material, White has problems with his ruptured pawns. In master games, Black has won more frequently than White. (For example,   18 c3 Rc8   19 a3 Rc4!   20 Rae1 b5 White has to worry about . . . a5 and . . . b4 as well as his weak pawns.)

White's f2-f3 Attack: The Rauzer Plan

Generally, when White's f2-f4 is effective the first player has castled on the kingside, but with f2-f3 White announces his intention to advance his g-pawn and h-pawn. His king then belongs on the opposite wing. His queen usually goes to d2 to support Bh6, attempting to exchange off the strong Black king bishop.

This scheme was popularized in the 1930s by Vsevolod Alfredovich Rauzer, a Soviet master whose creative career was cut short by the Nazi blockade of Leningrad in World War II. The simplicity of the plan was among its strengths, and before long the Rauzer attack had scored many quick victories. After f2-f3 Black did not have an attack against the White e-pawn, and he could not simplify the minor pieces with . . . Bg4 or . . . Ng4 as he could after f2-f4.

Further problems for Black are illustrated by the following example:

1 e4 c5   2 Nf3 d6   3 d4 cxd4   4 Nxd4 Nf6   5 Nc3 g6   6 Be3 Bg7   7 f3 Nc6   8 Qd2 0-0   9 Bc4 Na5 10 Bb3! Nxb3   11 axb3!

Position after 11 axb3!

Here Black has managed to simplify the situation a bit with an exchange of pieces, but this exchange has also helped White. White's castled position after 0-0-0 will be slightly stronger now since Black cannot occupy c4 with pieces and cannot easily exert pressure along the b-file toward b2. Also, while Black has eliminated some of White's control of d5, he is not ready for 11 . . . d5 because of 12 e5! (better than 12 Ndb5 a6! 13 exd5 Bd7 14 Nd4 b5 15 b4 a5) 12 . . . Ne8 13 f4 f6 14 exf6 Nxf6 15 0-0 and 16 Rad1.

Thus Black has nothing with which to impede White's basic attacking idea although he has a slight lead in development. On *11 . . . Bd7 12 h4 a6*, for example, we have reached a Spassky–Geller match game from 1965. Black, one of the most dangerous of modern attacking masters, found he had no counterplay and quickly drifted into a lost position: *13 h5 Rc8* (13 . . . Nxh5 14 g4 Nf6 15 Bh6 followed by Bxg7, Qh6+, and Nd5 is fatal) *14 Bh6 e5* (a sacrifice of pawn structure to stave off mate) *15 Nde2 Be6 16 g4 Qc7 17 Ng3 b5 18 b4 Qb7 19 Bxg7 Kxg7 20 hxg6 fxg6 21 Qxd6* and White won effortlessly.

(For similar examples of the speed with which White's rocklike pawn structure permits him to obtain a winning game see *Supplemental Games #2* and *#3* at the end of the chapter.)

The two most popular methods of obtaining counterplay for Black are the use of the c-file (with . . . Ne5-c4 or even . . . Rc8xc3) and the advance of the queenside pawns. An example of the latter is *1 e4 c5 2 Nf3 d6 3 d4 cxd4 4 Nxd4 Nf6 5 Nc3 g6 6 Be3 Bg7 7 f3 Nc6 8 Qd2 0-0 9 Bc4 Bd7 10 Bb3 Nxd4!? 11 Bxd4 b5*.

Position after 11 ... b5

Because of the slightly inaccurate 10 Bb3 (better is 10 h4 or 10 0-0-0), Black already has his queenside pawns rolling. It is easy to see that if White does nothing on the side where he intends to castle, Black's strategy will succeed. For instance, 12 0-0-0? can be met by 12 . . . a5 with a threat of . . . a4, trapping the bishop. A Yugoslav game in 1969 went 13 a3 b4! 14 Nd5 (14 axb4 axb4 15 Nb1 Qa5 is just as bad) 14 . . . Nxd5 15 Bxd5 e5! 16 Be3 bxa3 17 b3 a4 and Black took the queenside apart with a sacrifice of the exchange.

Lest the reader think that Rauzer's attack repeals Lasker's rule that every pawn move has its plusses and minuses, we should mention the endgame. While the White pawns are solid when they sit at e4, f3, g2, and h2, they are quite vulnerable when the g-pawn and h-pawn are advanced. The attacking mass can become a row of fragile tenpins, as in the case of Burgalat–Trifunovic, Mar del Plata 1953:

1 e4 c5   2 Nf3 d6   3 d4 cxd4   4 Nxd4 Nf6   5 Nc3 g6   6 f3 Bg7   7 Be3 0-0   8 Qd2 Nc6   9 0-0-0 Nxd4 10 Bxd4 Be6   11 Kb1 Qc7   12 g4 Rfc8   13 h4 Qa5

14 Nd5? Qxd2 15 Nxf6+ Bxf6 16 Rxd2 Bxd4
17 Rxd4 Kg7!

Position after 17 . . . Kg7!

In view of . . . b5-b4 White entered the endgame with his 14th move. His chances are dubious. Though his kingside pawns seem to control more terrain, they are also more vulnerable to attack, such as . . . Kf6-e5-f4!. If White stops the progress of the Black king with g4-g5 or f3-f4 he makes further concessions.

The result of White's *18 g5* was to face a new problem after *18 . . . h6!*. He could leave himself with a weak, isolated h-pawn after *19 gxh6+*, or he could play as he did with *19 Bh3 Bxh3 20 Rxh3 hxg5 21 hxg5*. The extent of his weakness was revealed by *21 . . . Rh8!*.

White must lose control of the only completely open file. This gives Black access to the weak White pawns. After *22 Rxh8 Rxh8 23 a4* (or 23 Rd1—to stop mate on the last rank— . . . Rh3 *24 Rf1 Rg3* winning a pawn) *23 . . . Rh5*, White had to lose material since *24 f4 Rh4 25 f5* is met by

25 ... gxf5. In the pawn race Black also loses: *24 Rc4 Rxg5*
25 Rc7 Rg3   26 Rxb7 Rxf3   27 Rxa7 g5!   28 Ra5 Kf6
29 Ra8 Kg7   30 Ka2 g4   31 Ra5 f5!   32 Rd5 g3   33 Rd1
f4   34 a5 g2 and White resigned because of 35 Rg1 Rg3
and ... f3-f2.

White's Positional Plan: Nd5

One of the easiest positions to play has a pawn structure like
the following diagram. White has ready pressure along the e-
file since Black's e-pawn cannot be supported by another
pawn. On the other hand, White's pawn at c4 can be bolstered
by b2-b3.

After the "Marco Hop"

This formation, which even many masters incorrectly
evaluate comes about in several modern openings: the
Alekhine Defense (1 e4 Nf6   2 e5 Nd5   3 d4 d6   4 Nf3
g6   5 Be2 Bg7   6 c4 Nb6   7 exd6 cxd6   8 h3 0-0
9 0-0 Nc6   10 Nc3 Bf5   11 Bf4 h6   12 Qd2 Kh7

13 d5!, for example), the King's Indian Defense, the English Opening, and various closed systems. But it is most common in the Sicilian when White moves his queen knight to d5 and Black captures it. The idea goes back to 1895, in the first decade of Dragon usage in international chess, when Georg Marco, the great Rumanian analyst, played it in a game with Max Weiss. After Nd5 and a capture on d5 White can use his f4-f5 attack most successfully, or he can use his queenside majority.

In its purest form—without minor pieces—White's advantage in space is great and so are his opportunities. The position below is Süchting–Chajes, Karlsbad 1911, which began
1 e4 c5   2 Nf3 Nc6   3 d4 cxd4   4 Nxd4 Nf6   5 Nc3 d6
6 Be2 g6   7 Be3 Bg7   8 0-0 0-0   9 h3 Bd7   10 Qd2 a6
11 a4 Rc8   12 Nxc6 Bxc6   13 Bf3 Nd7   14 Bd4 Ne5
15 Be2 Bd7   16 Nd5 Be6   17 f4 Bxd5?   18 exd5 Nc4
19 Bxc4 Rxc4   20 Bxg7 Kxg7   21 b3! Qb6+   22 Kh2 Qd4
23 Qe2 Rc7.

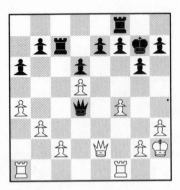

Position after 23 ... Rc7

White's game almost plays itself. First, he establishes a solid pawn formation with *24 c4!* and then proceeds with a kingside advance (*24 . . . Qf6   25 Rae1 Rb8   26 f5*). In retrospect Black's best chance was to play 26 . . . Qd4, forget about . . . b5, and bring his rook back to f8 to protect f7. Then White would have to prove that the weakness of the e-pawn and the Black kingside was enough for a win.

Black made it easy with *26 . . . gxf5   27 Qd3 Rg8 28 Rxf5 Qg6   29 Ref1 Kh8   30 Qc3+ f6   31 R1f2 b5 32 R5f4 bxc4   33 Rg4! Qd3   34 Rxg8+ Kxg8   35 Qa5 Ra7   36 Rf3 Qe4   37 Rg3+ Kf7   38 Qd8!* and Black soon resigned. A comparable position, with colors reversed, is *Supplemental Game #5*.

Black's counterstrategies involve stopping Nd5, permitting it and later freeing his game with . . . b5 or . . . e6, and anticipating it with . . . d5.

The last named is well known in similar positions. In what is called the accelerated Dragon, Black can achieve . . . d5 very early; e.g., 1 e4 c5   2 Nf3 Nc6   3 d4 cxd4   4 Nxd4 g6   5 Nc3 Bg7   6 Be3 Nf6   7 Be2 0-0   8 0-0? d5!. This is one reason why 5 c4, leading into the Maroczy Bind formation, is so popular.

The Marco Hop works well when Black cannot play either . . . e6 or . . . b5 effectively after pieces are exchanged on the d5 square. A good illustration of this is Alekhine–Golombek, Montevideo 1939:

1 e4 c5   2 Nf3 d6   3 d4 cxd4   4 Nxd4 Nf6   5 Nc3 g6   6 Be2 Bg7   7 Nb3 Nc6   8 0-0 0-0   9 Kh1 a5!? 10 a4 Be6   11 f4 Qc8   12 Be3 Bg4?   13 Bg1 Rd8

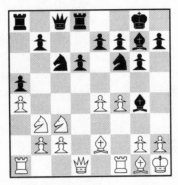

Position after 13 . . . Rd8

Note that White played 7 Nb3 to prevent . . . d5. Black countered with . . . a5, a move that threatened to weaken White's black squares with . . . a4-a3. When White stopped this with a2-a4 he permitted Black to occupy b4 indefinitely.

But Black's strategy is successful only if he prevents Nd5. He could have done this with 12 . . . Nb4! and 13 . . . Rd8, threatening . . . d5. But after the game continuation, 14 Nd5! Bxe2 15 Qxe2 Nxd5 16 exd5 Nb4 17 c4, Black was in a quandary. He has given up hope of . . . b5 with his . . . a5. His a-pawn is weak, and if he protects it with . . . b6, he concedes c6 to White pieces.

Alekhine played on both sides of the board, a luxury that the Marco Hop affords White. First he looked at the kingside, 17 . . . Qc7 18 Nd4 Rdc8 19 b3 Na6 20 Rae1 Re8 21 f5 Nc5 22 Qf3, but then he turned to the other wing where he began to win pawns: 22 . . . Rf8 23 Nb5 Qd7 24 Bxc5! dxc5 25 Qe3 Rfe8 26 Qxc5 gxf5 27 Qc7 Rad8 28 Qxa5. Black soon resigned.

The alternative break . . . e6 is highly risky because it can leave Black with two weak center pawns and a porous kingside after dxe6. A simple illustration of the dangers is Geller–Kan, Moscow, 1952:

1 e4 c5   2 Nf3 d6   3 d4 cxd4   4 Nxd4 Nf6   5 Nc3 a6   6 Be2 Qc7   7 0-0 g6?   8 Bg5 Nbd7   9 Nd5! Nxd5   10 exd5   Bg7   11 c3   Nf6   12 Bf3   0-0 13 Re1 Re8   14 Qd2 Bd7   15 h3 Rac8   16 Re2!

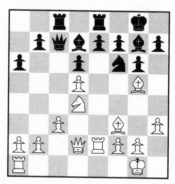

Position after 16 Re2!

Here is a case in which Black should have avoided the Dragon (7 . . . e6! instead of 7 . . . g6) because of the possibility of the Marco Hop. Black's e-pawn and kingside wait to be threatened. White has played c2-c3 instead of c2-c4, but the difference is slight since White's d-pawn cannot be attacked and c4 cannot be dangerously occupied.

Black's attempted solution to his constriction was 16 . . . e5?!, which, if it weren't for the en passant rule, would give

him a fine game after . . . f7-f5. As it is, Black pays a price for
the slight liberation of his pieces: *17 dxe6 fxe6   18 Rd1 Rcd8
19 Qf4! e5   20 Qh4*, and Black's pawns are badly fixed on
their squares.

He couldn't play 20 . . . exd4 because of 21 Bxf6 Bxf6
22 Qxf6 Rxe2   23 Bd5+. So he tried *20 . . . Rf8   21 Nc2!
Be6*, but after *22 Nb4* intending to occupy d5, Black made a
desperate bid for air and lost after *22 . . . d5   23 Qg3 Qf7
24 Rxe5 d4 25 cxd4 Kh8   26 d5 Bf5   27 d6*. (Black may
obtain greater piece activity if he recaptures on e6 with a piece,
but then his d-pawn is a deadly liability as in *Supplemental
Game #6*. See also *Supplemental Game #7*, which shows what
can happen with White's queenside majority in the Marco
Hop formation.)

Finally, we should mention that the Marco Hop formation
requires that White have an initiative to protect himself from
an incursion of Black pieces. Simply getting a knight to d5 will
not help if the opponent can drum up counterplay on the
queenside that makes both the newly created d-pawn and
other pawns subject to withering attack.

This is shown by a Soviet championship game from 1956,
Ragozin–Taimanov:

1 c4 Nf6   2 g3 d5   3 Bg2 e5   4 cxd5 Nxd5   5 Nc3
Be6   6 Nf3 Nc6   7 0-0 Nb6   8 a3 Be7   9 b4 0-0
10 d3 f6   11 Be3 Qd7   12 Ne4 Nd5   13 Rc1 Rfd8
14 Bc5 b6   15 Bxe7 Ndxe7   16 Qc2 Rac8   17 Rfd1

Position after 17 Rfd1

This is a routine Dragon position with colors reversed. The natural source of counterplay for Black is on the kingside and in the center with . . . Nd4. Probably the best idea is 17 . . . h6, stopping Ng5 and preparing 18 . . . f5; however, Black misjudged the formation and plunged forward with *17 . . . a5? 18 b5 Nd4 19 Nxd4 exd4*. Here the Marco Hop serves poorly because both the Black d-pawn and c-pawn are very weak. The best Black can do is exchange off his d-pawn with 20 Qb2 Nd5 21 Qxd4 Qxb5.

But Black made another error, *20 Qb2 Qe8?*, and simply lost a pawn after *21 a4 Bd5 22 Rd2 h6 23 Rdc2 f5 24 Nd2 Bxg2 25 Kxg2 Nd5 26 Nf3!*. Black struggled on gallantly with *26 . . . f4* (rather than 26 . . . Nc3 27 Nxd4! Nxa4? 28 Qb3+ and 29 Qxa4) *27 Nxd4 Qg6 28 Rc6 Qg4 29 Ne6 fxg3 30 hxg3 Re8 31 R1c4 Qg6 32 Nxc7*, but he could have resigned without missing much.

Supplemental Games

(1) White plays f4-f5 as part of an overall kingside advance.
Sigurjonsson–Kaufman, Chicago 1973; 1 e4 c5 2 Nf3 d6
3 d4 cxd4 4 Nxd4 Nf6 5 Nc3 a6 6 f4 Qc7 7 Bd3 g6
8 0-0 Bg7 9 Nf3 Bg4 10 h3 Bxf3 11 Qxf3 0-0
12 g4! Nc6 13 Be3 b5 14 Rae1 Rab8 15 Qg2 Rfc8?
(Since White is certain to continue his kingside attack, Black
should try . . . e6 and meet f4-f5 with . . . exf5 to open a file
for himself. The queenside counterplay is not enough.) 16 f5!
Qd8 17 Rf2 Ne5 (Nor is the e5 outpost or the exchange sacrifice that follows.) 18 Ref1 Rxc3 19 bxc3 Qa5 20 g5
Nfd7 21 Bd4 Qxa2 22 Kh1 Qa5 23 Rf4 Qd8 24 h4
(White's attack is based on obvious line-opening themes.) 24
. . . b4 25 fxg6 fxg6 26 Qh3 bxc3 27 h5 gxh5
28 Bc4+! Kh8 29 Qxh5 Nf8 30 Rh4 Rb1 31 Rxb1
Nxc4 32 Rf1 Resigns.

**(2) Black prevents h4-h5 in the Rauzer plan but makes fur-
ther concessions.** Moe–Whitely, Orebro 1966: 1 e4 c5
2 Nf3 d6 3 d4 cxd4 4 Nxd4 Nf6 5 Nc3 g6 6 Be3
Bg7 7 f3 Nc6 8 Qd2 0-0 9 Bc4 Bd7 10 0-0-0 Rc8
11 Bb3 Ne5 12 Qe2!? a6 13 h4 h5? (While this works in
some similar positions it is doubtful in most. By stopping h4-
h5 Black only encourages g2-g4.) 14 g4! hxg4 15 f4! Nf3
16 h5! (Black's strategy is proven bankrupt by this. The kingside is opened up faster now than if Black had permitted h4-
h5 at move 14.) 16 . . . Nxd4 17 Bxd4 Nxh5 18 f5! Bxd4
19 Qxg4! e6 20 Rxd4 Qf6 21 Rxd6 exf5? 22 Rxf6
fxg4 23 Rxg6+ Ng7 24 Rgh6 Resigns.

(3) Against the Rauzer plan, the . . . a5 strategy fails. Gip-slis–Bilek, Sousse 1967: 1 e4 c5   2 Nf3 d6   3 d4 cxd4   4 Nxd4 Nf6   5 Nc3 Nbd7   6 Bc4 g6   7 f3 Bg7   8 Be3 Ne5   9 Bb3 Bd7   10 h4 Rc8   11 Qd2 a5?   12 a4! Nc4 13 Bxc4   Rxc4   14 b3!   Rc8   15 0-0-0   0-0   16 Ndb5 (White's castled position is solid despite appearances because there is no easy way Black can initiate pawn action to open more lines. To prevent the simple plan of h4-h5 and Bh6 Black now takes desperate action.) 16 . . . h5   17 Bd4 e5?! 18 Be3 d5   19 Nxd5 Bxb5   20 axb5 Nxd5   21 Qxd5 Qc7   22 c4 a4   23 b6 Qe7   24 Qd6! (The ending after 24 . . . Qxd6 is won for White because of the queenside pawns.) 24 . . . Qe8   25 Kb2 axb3   26 Kxb3 Rxc4!? (Otherwise White consolidates comfortably and wins the end-ing.) 27 Kxc4   Qa4+   28 Kd3   Qb5+   29 Kd2   Ra8 30 Qd3 Qb2+   31 Ke1 Qxg2   32 Qf1 Qc2   33 Qe2 Qb3 34 Kf2 Bf8   35 Ra1 Rc8   36 Rhc1 Re8 37 Qc4 Qb2+ 38 Kg3 Resigns.

(4) Black's use of the c-file overwhelms a slow-moving Rauzer plan. Curdy–Keene, Orebro 1966:   1 e4 c5   2 Nf3 d6   3 d4 cxd4 4 Nxd4 Nf6.   5 Nc3 g6   6 Be3 Bg7   7 f3 Nc6   8 Bc4 0-0   9 Qd2 Bd7   10 0-0-0 Rc8   11 Bb3 Ne5 12 g4?! Nc4   13 Bxc4 Rxc4   14 h4 Qa5   15 Nb3 (or 15 h5 Rfc8 as in the game) 15 . . . Qa6   16 h5 Rfc8 17 Kb1? (A critical loss of time. With 17 hxg6 fxg6   18 e5! followed, for example, by 18 . . . dxe5?   19 g5 unclear compli-cations arise.) 17. . . Bxg4!   18 fxg4 Rxc3! (Triumph of c-file pressure:19 bxc3 Nxe4 and   20 . . . Nxd2+ or 20 . . . Nxc3+) 19 hxg Rxc2   20 gxf7+ Kf8   21 Qxc2 Rxc2   22 Kxc2 Qc4+   23 Kd2 Nxe4+   24 Ke1 Be5! White resigns.

(5)The Marco Hop formation favors the kingside attacker.
Larsen–Tal, Leningrad 1973: 1 c4 g6 2 Nc3 Bg7 3 Nf3
c5 4 g3 Nc6 5 Bg2 e6 6 0-0 Nge7 7 d3 0-0 8 Bd2
d5 9 Qc1 b6 10 Bh6 Bb7 11 Bxg7 Kxg7 12 cxd5
Nxd5! (After 12 ... exd5 13 d4! White has an easier
method of playing for a win, against the Isolani or hanging
pawns.) 13 h4?! Nd4! 14 Re1 h6 15 Ne5 Nxc3
16 Qxc3 (not 16 bxc3 Bxg2 17 Kxg2 Qd5+ or 17 cxd4
Qxd4) 16 ... Bxg2 17 Kxg2 Qd5+ 18 Nf3 Rad8!
19 Kg1 e5! 20 Nxd4 exd4! 21 Qc4 Qh5 (Black has free
run of the kingside, and White's only defense is a queenside
raid that may distract his opponent.) 22 Qa4 Rfe8
23 Qxa7 Rd6 24 b4 Rf6! 25 bxc5 Qf5! 26 f3 Qh3
27 Qc7 Rf5 28 cxb6 Rfe5! 29 e4 Qxg3+ 30 Kh1
Qxh4+ 31 Kg2 Rg5+ 32 Kf1 Qh3+ 33 Ke2 Rg2+
34 Kd1 Qxf3+ 35 Kc1 Qf2 White resigns.

**(6) Black breaks the Marco Hop formation with ... e6 and
accepts a weak d-pawn.** Boleslavsky–Suetin, Moscow 1952:
1 e4 c5 2 Nf3 Nc6 3 d4 cxd4 4 Nxd4 Nf6 5 Nc3 d6
6 g3 Bg4 7 f3 Bd7 8 Be3 g6 9 Bg2 Bg7 10 0-0 0-0
11 Nd5! Rc8 12 c3 Ne5 13 Qe2 Re8 14 Bf2 a6
15 Rfe1 b5 16 Rad1 Nc4 17 Ne3 Qc7 18 Nxc4 Qxc4
(Black has defended well by avoiding a capture on d5.
However ...) 19 Qd2 Red8 20 Bf1 Qc7 21 Nc2 a5
22 Ne3! Qb7 23 a3 Rb8 24 Nd5 Nxd5? (He can't resist
this time. Better was the durable defense 24 ... Bc6.)

25 exd5 e6   26 dxe6 Bxe6   27 Bg2 b4 (Black pinned his equalizing hopes on this. If several pawns on both sides are weakened, Black's d-pawn will not stand out.)   28 cxb4 axb4 29 f4 d5   30 Bd4! bxa3   31 bxa3 Bxd4+   32 Qxd4 Qb2 33 a4 Qxd4+   34 Rxd4 Rb2   35 Ra1 Rdb8   36 a5 Kf8 37 a6 Rb1+   38 Rd1! Rxd1+   39 Rxd1 Ra8   40 Ra1 Ke7   41 Kf2 Kd6   42 Ke3 Kc5   43 Bf1 Bd7   44 Rc1+ Kd6   45 Kd4 Bc6   46 Rb1 Re8   47 Bd3 Kc7   48 Bb5! (Decisive, since 48 . . . Rb8   49 Bxc6! Rxb1   50 a7 wins.) 48 . . . Re4+   49 Kc5 Ba8   50 Rc1 f5   51 Bd3 Re6 52 Kd4+ Kb8   53 Rc2 Re1   54 Re2 Rd1   55 Re8+ Ka7 56 Re7+ Kb6   57 Rxh7 Bc6   58 a7 Bb7   59 Rg7 Kxa7 60 Rxg6 Kb8   61 h4 Kc7   62 h5 Bc6   63 h6 Resigns.

(7) Black breaks the Marco Hop formation slightly with . . . b5, but White discovers his queen majority. Botvinnik–Kholodkevich, Moscow 1927:   1 d4 Nf6   2 c4 g6   3 Nc3 Bg7   4 e4 d6   5 g3 0-0   6 Bg2 Nbd7   7 Nge2 c5?! 8 0-0 cxd4   9 Nxd4 Ne5?   10 b3 Bd7   11 Bb2 Nc6 12 Nd5! Nxd5   13 exd5 Nxd4   14 Bxd4 b5   15 Bxg7 Kxg7   16 Qd4+ Kg8   17 cxb5! Bxb5   18 Rfe1   Qd7 19 Re3 f5?! (A strange method of defending his e-pawn against the doubling of White rooks.)   20 a4! Ba6 21 Rae1 Rf7   22 b4! Bb7   23 b5 a6   24 b6 Rc8   25 a5 Rc5   26 Rc3 Rxc3   27 Qxc3 Rf8   28 Qe3 Re8   29 Rc1 Rc8   30 Rxc8+ Bxc8   31 Qe6+! winning a piece and eventually the game.

C. MAROCZY UNBOUND

The Maroczy Bind

In the chess manuals of the last century there always seemed to be one proscription pressed upon new students of the game: "Do not take the queen's knight pawn with your queen." This parochial bit of wisdom has been replaced in the primers of the 20th century with another: "Do not permit the Maroczy Bind."

The dreaded Bind occurs in Open Sicilian formations when White can play both e2-e4 and c2-c4. Considering the last two chapters, we can appreciate why the Bind is a bind. Black has much greater difficulty in engineering either . . . d5 or . . . b5, his primary freeing moves. Black's use of the c-file is shortened by the presence of an easily protected White pawn on c4. Meanwhile, White can accomplish the Marco Hop, Nd5, early in the game and obtain either a dominating position for his knight or a transition into a more favorable pawn structure.

Oddly enough, Geza Maroczy (pronounced MAHRotsee) was not the originator of the pawn formation that bears his name. In fact, the first master game to gain recognition of the

Bind was Swiderski–Maroczy, Monte Carlo 1904, in which Maroczy, with Black in a Dragon formation, was the "bindee" rather than the "binder." It was his opponent who played c2-c4 and e2-e4. But for years later Maroczy, a great Hungarian grandmaster and chess journalist, repeatedly drew attention to the powers of the Bind, and, by the 1920s, permitting the Bind was equated with making a blunder. In our time, however, the Bind has been shorn of much of its reputation because of the many methods of freeing Black's game. In its purest form the Bind is still a very dangerous animal, but Black can avoid the pure form if he plays carefully.

The Maroczy Dragon

We'll consider two forms of the Bind depending on what Black does. The Maroczy Dragon occurs when Black fianchettoes his king bishop as in a normal Dragon. The Maroczy feature comes about in the Sicilian Defense (e.g., 1 e4 c5 2 Nf3 Nc6 3 d4 cxd4 4 Nxd4 g6 5 c4) and in a variety of King's Indian and English variations (e.g., 1 c4 Nf6 2 Nc3 c5 3 g3 d5 4 cxd5 Nxd5 5 Bg2 Nc7 followed by . . . Nc6 and . . . e5).

The primary advantage of the Bind is that if Black fails to fight the constriction of his pieces, he can be strangled. Passivity is fatal. A simple illustration of this is the game Botvinnik–Golombek from the 1956 Olympiad in Moscow:

1 c4 Nf6   2 Nf3 c5   3 g3 g6   4 b3 Bg7   5 Bb2 0-0
6 Bg2 Nc6   7 0-0 b6   8 d4 cxd4   9 Nxd4 Bb7
10 Nc3 Qc8   11 Nc2! d6   12 e4

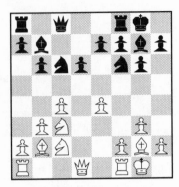

Position after 12 e4

Mikhail Botvinnik and Akiba Rubinstein first showed the supersolidity of the Bind in their games. The maneuver Nd4-c2 is a Rubinstein patent. White avoids an exchange of knights that might free Black's game, and he uses his knight to guard the key squares b4, d4, and e3.

What happens if Black doesn't initiate any pawn action, that is, if he leaves the Maroczy Bind formation intact? This game shows that mere maneuvers are insufficient. Black sought to exploit the hole on d4 with a shift of his king knight: *12 . . . Nd7   13 Qd2 Nc5   14 f4 Ne6?   15 Rad1 Ned4   16 Nxd4 Nxd4* and now *17 Nd5*.

After this simple move Black was reduced to passivity. To guard both his knight and e7 he should play *17 . . . Nc6* and await events after *18 Bxg7 Kxg7   19 Qc3+ Kg8*. White could then prepare for c4-c5, e4-e5, or f4-f5—all good plans, as we will see. In this 1956 game Black shortened the torture with *17 . . . Bxd5?*. This was immediately fatal because after *18 cxd5!* White penetrated along the c-file and won the adventurous knight: *18. . . Nb5* (or *18 . . . e5   19 dxe6* winning the d-pawn) *19 Bxg7 Kxg7   20 Rc1*, and Black resigned

in view of 20 . . . Qb7 21 a4 Nc7   22 Qc3+ and 23 Qxc7.
(See also *Supplemental Game #1*.)

White's Middlegame Plans

When White is given a free hand he can choose among three
good strategies: (1) playing f4-f5 as in the Dragon to secure
sole possession of d5 and to prepare a kingside attack, (2) playing c4-c5 to open up the side of the board on which he has superior pieces, and (3) playing e4-e5 to open the center for
assault.

The kingside attack in coordination with the Marco Hop
is so deadly that Black must make some provision for early
counterplay. This has been known for many years, but there
are still cases such as the following:

Portisch–Reshevsky, Petropolis 1973:

1 c4 c5   2 Nf3 g6   3 e4 Nc6   4 d4 cxd4   5 Nxd4
Nf6   6 Nc3 Nxd4   7 Qxd4 d6   8 Bg5 Bg7   9 Qd2
0-0   10 Bd3 a5   11 0-0 a4?   12 Rac1 Be6   13 Qc2
Nd7   14 f4! Rc8   15 b3 axb3   16 axb3

Position after 16 axb3

Black has invested valuable time in . . . a5-a4 to open up a file he doesn't really need. In the meantime White has built up a strong attacking formation. On 16 . . . Nc5, for instance, he would continue 17 f5 Bd7   18 Nd5 f6   19 Be3 with a great advantage.

Black returned his knight to the kingside for defense, but after *16 . . . Nf6   17 Kh1 Qa5?* (pointless) *18 f5! Bd7 19 Nd5!* he was in very bad shape; e.g., 19 . . . Nxd5 20 exd5 Bf6   21 Bxf6 exf6   22 fxg6 fxg6   23 Bxg6! or 20 . . . Rce8   21 Rce1 Qd8   22 Qf2 and 23 Qh4.

Black deferred the capture on d5, but the transfer of White's queen to the kingside was too much. After *19 . . . Qd8 20 Qf2! Bc6   21 Qh4 Bxd5   22 exd5* it is clear that White has a murderous attack coming up with Rf3-h3.

Position after 22 exd5

The game ended with a sparkle: *22 . . . Re8   23 Rf3 Nd7 24 Rcf1 Bf6   25 Rh3 Nf8   26 fxg6 fxg6   27 Bxg6! hxg6 28 Rxf6 Resigns* (in view of 28 . . . exf6   29 Qh8+ Kf7 30 Rh7+ Nxh7   31 Qxh7+ Kf8   32 Bh6 mate).

Another plan, c4-c5, requires the right combination of elements for success. If White hurries c4-c5 he will reduce the position to one of pawn symmetry and positional equality. But c4-c5 can be powerful if Black's pieces are confused on the d-file (see *Supplemental Game #2*). Then the confusion is exposed to White's power.

The simplest form of this idea is shown by *Supplemental Game #3* and by the following:

Pachman–Gunnarson, Vrnjacka Banja 1967:

1 c4 Nf6	2 Nc3 c5	3 Nf3 g6	4 d4 cxd4	5 Nxd4
Bg7	6 e4 d6	7 Be2 0-0	8 0-0 Nc6	9 Be3 Bd7
10 Qd2	Ng4	11 Bxg4	Bxg4	12 Rac1 Nxd4
13 Bxd4 Be6	14 f4 Bxd4+	15 Qxd4 Qc8	16 b3 f6	

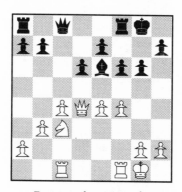

Position after 16 . . . f6

White could, of course, continue with 17 f5, but Black is prepared to exchange queens or occupy e5 in that event; e.g., 17 f5 Bf7 18 Rf3 Qc5 or 18 Kh1 Qc5 19 Qd2 Kg7 and 20 . . . Qe5. The superior plan was *17 Nd5 Bxd5 18 Qxd5+* (better than 17 exd5 Qc5 when Black could defend his e-pawn in the endgame with . . . Kf7) *18 . . . Kg7 19 c5!*.

The preponderance of White's heavy pieces in the center makes c4-c5 the right idea. After *19 . . . dxc5   20 Rxc5* Black could not abdicate the center completely (20 . . . Qb8   21 Qd7 and Rc7); so he played *20 . . . e6   21 Qc4 Qe8* and tried to hold on after *22 e5 f5* (22 . . . fxe5   23 Rxe5 dooms the e-pawn.)

But the open lines belonged to White and he won casually: *23 Rd1 Rf7   24 Rd6 Rd8!?* (hoping for 25 Qxe6 Qxe6 26 Rxe6 Rd2 or 25 Rxe6 Rd1+   26 Kf2 Qd7 with some play for a pawn) *25 Rc7! Rfd7   26 Rdxd7 Rxd7   27 Qb5!* and Black resigned because he loses the equivalent of a rook in the double pin.

The third idea, e4-e5, is relatively rare, but it occasionally damages Black when White has obtained a pin along the d-file, as in *Supplemental Game #4* and Portisch–Larsen, Lugano 1968:

1 Nf3 c5   2 c4 g6   3 d4 cxd4   4 Nxd4 Bg7   5 e4
Nc6   6 Be3   Nf6   7 Nc3   Ng4!   8 Qxg4   Nxd4
9 Qd1 Ne6   10 Rc1 d6   11 Bd3 Bd7   12 0-0 a5
13 f4 Bc6   14 Bb1 Nc5?   15 Qe2

Position after 15 Qe2

Black's exchange of pieces at move seven averted the Rubinstein maneuver, Nc2, but in the last few moves Black has created tactical problems for himself. Here he cannot play 15 . . . Bxc3   16 Rxc3 Nxe4 because of 17 Bxe4 Bxe4 18 Bd4. To allay his fears Black should try 15 . . . b6, but he went in for *15 . . . 0-0* and now 16 e5! embarrassed him.

Black cannot take the e-pawn without losing his knight. He had to acquiesce in the isolation of his d-pawn: *16 . . . Na4 17 Nxa4 Bxa4   18 b3 Bc6   19 Rcd1 Qc7   20 exd6 exd6.*

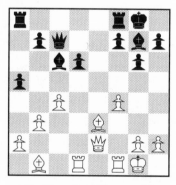

Position after 20 . . . exd6

Black's d-pawn is weak, but his game suffers because of the presence of another problem, his vulnerable king position. With one weakness, he might defend easily. With two, his chances are dubious.

This was the case after *21 f5! Rfe8   22 Qf2 a4   23 Bb6 Qd7   24 Bd4 axb3   25 axb3 Bxd4   26 Rxd4 Re5   27 Bd3 Qe7?* (27 . . . Rae8) 28 Rf4!. Confronted with the threat of

29 fxg6 fxg6   30 Rf7 Black's only hope was 28 . . . Be8, and
so his 28 . . . g5? was the final mistake: 29 f6! Qe6   30 Bf5!
Qe8   31 Rg4 h6   32 Qf4! Rxf5 (otherwise 33 Rxg5+)
33 Qxf5 Qe3+   34 Kh1 Re8   35 Rg3 Qd2   36 h4 Re2
37 Qh3 Qd4   38 hxg5 h5   39 g6 Resigns.

Black's Counterstrategies: . . . b5

What makes the Maroczy Bind such a difficult structure to
handle—by either side—is that most of the dynamic possibilities lie with Black. It is he who threatens pawn action
most frequently in the early stages of the game—on the
queenside with . . . b5, on the kingside with . . . f5, and in
the center with . . . d5. It is only after these ideas are prevented that White has the time for his own designs. Thus,
White's basic task is consolidation and confinement while
Black's is liberation.

When Black plays . . . b5 he accomplishes several things:
he will open at least one more line for his pieces; he sets up
White's queenside pawns for pressure; and he may threaten
the enemy e-pawn via . . . b4. Successful examples of this
can be found in *Supplemental Games #5* and #6 at the end of
this section, but the subtlety of the play surrounding . . . b5
is best known by a typical position of the modern Sicilian
Defense:

1 e4 c5   2 Nf3 Nc6   3 d4 cxd4   4 Nxd4 g6   5 c4
Nf6   6 Nc3 Nxd4   7 Qxd4 d6   8 Be2 Bg7   9 Be3
0-0   10 Qd2 Be6   11 Rc1 Qa5

Position after 11 . . . Qa5

Let's examine three different lines of play from the diagram:

(1) Suppose White proceeds as if nothing is happening and continues with 12 0-0 a6 13 f4. He is then ready to continue with kingside play (f4-f5) and to consolidate on the queenside (13 . . . Rfc8 14 b3). But Black acts first with 13 . . . b5!. After 14 cxb5 axb5 White will have a bad game after 15 Bxb5 Nxe4! 16 Nxe4 Qxb5. This use of the temporary weakness of the White e-pawn in order to promote . . . b5 is a common theme in the Open Sicilian and is especially useful here.

In one spectacular game, Cardoso–Adorjan, Lanzarote 1975, White continued 15 b4 (to stop . . . b4) Qxb4 16 Rb1 Qa3 17 Rxb5 Rfc8 18 Bd4, but Black found a fine queen sacrifice in 18 . . . Rxc3 19 Qxc3 Nxe4 20 Rb8+ (20 Qxa3 Bxd4+ or 20 Qa1 Bxd4+ 21 Qxd4 Nc3 wins for Black) 20 . . . Rxb8 21 Qxa3 Bxd4+ 22 Kh1 Nf2+ 23 Rxf2 Bxf2. Despite his material minus Black held the advantage and he eventually won after 24 h3 h5 25 Qf3 Rb1+ 26 Kh2 Bg1+ 27 Kg3 Rb2 28 Qe4 Rxa2.

(2) A more exact procedure for White is 12 b3! which guards against . . . b5. Now if Black prepares for . . . b5 with 12 . . . Rfc8   13 0-0 a6 White has time for 14 f4! b5   15 f5! Bd7   16 fxg6 hxg6   17 c5!.

Position after 17 c5!

This follows a fine tactical encounter, Tal–Parma, Bled 1961. Black cannot play 17 . . . dxc5 because of 18 Rxf6 and Qxd7. With 17 . . . b4 Black avoids this danger, but White can sacrifice a pawn with 18 Nd5! Nxd5   19 exd5 dxc5   20 Bc4. He then threatens to assault Black's kingside (d5-d6) very strongly.

In the game Black played very sharply and lost in a flurry of excellent responses: 17 . . . Be6   18 Bf3! dxc5!   19 e5 Ng4   20 Bxa8   Bxe5!?   21 Bd5 Nxe3   22 Bxe6 Rd8   23 Qf2 Nf5   24 Qe2! Bd4+   25 Kh1 fxe6   26 Qxe6+ Kg7   27 Ne4 Qc7   28 Ng5 Rf8   29 Qxf5! Resigns.

(3) The most accurate play for Black after 12 b3! is 12 . . . a6, threatening 13 . . . b5. Then White can put a stop to the idea with 13 f3 Rfc8   14 a4, but White has delayed indefinitely his kingside plans of f4-f5 and has created a new queen-

side weakness, which can be investigated by 14 . . . Qb4. Black is not yet equal, but he has taken the greatest sting out of the Bind.

Simagin's . . . f5

On the other wing Black has a break that is much easier to achieve but more dangerous to him as a weakness. This is . . . f5, an idea popularized by the late Soviet master Vladimir Simagin. Simagin showed during the 1950s that by advancing his f-pawn Black can probe White's king position and remove one of the pillars of the Maroczy center, the White e-pawn.

In its best light Simagin's plan is the signal for a flash attack. White takes pains to stop . . . b5 but he cannot prevent . . . f5. Case in point:

1 c4 Nf6   2 Nc3 c5   3 Nf3 Nc6   4 g3 g6   5 Bg2 Bg7   6 0-0 0-0   7 d4 cxd4   8 Nxd4 Nxd4!   9 Qxd4 d6   10 Qd3 a6   11 Bd2 Bf5!?   12 e4 Be6   13 b3 Qd7

Position after 13 . . . Qd7

Black's 11th move seems illogical. He gives White an extra move to establish the Maroczy formation. But this serves to block the long diagonal of White's fianchettoed bishop, to weaken the squares d3 and f3, and to give . . . f5 real strength.

In the game cited White continued as if all he had to worry about were . . . b5. He played *14 Rfd1? Ng4! 15 a4?*, but now *15 . . . f5! 16 Rf1 Ne5* gives Black a strong initiative. His knight eyes the weakened d3 and f3 squares while his rooks are about to seize the f-file. The game continued: *17 Qe3 fxe4 18 Bxe4 Bh3! 19 Bg2* (19 Rfe1 Ng4) *Bxg2 20 Kxg2 Rf3 21 Qe4 Raf8.*

Position after 21. . . Raf8

Black's pieces are reaching their maximum strength; all but the queen and king bishop are poised for attack against the kingside. It is no surprise that Black won swiftly: *22 Rae1 Nd3! 23 Re2 Nc5 24 Qc2 Bd4! 25 Nd5 e6 26 Ne3 Qc6 27 Kg1 Ne4 28 Ng4 Nxg3!* White resigns.

The problems created for Black by . . . f5 are those of king safety and vulnerability of his central pawns. After an exchange of pawns White obtains the use of the e-file and perhaps the e4 square. Black gets f5 for a piece or pawn. But his use of the f-file can be reduced sharply by White's f2-f4!.

1 e4 c5   2 Nf3 Nc6   3 d4 cxd4   4 Nxd4 g6   5 c4
Bg7   6 Be3 Nh6   7 Nc3 0-0   8 Be2 d6   9 0-0 f5

Position after 9 . . . f5

After 10 exf5 Black has a broad choice of recaptures. He can exchange two pieces on d4 and then recapture on f5 with a bishop, but then White's minor pieces will be superior to Black's after f2-f4! and Bf3. Another idea is 10 . . . Nxf5 11 Nxf5 Bxf5, but here again White would obtain the better of the middlegame play with 12 Qd2, 13 f4! and 14 Bf3. Most interesting of all is 10 . . . gxf5, a move that gives up the play along the f-file in exchange for pawn control of e4. Once again, White should play 11 f4! Bd7 12 Qd2. It is true that White will not be able to play Ne4-g5-e6 as he might if Black recaptures on f5 with a minor piece, but the dangers for Black of having his center pummeled by c4-c5, Nd5, and the placing of rooks on c1 and e1 are still there.

Black's counterplay is not quite adequate, and this may explain why in Szabo–Larsen, Vinkovci 1970, Black sought complications with *12 . . . Ng4* (before 13 h3!) *13 Bxg4 fxg4*. This solved one problem—the inferiority of Black's king knight compared with the good White king bishop—but it created an imbalance of pieces in the center, which White soon exploited: *14 Nd5 Rf7   15 f5!* (based on 15 . . . Nxd4 16 Bxd4 Bxf5   17 Bxg7 Kxg7   18 Qg5+ Bg6   19 Rxf7+ and 20 Rf1+ with a quick win) *15 . . . Kh8   16 Ne6! Qg8* (or 16 . . . Bxe6   17 fxe6 Rxf1+   18 Rxf1 and Rf7) *17 Nxg7 Qxg7   18 Nxe7!*.

Black's game was lost because of *18 . . . Nxe7   19 f6*; e.g., 19. . . Rxf6   20 Rxf6 Qxf6   21 Bd4. Black tried to prolong the game with *19 . . . Qg6*, but it was a losing effort (*20 fxe7 Rxe7   21 Bd4+ Kg8   22 Rf6 Qh5   23 Raf1 g3   24 hxg3 Be6   25 Qf4 Rf7   26 g4* Resigns).

Black's . . . d5, . . . Bxc3+, and . . . e5 Ideas

Black's counterstrategies are by no means limited to the flanking breaks . . . b5 and . . . f5. What is important to his game is that he has several plans, any one of which may be most appropriate in a given situation. Black actually has more freedom of choice in the Bind than in many other formations.

Because of the position of his king bishop Black rarely tries for . . . e6 and . . . d5 in the Dragon Maroczy. His d-pawn would become too vulnerable too soon. This idea is most commonly seen in the Scheveningen Maroczy in the pages that follow. But there are instances when it can work—usually with colors reversed as in *Supplemental Game #8*.

Not really a pawn action but one that effects the pawn structure is the exchange of Black's fianchettoed bishop for a knight on c3. This doubles White's c-pawns but gives him some attacking chances in compensation. On the whole the exchange of pieces eases the Bind by giving Black counterplay. With colors reversed this can come about in this manner:

1 c4 c5   2 Nc3 Nf6   3 g3 d5   4 cxd5 Nxd5   5 Bg2 Nc7   6 Nf3 Nc6   7 d3 e5   8 Nd2!

Position after 8 Nd2!

White's maneuver Nd2-c4 serves several purposes, such as freeing his fianchettoed bishop and preparing for Simagin's f2-f4. Immediately it has a positional threat (Bxc6+) in store for Black. After 8 ... Be7?, for example, White can play 9 Bxc6+! bxc6   10 Nc4 f6   11 Qa4 with a rare situation. White can delay castling for several moves as he prepares for the attack on the Black queenside. In one Soviet game, Sokolsky–Arulaid, Tallinn 1959, White already had a winning position before he took time to castle: 11 ... Bd7   12 Na5 Nd5   13 Bd2 Qb6   14 Nc4 Qb7   15 Ne4 0-0   16 Qa5 Qb5

17 Rc1 Nb6 18 b3! f5 19 Ned6 Nxc4 20 Nxc4 e4? 21 Qc7 Rad8 22 Ne5 winning a piece. Had Black not rushed his pawns forward in the center he would still have lost at least a pawn on the queenside, e.g, 20 . . . Bf6 21 Be3 and 22 Bxc5.

It should be noted that the main purpose of the bishop-takes-knight idea is to cripple the enemy pawns. If the pawns are not crippled the exchange is highly dubious—even if a pawn is won in the process! For instance, in the diagram above if Black had played 8 . . . Bd7 9 Nc4 Be7 10 0-0 0-0!?, he would be making a speculative sacrifice of a pawn, but this would be superior to 8 . . . Be7. An example of the pawn sacrifice is Commons–Gheorghiu, Lone Pine 1975, which went 11 Bxc6 Bxc6 12 Nxe5 Be8 13 Qb3 b6 14 Be3 Kh8 15 Rfd1 f6 16 Nf3 Bf7 17 Qa4 Nd5 18 Nxd5 Bxd5 19 a3 a6 20 Nd2? Qc8! 21 f3 Qe6 22 Kf2 f5 23 Re1 Bf6 24 Qc2 f4! 25 Bxf4 g5 26 e4 gxf4 27 exd5 Qh3 28 Nf1 Bd4+ 29 Ke2 Rae8+ 30 Kd1 Rxe1+ 31 Kxe1 Re8+ and White resigned. Sometimes it is worse to have bad pawns than to have fewer pawns.

Another point worth mentioning is that the Bxc6/ . . . Bxc3 idea goes hand in hand with Simagin's plan and with a frontal attack on the Bind pillar at c4/c5. *Supplemental Game #9* is one good example, and the following Bielicki–Evans, Havana 1964, is ideal:

1 c4 Nf6 2 Nc3 d5 3 cxd5 Nxd5 4 g3 c5 5 Bg2 Nc7 6 Nf3 Nc6 7 0-0 e5 8 b3 Be7 9 Bb2 0-0 10 Rc1 f6 11 Ne1!?

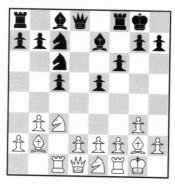

Position after 11 Ne1!?

White's idea runs something like this: he will threaten the Black queenside with Nd3 and/or Bxc6; then, when Black is preoccupied with the queenside pressure, he will be vulnerable to f2-f4.

His last move is superior to 11 Na4 which could be met by 11 ... b6; e.g., 12 Nxe5 Nxe5 13 Bxa8 Nxa8 or 12 Nh4 Bd7.

11	...	Bd7!?

Here is a case when the threat of Bxc6 is stronger than its execution. In the 1930s Botvinnik played 11 ... Bf5 to stop 12 Nd3. He didn't mind 12 Bxc6 bxc6 because with b2-b3 and Ne1 already played, White's queenside exploitation is a little slow (13 Na4 Ne6 14 Ba3 Qd5 or 14 ... Qa5), and without Bxc6, Black can develop smoothly; e.g., 12 Na4 Na6 13 Ba3 Qa5 14 Nc2 Rfd8 15 Ne3 Be6 16 d3 Rac8 17 Nc4 Qc7 18 Nd2 b6 19 Bb2 Qd7 20 Re1 Nd4 21 Nc3 Nb4! 22 Nf3 Nxa2! and wins (Kirilov–Botvinnik,

Moscow 1931). Once a player has time to establish the Bind his game plays itself.

12	Na4	Na6
13	Nd3!	Qa5
14	f4!	

With Black's attention elsewhere the Simagin thrust opens up a dangerous kingside initiative. Black is unprepared for 14 ... Bd6   15 fxe5 fxe5   16 Qc2 threatening Qc4+-d5, and so he plays *14 . . . exf4   15 Nxf4 Bd6   16 e3!*.

Position after 16 e3!

White's advantage is considerable. The Bind has failed to bind, and White already threatens mate with 17 Bd5+ Kh8 18 Ng6+ hxg6   19 Rc4. Black lacks the time to cover his kingside weaknesses with . . . f5. He is simply outgunned on the kingside: *16 . . . Bxf4   17 Rxf4 Rad8   18 Bd5+ Kh8 19 Rh4 h6   20 Rcc4 Bf5?* (*20 . . . Be8!*) *21 Bxc6 bxc6 22 Bc3 Qb5   23 Rxh6+! gxh6   24 Qh5 Nc7   25 Qxh6+ Kg8   26 Bxf6 Ne6* (*26 . . . Rxf6   27 Qxh6 Rf8   28 Qg5+ Kh8   29 Rh4+ Bh7   30 Qe5+* wins also) *27 Rg4+* and Black resigned.

There is one final Black strategy to note before we leave the Dragon version of the Maroczy Bind. The logic behind it goes this way: If White has created a hole on d4 with his e2-e4 and c2-c4 moves, why not exploit it with . . . e5? True, Black creates a big hole of his own at d5 and makes his d-pawn horribly backward, but if he occupies d4 with minor pieces, the d-file will be blocked.

This is another idea popularized by Simagin but usually attributed to David Bronstein, the veteran Russian grandmaster. Simagin's game with V. Bivshev in the 1952 U.S.S.R. Championship illustrates the need for finding an appropriate plan to counter . . . e5.

1 e4 c5 2 Nf3 Nc6 3 d4 cxd4 4 Nxd4 g6 5 c4
Bg7 6 Be3 Nf6 7 Nc3 Ng4 8 Qxg4 Nxd4 9 Qd1
e5!? 10 Bd3 0-0 11 0-0 b6

Position after 11 . . . b6

White should handle the position in the first diagram slowly, seeking to exchange off pieces with Ne2 after some preparation. But in the 1954 game White made the error of trying to force the matter and to open up the position: *12 Nd5?! Bb7 13 f4? exf4! 14 Bxf4 d6 15 Qd2 Ne6*. It is true that Black has an isolated d-pawn now, but it is offset by the freedom of his minor pieces on the black squares and by the isolation of White's e-pawn. White compounded his previous errors with *16 Bh6? Bxh6!* and after *17 Qxh6 Bxd5 18 exd5 Nc5* he reached the following position.

Position after 18 . . . Nc5

Suddenly White has a bad bishop facing an excellent Black knight. The minor pieces and pawn structure now favor Black because he can seize control of the black squares and mobilize his kingside majority. White's pieces appear more aggressively placed, but a superior pawn structure will inevitably change that. The game continued *19 Rf3 f5! 20 Re1 Qf6 21 Rh3 Rf7 22 b3 f4! 23 Bb1 a5! 24 Qh4 Qxh4*, and Black won the ending following *25 Rxh4 Raf8 26 Kf2 Nd7 27 Re6 Rf6 28 Re7 R8f7 29 Rxf7 Rxf7 30 Bd3 Kg7 31 Be2 Ne5 32 Rh3 g5 33 Rc3 g4 34 a3 h5 35 b4 axb4 36 axb4 Rc7*.

Scheveningen Maroczy

While the Bind in the Dragon formation enjoyed an unsullied reputation until the 1950s, its counterpart in the Scheveningen kept its luster into the 1970s. At the height of its popularity the Bind was thought to be much stronger against a Sicilian formation in which Black has weakened his d-pawn with . . . e6. It appeared that Black had fewer chances of counterplay since . . . f5 was more weakening than normal, that . . . Bxc3 was hard to achieve since Black's bishop sat on e7, and that White could stop . . . b5 quite easily.

A simple example of containing the Scheveningen while building up pressure against the d-pawn is Tal–Korchnoi, Leningrad 1973, a game that developed out of a normal Dragon formation:

1 Nf3 Nf6   2 c4 b6   3 g3 c5   4 Bg2 Bb7   5 0-0 g6
6 b3 Bg7   7 Bb2 0-0   8 Nc3 Ne4!   9 Na4 Bxb2
10 Nxb2 d5   11 cxd5 Bxd5   12 Qc1 Nc6   13 d3
Nd6!

Position after 13 . . . Nd6!

With colors reversed this is a Dragon in which Black threatens to create a Maroczy Bind with . . . e5 and . . . Nf5. Here White offered a draw as he played *14 e3?*, a highly dubious move that commits White to either advancing his d-pawn or defending it.

In the diagram it doesn't appear that Black is ready to exert power along the d-file, but he obtained an ideal position in three logical stages:

(1) Establishing the Bind: *14 . . . e5! 15 Nc4 f6 16 Rd1 Nf7*. This insured that Black could meet d3-d4 with . . . cxd4 and . . . e4!, a typical idea that keeps the White d-pawn under attack and gives Black chances against the kingside.

(2) Restraining b3-b4: *17 Qc3 Qd7 18 a3 Rac8 19 Qb2 Rfd8 20 Rac1 Qe7! 21 Rb1*. Note that 19 b4 would have been met by 19 . . . cxb4 and 20 . . . b5!. White is not in sufficient control of the queenside lines to engineer b3-b4 safely.

(3) Taking aim at d6: *21 . . . Rc7! 22 Ncd2* (22 b4 e4!) *Be6! 23 Bf1 Bf5 24 Ne4 Bg4* (threatening . . . f5 and . . . e4) *25 Ned2 Ng5 26 Be2 Rcd7*.

Position after 26 . . . Rcd7

Black has handled the position masterfully. At no time could White have freed his game with b3-b4. Now Black threatens ... e4; e.g., 27 Qc2 e4! 28 dxe4 Rxd2. While White eliminated this possibility with *27 Re1 Nxf3+ 28 Nxf3*, he had to concede a pawn after *28 . . . Bf5!* (29 e4 Bg4) and eventually this cost him the game.

As in the Dragon, Black can obtain the amount of freedom he needs with ... b5 and ... f5 (*Supplemental Games #10 and #11*), but the main focus of the Scheveningen Maroczy is on ... d5. The other pawn breaks are secondary ideas that can be quite useful, but if Black successfully advances his d-pawn, the Bind is broken.

"Successfully" is the key word. It does not necessarily mean that Black exchanges off several pawns after ... d5 and can recapture material on d5. Frequently ... d5 is a temporary sacrifice which gives Black a quick counterattack along the c-file, the e-file, and the diagonal leading to the White king. This sacrifice can be sound because White usually takes certain protective steps in his own camp. These steps may be seen as weakening only if the pawn center is liquidated. Therefore, after ... d5 Black can probe the extent of these weaknesses in the White stronghold. This is shown by Adorjan–Portisch, Wijk aan Zee 1972:

1 e4 c5   2 Nf3 e6   3 d4 cxd4   4 Nxd4 Nc6   5 Nb5 d6   6 c4 Nf6   7 N1c3 a6   8 Na3 Be7   9 Be2 0-0 10 0-0 b6   11 Be3 Bb7   12 Qd2 Ne5   13 Qd4?! Ned7   14 Rfd1 Re8   15 Nc2 Qc7   16 Rac1 Rac8

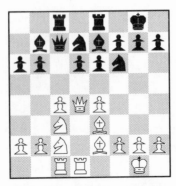

Position after 16 ... Rac8

White appears to have contained Black nicely so far. His queen is posted strongly in the center and his bishops are directed against the queenside. But in fact Black has at least equalized. He can bring his queen to a8 where it threatens the White e-pawn and prepares for ... d5. Of course, White can always play f2-f3; although this is a weakening move, that can only be proven by counterattack.

Which is just what happened after *17 f3? d5!*. Black makes a temporary sacrifice of a pawn to open up his two files and give his king bishop life. After *18 cxd5 exd5* White must avoid 19 exd5 because then the Black bishop wins with 19 ... Bc5 20 Qd2 Rxe3! 21 Nxe3 Re8.

A better defense is *19 Nxd5 Nxd5 20 exd5* so that on 20 ... Bc5 White can respond 21 Qd2 Rxe3 22 Nxe3 Re8 23 b4 or 22 ... Qe5 23 Rxc5. But Black used the bishop differently: *20 ... Bf6 21 Qb4* (21 Qd2 Bxb2 or 21 Qg4 Bxb2 22 d6 Qd8 23 Bd4 Bxd4+ 24 Nxd4 Rxc1 25 Rxc1 Ne5 favors Black's safer pawns and active pieces) *21 ... Qe5!*. White could not avoid 22 ... Qxb2 (or 22 b3 Qb2), and he fell apart speedily with *22 f4? Qxb2 23 Bg4 Rxc2*

24 Qxb2 Rxb2   25 Bxd7 Rxe3   26 Rc7 Bd4!   27 Kh1
(27 Rxd4 Re1 mate) *Rd2!   28 Rb1 g6   29 Rxb7 Bc5*
30 Bc6 Ree2   31 d6 Rxd6   32 Bf3 Rxa2   33 f5 a5 and
White resigned.

Supplemental Games

(1) Passivity is punished by a kingside attack. Darga–Yanofsky, Winnipeg 1967: 1 c4 Nf6   2 Nc3 g6   3 e4 d6   4 d4 Bg7   5 f3 0-0   6 Be3 b6   7 Bd3 Nbd7   8 Nge2 c5   9 0-0 Bb7   10 Qd2 Re8   11 Rad1 Qc8   12 b3 cxd4 (an unpleasant decision, but Black has no constructive alternative plan) 13 Nxd4 Nc5   14 Bb1   Ne6   15 Kh1   Nh5   16 Nde2! Nf6   17 Rfe1 Bc6   18 a4 Nc5   19 Bc2 a5 (recognition that ... b5 is impossible and that b2-b4 had to be prevented) 20 Nd4 Qb7   21 Nd5 Nfd7   22 Bh6 Ne6   23 Nf5!! (to meet 23 ... gxf5 with 24 exf5 Bxh6 25 Qxh6 Nef8   26 Nxe7+ Rxe7   27 Rxe7 with a winning attack) 23   ...   Bf8   24 Bxf8 Ndxf8   25 Nh6+ Kg7   26 Ng4 f6   27 Qh6+ Kf7   28 f4 Ng7   29 Qh4 Nh5   30 e5! Bxd5   31 Rxd5 dxe5   32 fxe5 Kg7   33 e6 Rad8   34 Rxh5 gxh5   35 Qxh5 Qc6   36 Qf7+ Kh8   37 Nh6 Ng6   38 Bxg6 hxg6   39 Qxg6 Qxe6!?   40 Nf7+ Resigns.

(2) Passivity is fatal in the endgame. Kiselev–Cherniaev, Povedniki 1992:   1 d4 Nf6   2 c4 g6   3 Nc3 Bg7   4 e4 d6   5 Bd3 0-0   6 Nge2 Nbd7   (A dubious plan here, compared with 6 ... e5! and 7 ... Nc6)   7 f3 c5   8 Be3 cxd4 9 Nxd4 Ne5   10 Be2 Bd7   11 Qd2 Qa5   12 Nd5! (In the endgame, White's spatial edge is considerable) Qxd2+ 13 Kxd2 e6   (Or 13 ... Nxd5   14 exd5, exposing e7 to later attack) 14 Nc3! a6 15 Rhd1 Rac8 16 b3 Rfe8 17 Rac1 Rcd8 18 g4! (Underlining Black's lack of space with a threat of 19 g5 Nh5 20 f4 and Bxh5) Nc6 19 Kc2 h6 20 Nxc6 Bxc6 21 Bb6 Rd7 (Otherwise the d-pawn falls) 22 b4! Rc8 23 Kb3 (No defense now to 24 b5) Rdd8 24 Bxd8 Rxd8 25 e5 Resigns.

(3) A brilliant illustration of White's using his c4-c5 and e4-e5 breaks. Korchnoi–Huebner, Leningrad 1973: 1 c4 Nf6 2 Nc3 c5 3 Nf3 g6 4 e4! Bg7 5 d4 cxd4 6 Nxd4 Nc6 7 Nc2 d6 8 Be2 Nd7 9 Bd2 (to take the sting out of ... Bxc3) 9 ... Nc5 10 b4 Ne6 11 Rc1 0-0 12 Nd5 Ned4 13 Nxd4 Nxd4 14 Bg5 Re8 15 0-0 Be6 16 Re1 Nxe2+ 17 Rxe2 Qd7 18 Rd2 Bxd5 19 Rxd5!? (preparing to keep the position closed until he can play c4-c5 or e4-e5 with greatest effect) 19 ... Qe6 20 Qd3 Rac8 21 Be3 a6 22 h3 Rf8 23 g4! (to stop ... f5) 23 ... Qf6 24 Bg5 Qb2 25 a3 Rc7 26 c5! Rfc8 27 Kg2! Bf8 28 cxd6! (based on the variation 28 ... Rxc1 29 d7! Rd8 30 Bxc1 Qxc1 31 Rc5 Qf4 32 Rc8 Rxd7 33 Qxd7 Qxe4+ 34 Kg3 and White avoids perpetual check) 28 ... exd6 29 Rxc7 Rxc7 30 e5! Rc2 31 Bd2! dxe5 32 Rd8 Kg7 33 Qe3! Be7 34 Qh6+ Kf6 35 Qh4+ Ke6 36 Re8 Rxd2 37 Qxe7+ Kd5 38 Rd8+ and Black resigned in face of 38 ... Kc4 39 Qc5+ Kb3 40 Qe3+.

(4) The e4-e5 plan executed perfectly. Capablanca–Yates, Bad Kissingen 1928: 1 e4 c5 2 Nf3 d6 3 d4 cxd4 4 Nxd4 g6 5 c4 Bg7 6 Nc3 Nf6 7 Be2 0-0 8 0-0 Nbd7?! 9 Be3 Nc5 10 f3! Bd7 11 Qd2 Rc8 12 Rfd1 a6 13 Rac1 (Both sides have completed their development, but because of the pawn structure Black has run out of ideas whereas White can decide among several.) 13 ... Ne6 14 b3 Nh5?! 15 Nxe6 Bxe6 16 Na4 (with the idea of 17 Bb6 and 18 c5) 16 ... Rc6 17 f4 Nf6 18 Bf3 Ng4 19 e5! Nxe3 20 Qxe3 Rc7 (Now with some luck Black can hold his losses to a bad d-pawn.) 21 c5! Qb8 22 exd6 exd6 23 Rxd6 Re8 24 Qd2 b5 25 Nb6! Bf8 26 Nd5 (not 26 Rc6? Rxc6 27 Bxc6 Bxc5+!) 26 ... Rxc5?! 27 Nf6+ Kh8 28 Nxe8 Rxc1+ 29 Qxc1 Qxe8 30 Rxa6 Qe7 31 Qc3+ Kg8 32 Qe5! b4 33 Be4 Qd8 34 h3 Bxh3 35 Bd5 Qh4 36 Qf6 Bc5+ 37 Kh2! Resigns.

(5) An ideal version of . . . b5 tactical play. Bobekov–Joppen, Amsterdam 1954: 1 d4 Nf6 2 c4 g6 3 Nc3 Bg7 4 e4 d6 5 f3 0-0 6 Be3 Nbd7 7 Qd2 c5 8 Nge2 a6 9 Ng3? (better is 9 0-0-0 or 9 Nc1 and Nb3) 9 ... cxd4 10 Bxd4 Ne5! (Black should not fear 11 Bxe5 dxe5, which gives him pawn control of d4 and the chance to occupy that square with a knight.) 11 Be2 Qa5 12 Rc1 Be6 13 b3 Rfc8 14 0-0 b5! 15 f4 (not 15 cxb5 axb5 16 Bxb5 Rxc3 or 15 c5 Nc6!) 15 ... Nc6! 16 Be3 bxc4 17 f5 Bd7 18 Bxc4 Ne5 (Black has a fine game now that lines are open and e5 is secure.) 19 Nd5? Qxd2 20 Bxd2 Nxc4 21 Nxe7+ Kf8 22 Nxc8 Nxd2 23 Rfd1 Bxc8! 24 Rxd2 Bh6 25 Rxc8+ Rxc8 26 Rxd6 Ng4! White resigns.

(6) With colors reversed, the b2-b4 stroke gives White open lines for bishop and rook. Schmidt–O'Kelly, Sarrbrucken 1950: 1 Nf3 Nf6 2 c4 c5 3 Nc3 Nc6 4 g3 d5 5 cxd5 Nxd5 6 Bg2 Nc7 7 0-0 e5 8 a3 Be7? 9 b4!

(the familiar trick of 9 . . . cxb4   10 axb4 Bxb4   11 Nxe5!
Nxe5   12 Qa4+)   9 . . . f6   10 bxc5 Ne6? (simply 10 . . .
Bxc5 is more efficient)   11 Nh4!   0-0   12 Nf5 Nxc5
13 Nxe7+ Nxe7   14 a4! Rb8   15 Nb5 a6   16 Ba3 b6
17 d4!   exd4   18 Nxd4 Bb7   19 Bxc5 bxc5   20 Ne6
Qxd1   21 Rfxd1 Rfc8   22 Rd7 Bxg2   23 Kxg2 Kf7
24 Nxg7 Kxg7   25 Rxe7+ Kg6   26 Rd1 Rb4   27 Rdd7
Rxa4   28 e4! Rg8   29 g4! h6   30 h4 h5   31 g5 and
Black resigned in view of f4-f5 mate.

(7) Exploitation of Simagin's . . . f5. Milic–Irc, Ljubljana
1955; 1 e4 c5   2 Nf3 Nc6   3 d4 cxd4   4 Nxd4 g6
5 c4 Bg7   6 Nc2 Nf6   7 Nc3 d6   8 Be2 Nd7   9 0-0?!
Nc5?   (9 . . . Bxc3!)   10 f3 0-0   11 Be3 f5   12 Qd2 Ne6
13 exf5! gxf5   14 f4! (Having missed chances for . . . Bxc3,
Black now must defend his center pawns against pressure along
the open files—without counterplay.)   14 . . . Kh8
15 Rad1 b6   16 Bf3 Bb7   17 b3 Qd7   18 Nb5 Nc5
19 Ncd4! Nd8   20 Bxb7 Ndxb7   21 Nc3 Rac8   22 Nf3
Nd8   23 Bd4 Rg8   24 Rfe1 Nce6   25 Bxg7+ Rxg7
26 Nd5 Nc5   27 Qb2 Nde6   28 Ng5 Kg8   29 Nxe6
Nxe6   30 Qe2! Rg6   31 Rd3! (Black's weakest point is e7,
and in the simplified situation now arising he cannot defend
it.)   31 . . . Re8   32 Re3 Nd4   33 Qb2 Nc6   34 b4 e5
(otherwise the e-pawn falls to b4-b5)   35 b5 Na5   36 fxe5
Nxc4   37 Qb3 Qc8   38 Rc1 f4   39 Rxc4 Qg4   40 Nxf4
d5   41 Rd4 Resigns.

**(8) A lightning example of e2-e3 and d2-d4 in the reversed
Dragon.** Keres–Smyslov, Leningrad 1947: 1 c4 Nf6
2 Nc3 c5   3 Nf3 e6   4 g3 d5   5 cxd5 Nxd5   6 Bg2 Nc6
7 0-0 Nc7 (A little overambitious here. Black has lost a move

with ... e6 if he intended ... e5.)   8 b3 Be7   9 Bb2 e5
10 Rc1 f6   11 Na4 b6?   12 Nh4! (Black's problems now
become apparent, e.g.,   12 ... Bb7   13 b4!.) 12 ... Bd7
13 e3! (with a primary threat of Qh5+)   13 ... 0-0   14 d4!
exd4   (here the major threat was d4-d5)   15 exd4 Rc8
16 dxc5 b5   17 Nc3 f5   18 Rc2 Bxh4   19 Rd2! Rf7
20 gxh4!   (not allowing Black to give up his queen with
20 Bxc6 Bxc6)   20 ... Ne6   21 Nxb5 Nxc5   22 Nd6
Re7   23 Nxc8   Qxc8   24 Ba3   Ne4   25 Bxe4   fxe4
26 Bxe7 Nxe7   27 Rxd7 Resigns.

**(9) Simagin's f2-f4 and Bxc6 lead to a different kind of
attack.** Matulovic–Janosevic, Ljubljana 1959:   1 c4 Nf6
2 Nc3 c5   3 g3 d5   4 cxd5 Nxd5   5 Bg2 Nc7   6 Nf3
Nc6   7 Qa4 Qd7   8 d3 e5   9 0-0 Be7   10 Nd2 0-0
(10 ... Nd4 avoids the impending problems)   11 Nc4 f6
12 f4 Qe6   13 f5! (a strong idea that secures e4 indefinitely for a White minor piece)   13 ... Qd7   14 Be3 Rb8
15 Bxc6! bxc6   16 Ne4 Na6   17 a3 Rb5   18 Qc2 Qc7
19 Rf3 Bd7   20 g4! Be8   21 Raf1 (White's plan of g4-
g5 shows he can win on either wing)   21 ... Qd8
22 Qc1 Rb7   23 g5 Bh5   24 R3f2 Kh8   25 Rg2 Rd7
26 Qe1 Qe8   27 Qh4 fxg5   28 Bxg5 g6   29 f6 Bd8
30 Bh6 Rff7   31 Ned6 Qe6   32 Nxf7+ Rxf7   33 Bg7+
Kg8   34 Qe4   Bc7   35 Rg5   h6   36 Bxh6   Rxf6
37 Rxf6   Qxf6   38 Nxe5   Kh7   39 Rxh5   Bxe5
40 Bg5+ Resigns.

(10) The ... b5 break in the Scheveningen Maroczy.
Keene–Karpov, Hastings 1971–2:   1 Nf3 c5   2 e4 e6   3 d4
cxd4 4 Nxd4 Nc6   5 Nc3 a6 6 g3 Nge7   7 Nb3 Na5!
8 Bg2 Nec6   9 0-0 d6   10 Nxa5 Qxa5   11 Ne2 (to es-

tablish the Bind with b2-b3, Bb2 and c3-c4) 11 ... Be7
12 b3 0-0 13 Bb2 Bd7 14 c4 Rfd8 (not yet 14 ... b5 because of 15 c5!) 15 a4 Rac8 16 Bc3 Qc7 17 Qd2 b6
18 Qb2 Bf8 19 f4? (White rushes into a kingside attack
that allows Black to play ... b5 through tactical means. The
opening of the position favors Black now that White's queenside has been grossly compromised by b2-b3 and a2-a4.) 19
... b5! 20 axb5 axb5 21 cxb5 Qb6+ 22 Kh1 Qxb5
23 b4 d5! 24 Rab1 Rb8 25 exd5 exd5 26 f5? Nxb4
27 Qd2 Re8 28 Nd4 Qc4 29 Rbd1 Rbc8 (Black's pieces
control the board now) 30 Ba1 Ra8 31 Rc1 Ra2
32 Qg5 Qa6 33 Ne6!? h6! 34 Qg4 Bxe6! 35 Bxg7
Qe2! 36 Qxe2 Rxe2 37 Bxf8 Rxf8 38 fxe6 fxe6
39 Rfe1 Rff2 40 Rxe2 Rxe2 White resigns.

(11) And the ... f5 idea. Dely–Suetin, Kecskemet 1972:
1 e4 c5 2 Nf3 Nc6 3 d4 cxd4 4 Nxd4 e6 5 Nb5 d6
6 c4 Nf6 7 N5c3 Be7 8 Be2 0-0 9 0-0 b6 10 b3 Bb7
11 Bb2 Nd7! 12 Na3 Nc5 13 Qd2 Bf6! 14 Rfe1 Be5!
(This maneuver is designed to provoke f2-f4, a move that
would seriously undermine the White e-pawn, and to provide
room for ... f5, an attacking idea.) 15 Bf1 f5! 16 exf5
Rxf5 17 Nd1 Qh4 18 g3 Qf6 19 Bg2 Rf8 20 Rb1
Bxb2 21 Rxb2 Ne5! 22 Re3 Bxg2 23 Kxg2 Ng4
24 Re1 Rh5! and White resigned because of 25 h3 Qf3+
26 Kg1 Rxh3 or 25 h4 Qf3+ 26 Kg1 Nd3.

D. THE BOLESLAVSKY HOLE

The idea that Black can play ... e5 to obtain active piece
play—and enough of it to compensate for his backward

d-pawn—is considered a relatively new idea in the Open Sicilian-English. Actually it is one of the oldest. Louis Charles Mahe de LaBourdonnais, who died in 1840, tried it in his marathon match with Alexander MacDonnell. In that famous encounter, a predecessor of today's world championships, the French champion played 1 e4 c5　2 Nf3 Nc6　3 d4 cxd4 4 Nxd4 e5 in order to bring out his king bishop with a gain of time. (MacDonnell considerably eased Black's game with 5 Nxc6?, a typical positional error, and lost a fine brilliancy—*Supplemental Game #1.*)

The modern version of this has been attributed to Louis Paulsen and Isaac Boleslavsky, two masters separated by 70 years of chess theory who appreciated the dynamic qualities of . . . e5. Even if Black's king bishop is locked inside with . . . d6 Black's game threatens to blossom with . . . d5. Unlike the Dragon and Scheveningen formations, Black has a center pawn on the fifth rank here, and he is always preparing to push another one to the fifth. He has a bad d-pawn and concedes a hole on d5, but this is not enough to give White an advantage. (We call this the Boleslavsky Hole to distinguish it from the Boleslavsky Wall of Chapter 6.)

In the Sicilian Defense we see this idea in a variety of lines: 1 e4 c5　2 Nf3 d6　3 d4 cxd4　4 Nxd4 Nf6　5 Nc3 a6 (the Najdorf Variation), 1 e4 c5　2 Nf3 a6　3 d4 cxd4 4 Nxd4 Nf6　5 Nc3 e5 (the O'Kelly Variation), and 1 e4 c5 2 Nf3 d6　3 d4 cxd4　4 Nxd4 Nf6　5 Nc3 Nc6　6 Be2 e5 (the Boleslavsky Variation).

The dynamism inherent in Black's formation can be shown by examples such as this, one of many games of this nature and brevity played between masters shortly after World War II.

Novotelnov–Petrosian, Moscow 1951:

1 e4 c5   2 Nf3 d6   3 d4 cxd4   4 Nxd4 Nf6   5 Nc3
a6   6 Be2 e5   7 Nb3 Be7   8 0-0 0-0   9 f4 Nbd7
10 Qe1? b5   11 a3 Bb7   12 Bf3 Rc8   13 Kh1 Re8
14 Qf2? Bf8   15 Bd2

Position after 15 Bd2

Black has a perfect position for *15 . . . d5!*. Much earlier he
could have been restrained with a2-a4 and by Bg5xf6, as we'll
see, but once . . . d5 is played here the comparison between
Black's coordination and White's aimlessness becomes overwhelming.

This is clear from either 16 fxe5 dxe4 or 16 exd5 e4, after
which Black's pieces simply control more squares than
White's. White's preference was *16 Nxd5*, but this lost at least
a pawn (*16 . . .Rxc2   17 fxe5 Nxd5   18 exd5 Nxe5*) and, after *19 Nd4? Nd3!*, the game. Another illustration of the pent-
up power of . . . d5 can be found in *Supplemental Game #2* at
the end of the chapter.

Stopping . . . d5 by Control of d5

It is no secret then that White's first priority is stopping . . . d5. He can do this mechanically with Nd5 or by dropping some other piece onto d5, but this can lead to exchanges that result in White's eventually recapturing with a pawn on d5. This pawn would then block the d-file, correct the Black pawn structure, and give Black a ready-made kingside attack with . . . f5.

If possible it is desirable to recapture on d5 with a piece, which means that White must control the square with one more piece than Black. The battle for d5 begins with four minor pieces each, however. The early skirmishing requires a subtle appreciation of how to coordinate pieces and pawns to one strategic end. In one modern opening system—*1 e4 c5 2 Nf3 d6 3 d4 cxd4 4 Nxd4 Nf6 5 Nc3 a6 6 Be2 e5 7 Nb3 Be7 8 0-0 Qc7*—this is obvious.

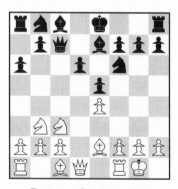

Position after 8 . . . Qc7

9 a4!

This is part of the battle plan because it stops . . . b5, a move that prepares . . . d5 with . . . Bb7 and . . . b4. In Boleslavsky's own variation Black plays . . . a5, threatening to disrupt the queenside with further advances. When White responds a 2-a4 Black can put his queen knight on b4 to promote . . . d5. This is one reason why White's 9 a4 in the diagram can be considered double edged. If Black can bring his queen knight to b4 quickly he will have a well-placed piece and probable equality, but right now 9 a4 Nc6 runs into 10 Nd5! Nxd5 11 exd5 Nb4 12 c3.

9 . . .   **b6?**

Black can find a different place for his queen bishop to watch d5 by playing . . . Be6. This is the most accurate even though White can harass the bishop with f4-f5. One of the most heavily analyzed variations in recent years continues 9 . . . Be6 10 f4 0-0 11 f5 Bc4 12 a5 Nbd7 13 Be3 b5! 14 axb6 Nxb6, and Black is regarded as close to equality despite his new weakness, the a-pawn.

10   Bg5

In the battle of minor pieces it is obvious that a Black knight can control d5 but a White queen bishop cannot. White prepares to make a favorable exchange—favorable because it secures d5 control and because Black is left with a bishop on e7 that is hemmed in by its own pawns.

10	. . .	Nbd7
11	Nd2!	Bb7
12	Nc4	

This knight heads for e3 after which all four White pieces will be able to establish d5 control. Note that on 12 . . . Nxe4

White can play 13 Nd5! with a winning game for tactical rather than positional reasons. After *12 . . . 0-0* White completed his strategic plan with *13 Ne3 Rfc8   14 Bc4 Qc5   15 Bxf6 Nxf6   16 Ncd5!*.

Position after 16 Ncd5!

Black has an awful game whether he leaves himself with a bad-bishop-vs.-good-knight middlegame (16 ... Nxd5 17 Bxd5 Bxd5   18 Nxd5) or avoids exchanges. In the game Bogdanovic–Buljovcic, Kraljevo 1967, White secured a won game as pieces were traded off: *16 . . . Bxd5   !7 Bxd5 Ra7 18 c3 g6   19 g3 Bf8   20 Qf3 Bg7   21 Rfd1 b5   22 axb5 axb5   23 Rxa7   Qxa7   24 Qe2   Rb8   25 Nc2!   Nxd5 26 Rxd5 Qd7   27 Qd3 Rb6   28 Kg2 f5   29 f3.*

The pawn structure provides the basis for attacking play also because d5 is a very useful square for pieces directed against the kingside. In the Scheveningen formation we saw how f4-f5 by White often forces . . . e5. White's kingside attack grew naturally out of the center pawn situation. Here is another example:

Torre–O'Kelly, Malaga 1973:

1 e4 c5　2 Nf3 d6　3 Bb5+ Nd7　4 d4 Nf6　5 Nc3
cxd4　6 Qxd4 e5!?　7 Qd3 h6!　8 Nd2! Be7　9 Nc4
0-0

Position after 9 . . . 0-0

Black has taken a move to stop Bg5, and White has used
that tempo to execute a knight maneuver to control d5. White
cannot win a pawn with 10 Nxd6 because of 10 . . . Nc5, but
10 Bxd7! prevents Black from immediately unraveling his
pieces with . . . Nc5 and . . . a6.

Subsequent analysis suggests that 10 . . . Bxd7! is best although it involves a pawn sacrifice (11 Nxd6 Qc7　12 Nf5
Bxf5　13 exf5 e4 or 12 Ndb5 Bxb5　13 Nxb5 Qc6
14 Nc3 Bb4). White can also ignore the sacrifice and play
11 Ne3. However, *10 . . . Qxd7?* was played, and after
11 Ne3 Qc6 White began an effortless attack with *12 g4!*.
This works tactically because Black cannot survive long with
an open g-file since after 12 . . . Nxg4　13 Nxg4 Bxg4
14 Rg1 h5　15 h3 Be6　16 Bh6 Bf6　17 Bxg7! and

18 Qg3. It works strategically because the natural response to g2-g4 in Scheveningen positions (. . . d5) is out of the question here.

The attack rolled on: *12 . . . Be6   13 Rg1 Nd7   14 Nf5 Bxf5   15 gxf5 Kh7   16 Qh3 Rg8   17 Nd5 Bf6   18 c3 Raf8   19 Qh5.*

Position after 19 Qh5

The significance of a favorable pawn structure is obvious here. White only has three developed pieces and an uncastled king. But his pieces count more and he threatens to win with 20 Rg6 followed by 21 Rxh6+ (e.g., 20 . . . fxg6   21 fxg6+ Kh8   22 Bxh6). The game ended with *19 . . . Rh8   20 Be3 Qa4   21 Kd2 Rhg8* (or *21 . . . Qxe4   22 Nxf6+ Nxf6 23 Rxg7+ and 24 Rg1+*)   *22 Rg6!* and Black resigned.

Stopping . . . d5 Mechanically

As mentioned earlier the occupation of d5 by a pawn is not as desirable as by a piece. But in coordination with c2-c4 and b2-

b4, a pawn on d5 can help promote a general queenside advance involving c4-c5. Then White will have a mobile majority and a great advantage in space.

The drastic defeat of Bobby Fischer by Yefim Geller in 1962 (*Supplemental Game #3*) perhaps best illustrates the problems of defense. A more recent example, a 1970 game between Leonid Stein and Isaac Boleslavsky himself, shows the constriction placed on Black's game.

1 e4 c5   2 Nf3 d6   3 d4 cxd4   4 Nxd4 Nf6   5 Nc3 a6   6 Be2 e5   7 Nb3 Be7   8 0-0 0-0   9 Be3 Qc7 10 a4 Be6   11 a5 Qc6   12 Bf3 Nbd7

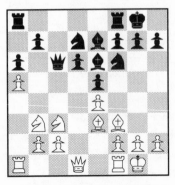

Position after 12 ... Nbd7

Black appears to have a fine game. His bishop, for instance, can remain indefinitely on e6 because f2-f4-f5 has been delayed. If White proceeds routinely with 13 Qd2 Rfd8 14 Rfd1 b5 Black should equalize easily. But *13 Nd5! Bxd5 14 exd5* upsets his plans. Now it is White who has a grand design—preparing for c4-c5 with Qd3, c2-c4, and Rfc1. Black

tried to forestall this plan with *14. . . Qc4*, but White proceeded forward with *15 Nd2 Qb5   16 Qb1!*.

Position after 16 Qb1!

Now what? Not only are b2-b4 and c2-c4 part of a positional plan but they also threaten to trap the Black queen. If
Black has to provide a retreat such as *16 . . . Rfc8   17 b4 Nf8*,
it is easy to see White's grand design coming true with *18 c4
Qd7   19 Rd1 Ng6   20 c5 dxc5   21 Nc4* followed by Nb6
or bxc5.

In the actual game Black made a bid for freedom with *16
. . . e4*, but this pawn sacrifice was insufficient after *17 c4 Qb4
18 Bxe4 Nxe4   19 Qxe4 Bf6   20 Qc2!* (*20 . . . Qxb2
21 Qxb2* and *22 Rab1*) threatening *21 Ra4*. The game was
beyond salvation after *20 . . . a6   21 axb6 Nxb6   22 Ra3!*
(intending Rb3 whether or not Black takes the b-pawn) *Nd7
23 Ne4 Be5   24 Ra4 Qb8   25 f4 Bf6   26 Nxf6+ Nxf6
27 Bd4*.

Perhaps the chief drawback to Nd5 in these instances is the
mobile Black kingside that is created. Black's e-pawn is joined

by the f-pawn on the fourth rank and together they build up an aggressive momentum.

Often the middlegame becomes a race between White's grand design on the queenside and Black's on the kingside, but if White is slowed up, Black's game plays itself, as in Pilnik–Geller, Göteborg 1955:

1 e4 c5 2 Nf3 Nc6 3 d4 cxd4 4 Nxd4 Nf6
5 Nc3 d6 6 Be2 e5 7 Nb3 Be7 8 0-0 0-0 9 Be3
Be6 10 Bf3 a5 11 Nd5 Bxd5 12 exd5 Nb8
13 c4

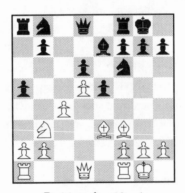

Position after 13 c4

White was provoked into 11 Nd5 by the threat of 11 . . . a4 12 Nd2 d5 or 12 Nc1 Qa5 followed by . . . a3. White rejected 11 a4 because of the outpost this would grant Black's queen knight on b4.

In the above diagram we can see that *13 . . . Na6!* puts White's plan of c4-c5 out of reach. Black can establish solid control of the key square with . . . b6 and . . . Nc5. For this reason White abruptly changed direction and tried to reposition his pieces: *14 Bd2 b6 15 Bc3 Nc5 16 Nxc5 bxc5 17 Qe1 Nd7 18 Bd1 a4!* (stopping Ba4) *19 Bc2 f5! 20 Rd1 g6 21 Qe2 Bf6 22 f3.*

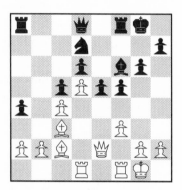

Position after 22 f3

Black's pawns in the center appear to be static. They control squares but apparently cannot advance without conceding weaknesses; for example, 22 . . . f4? would give White e4 for his bad bishop. But Black created a pawn formation that was highly favorable for a kingside attack: *22 . . . e4!! 23 Bxf6 Qxf6 24 fxe4 f4!.*

In the final stage Black's knight reigns supreme on e5 while his heavy pieces prepare for . . . g5-4-3. White had no perceptible counterplay: *25 Rf2 Ne5 26 Rdf1 Qh4 27 Bd1 Rf7 28 Qc2 g5! 29 Qc3 Raf8 30 h3 h5 31 Be2 g4! 32 Rxf4 Rxf4 33 Rxf4 Rxf4 34 g3 Nf3+ 35 Kf2 Qxh3 36 gxf4 g3+ 37 Kxf3 g2+ 38 Kf2 Qh2* and White resigned.

The f2-f4 Problem

The final complication to the Boleslavsky Hole comes about when White plays f2-f4 and Black responds . . . exf4. This creates two isolated pawns in the center, White's at e4, Black's at d6. White's prospects are inherently superior because of the difference in pawns. Both are easily defended but White's gives him better use of the f5 square as an outpost. Although Black gets e5 as an outpost square he gives White another outpost at d4.

It is not surprising that the best illustration of Black's problems is a 1961 game between Geller and Lev Polugaevsky. Geller played the position with White or Black as well as anyone in the world, and Polugaevsky has consistently tried to defend the Black position after . . . exf4. (He scored one-half point in four games of a 1974 match with Anatoly Karpov in this variation.) The 1961 game began *1 e4 c5   2 Nf3 d6   3 d4 cxd4   4 Nxd4 Nf6   5 Nc3 a6   6 Be2 e5   7 Nb3 Be7   8 0-0 0-0   9 Be3 Qc7   10 Qd2 Be6   11 f4 exf4   12 Rxf4 Nbd7.*

Position after 12 . . . Nbd7

Black didn't have much choice about . . . exf4 because he was threatened with 12 f5 Bc4 13 g4! and a rush of kingside pawns. White's recapture with a rook on f4 seems unnatural but is more logical then 12 Bxf4. The bishop does its best work along the g1-a7 diagonal, and the rook is needed to control the outpost square at f5.

The White pieces began to take charge with *13 Nd4! Ne5 14 Nf5*. Black could exchange minor pieces now or later, but after 14 . . . Bxf5 15 Rxf5 Nc4 16 Bxc4 Qxc4 17 Bd4 the comparison of the remaining minor pieces must favor White. However, without exchanges Black has nothing much to do whereas White brings his heavy pieces to the kingside theater.

This is what happened: *14 . . . Rac8 15 Raf1 Rfe8 16 Bd4! Bf8 17 Bd3 Nfd7 18 Rh4! Ng6 19 Rh3 Nde5 20 Qd1! b5 21 Qh5 h6 22 Rg3 Kh7 23 Nd5 Bxd5 24 exd5 Nxd3 25 cxd3 Qb7 26 Kh1 Rc2 27 Ne3*. White threatens sacrifices on h6, f6, and g7 when this knight reaches g4. With *27 . . . Rd2 28 Ng4 Qd7 29 h4!* (better than the immediate 29 Qxh6+ gxh6 30 Nf6+) *29 . . . Qe7* (or 29 . . . Kg8 30 Nxh6+ gxh6 31 Rxg6+ fxg6 32 Qxg6+ and 33 Bxg7) *30 Re3! Qd7 31 Qxh6+* Black could safely resign because he loses a rook after 31 . . . gxh6 32 Nf6+. He actually played *31 . . . Kg8* and gave up after *32 Rxe8* which exposes the Black rook on d2.

Supplemental Games

(1) An early example with an antipositional Nxc6. Mac-Donnell–LaBourdonnais, match 1834: 1 e4 c5 2 Nf3 Nc6 3 d4 cxd4 4 Nxd4 e5 5 Nxc6?! (With 5 Nb5, threatening 6 Nd6+, White has much better chances for an advantage.) 5 ... bxc6 6 Bc4 Nf6 7 Bg5 Be7 8 Qe2 d5 9 Bxf6 Bxf6 10 Bb3 0-0 11 0-0 a5 12 exd5 cxd5 13 Rd1 d4 14 c4 (better is 14 Nd2 and Ne4) 14 ... Qb6 15 Bc2 Bb7 16 Nd2 Rae8 17 Ne4 Bd8 18 c5 Qc6 19 f3 Be7 20 Rac1 f5! 21 Qc4+ Kh8 22 Ba4 Qh6! 23 Bxe8 fxe4 24 c6 exf3 25 Rc2 (on 25 cxb7 Qe3+ 26 Kh1 fxg2+ and ... Rf2+ win for Black) 25 ... Qe3+ 26 Kh1 Bc8 27 Bd7 f2 28 Rf1 d3 29 Rc3 Bxd7 30 exd7 e4! (The error of 5 Nxc6 shows up in Black's astonishing center. Watch it advance.) 31 Qc8 Bd8 32 Qc4 Qe1 33 Rc1 d2! 34 Qc5 Rg8 35 Rd1 e3 36 Qc3 Qxd1! 37 Rxd1 e2!! White resigns.

(2) White's dalliance permits ... d5 to give Black pieces the lion's share of the board. Unzicker–Bronstein, Göoteborg 1955: 1 e4 c5 2 Nf3 d6 3 d4 cxd4 4 Nxd4 Nf6 5 Nc3 a6 6 Be2 e5 7 Nb3 Be7 8 0-0 0-0 9 Be3 Qc7 10 a4 b6 11 Qd2 (11 Bg5 is a move slower than in the example cited earlier because White has already played Be3) 11 ... Be6 12 Rfd1 Rc8 13 Qe1? (A much better idea is 13 Nc1 with the maneuver Na2-b4 to control d5.) 13 ... Qb7! (Black threatens ... Rxc3 and ... Nxe4 or ... d5.) 14 Rd2 Nbd7 15 f3 d5 16 exd5 Nxd5 17 Nxd5 Bxd5 18 Rad1 Nf6 19 Nc1 e4! 20 Qf2 Bc5 21 Bxc5 bxc5 22 Qe3 Re8 23 f4 c4 24 b3 Rac8 25 h3 Be6 26 Kh2 Qc7 27 Rd6 a5 28 bxc4 Bxc4 29 Nb3 Bxe2 30 Qxe2 e3 31 R6d4 Ne4 32 Qf3 Ng5 33 Qg4 Ne6 34 Re4 h5! 35 Qf3 Ng5 36 Rxe8+ Rxe8 37 Qg3 Qxc2 38 Rd5 e2!? (leading to an exciting finish although 38 ... Qxb3 39 Rxg5 Qb2 was simpler) 39 Rxg5 e1(Q)

40 Rxg7+ Kh8 41 Qg5 Qxg2+! 42 Qxg2 Re2 and White resigned because the Black king escapes perpetual check at h6.

(3) White cripples the Black queenside with c4-c5. Geller–Fischer, Curaçao 1962: 1 e4 c5 2 Nf3 d6 3 d4 cxd4 4 Nxd4 Nf6 5 Nc3 a6 6 Be2 e5 7 Nb3 Be7 8 0-0 0-0 9 Be3 Qc7?! (The queen move is usually needed only after . . . Be6 to meet f4-f5. Here it loses a tempo that might be better spent on an immediate . . . Be6.) 10 a4 Be6 11 a5 Nbd7 12 Nd5! (not 12 f3 because then 12 . . . b5! offers good play) 12 . . . Nxd5 13 exd5 Bf5 14 c4 Bg6 (Black hurries toward . . . f5, but his best chance is 14 . . . Rfc8 followed by . . . Qd8 and . . . Bg5.) 15 Rc1 Nc5? (Black correctly fears c4-c5 but he could have preserved better chances with 15 . . . f5 16 c5 dxc5 17 Nxc5 Nxc5 18 b4 f4! 19 Bxc5 Bd6.) 16 Nxc5 dxc5 17 b4! (From here on White threatens to obtain two mobile pawns at c5 and d5, e.g. 17 . . . cxb4 18 Bb6 and 19 c5.) 17 . . . Rac8 18 Qb3 Bd6 19 Rfd1 Qe7 20 bxc5 Bxc5 21 Bxc5 Rxc5 22 Ra1 Rd8 23 Ra4! Bf5 24 Rb4 Bc8 25 Rb6! Rd6 26 Qb4 Qc7 27 Rxd6 Qxd6 28 Rb1 Qc7 (White was threatening Qb6, to break the blockade. Positionally, the game has been over since 17 b4!.) 29 Qa4! Bd7 30 Qa3! Rxa5 31 Rxb7 Qxb7 32 Qxa5 g6 33 h3 Qb1+ 34 Kh2 Bf5 35 Qc3 Qe4 36 Bf3 Qd4 37 Qxd4 exd4 38 g4 Bc8 39 c5! a5 40 c6 Kf8, and Black resigned because after 41 d6 the pawns can't be stopped, e.g., 41 . . . a4 42 c7 a3 43 Bc6 a2 44 d7 Bxd7 45 Bxd7 a1(Q) 46 c8(Q)+ or 41 . . . Ke8 42 Bd1! Ba6 43 g5 Bb5 44 c7 Bd7 45 Ba4.

CHAIN REACTIONS

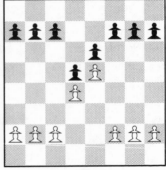

The d5 Chain   The e5 Chain

PAWNS ARE BORN FREE BUT ARE EVERYWHERE IN CHAINS. IN THE French Defense, in the Nimzo-Indian and King's Indian defenses, and in assorted Benoni openings pawn chains are familiar parts of the topography. They provide the most sophisticated strategies of closed formations. It is hardly an exaggeration to say that no one can achieve the status of master without acquiring a mastery of chains.

In the period of chess history immediately preceding the rise of Paul Morphy, closed positions with chains were common; however, it is fair to say that pawn chains were really "discovered" by Aron Nimzovich, the polemical Latvian master and analyst. With typical modesty Nimzovich wrote in the 1930s: "Today . . . everyone knows that all the things I then [before 1913] said about the Pawn-chain are uncontestable truths." And what Nimzovich said has pretty much held up.

Nimzovich described the chain as partly but not only a "cramping problem," and we should take note of this first. A pawn chain can be large (c3, d4, e5, f6 vs. c4, d5, e6, f7) or small (d4, e5 vs. d5, e6). But in either case the center is closed, enticing pawn marches on the opposite wings. In the smaller case the White f-pawn heads to f5 to attack the "base" of Black's chain at e6. Black attacks the White base at d4 with . . . c5.

The chain can have a great cramping and constricting impact on the enemy pawns and pieces. A pawn chain headed by a pawn at e5 prevents the enemy king knight from developing to its most natural square, for example. Nimzovich spoke of the cramping effect on the enemy pawns, but we are more concerned with the impact on pieces. Consider the following:

Position after 9 . . . Kf7!

This and the following position occurred in Rivera–Suttles, San Juan 1965, and show the extreme cramping effect of Black's chain on the White kingside. The initial position is reached by 1 d4 g6 2 e4 Bg7 3 c4 d6 4 Nc3 Nc6 5 Be3 e5 6 d5 Nce7 7 f3 f5 8 c5! Nf6 9 Bb5+ Kf7!. Both players have logically attacked the base of the enemy chain—White with c4-c5, Black with . . . f5. Black's last move avoids the exchange of his good bishop, the loss of which would make e6 highly vulnerable to enemy pieces.

White now played 10 h3??, a natural move with the idea of preparing 11 g4, which blocks the kingside, and of stopping 10 . . . fxe4 11 fxe4 Ng4. But White lost his chance for g2-g4 because Black immediately responded 10 . . . f4! 11 Bf2 g5. To use Nimzovich's phrase, Black transferred his attack on the base from e4 to f3. If White plays 12 g4 Black captures en passant and bombards the hopelessly weak f-pawn.

The game proceeded with 12 Nge2 h5 13 cxd6 cxd6 14 Qb3 g4 15 0-0-0 g3! 16 Be1 (16 Bg1?? would entomb the White queen bishop and king rook for the foreseeable future) Ng6.

Position after 16 . . . Ng6

Black decided not to open the kingside but rather to attack the ultimate base, g2, with pieces instead. After 17. . . Nh4 White can cover g2 with 18 Rg1. But because of the extended position of his kingside pawns and his superior pieces on the kingside, Black has a simple winning plan of preparing to sacrifice his knight for the g-pawn and h-pawn. (For an illustration of this idea on the queenside see *Supplemental Game #1*.)

As the game went White chose to defend g2 with a bishop, hoping that he would be able to free his kingside once he had taken the initiative on the queenside. But it was Black who seized power on that wing: 17 Ng1? Nh4 18 Bf1 a6 19 Kb1 b5 20 Nge2 Nd7 21 Nc1 Nc5 22 Qc2 Bd7 23 b4 Na4 24 Nb3 Nxc3+ 25 Bxc3 Qb6 26 Na5 Rhc8 27 Qd2 Ra7 28 Bb2 Bf6 29 Rc1 Rxc1+ 30 Bxc1 Bd8 31 Kc2 Rc7+ 32 Kd1 Rc8 33 Nb3 Qa7 34 Bd3 Bb6 35 Re1 Bf2! 36 Bf1 Bxe1 37 Qxe1 Qg1 38 Qe2 Bxh3 White resigns.

The inhibiting effect of a chain is especially powerful when the defender has nothing to show on another wing of the chain. If White could use the c-file in the preceding example then Black's exercise with his g-pawn would look silly. An equally extreme but also instructive example of this is Korchnoi–Barcza, Sochi 1966:

1 c4 e6 2 d4 Bb4+ 3 Nc3 c5 4 d5?! d6 5 e4 Nf6 6 Bd3 Nbd7? 7 Ne2 e5? 8 0-0 Bxc3 9 Nxc3 0-0 10 g3!

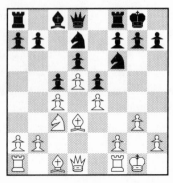

Position after 10 g3!

Black deserves enslavement for his opening play. He could have doubled White's c-pawns with . . . Bxc3+ on the fourth, fifth, or sixth moves. After Ne2 White can always recapture with his knight. After White castles he threatens to embarrass the bishop with Na4 and with preparations for b2-b4 (a2-a3, Rb1). So Black gives up this bishop and then tries to keep the center closed (7 . . . e5). How Black hoped to obtain counterplay, we'll never know.

White has a simple plan. He prepares for f2-f4 and makes sure that he will be able to recapture on f4 with a pawn. (10 f4? exf4! 11 Bxf4 Qe7 and . . . Ne5 would ease Black's game considerably.) White can control events on both sides of the board, and that explains the following: 10 . . . Ne8   11 Kh1 f6   12 f4 Rf7   13 Qe2 Nf8   14 Bd2 Qe7   15 Rae1 Rb8 16 a3 b6   17 Rf2 Rb7   18 Nd1! Qd8   19 Ne3 Rbe7.

White easily restrained his opponent's . . . f5 and . . . b5, the two pawn breaks that Black needs for counterplay. Meanwhile, he prepares for breaks of his own (b4xc5 or fxe5). Black's inability to do anything led White to suddenly transfer the attack to the kingside base: 20 f5! Rb7   21 h4 Bd7   22 g4 h6

23 Rh2 Nh7   24 Rg1 Kf8 (hoping to reach the queenside before the storm breaks on g5) *25 Ng2! Qb8   26 b4 Ke7 27 Ne1 Kd8   28 Nf3! Kc8   29 g5 fxg5   30 hxg5 Nxg5 31 Nxg5 hxg5   32 Rh8! Kc7.*

Position after 32 . . . Kc7

Black's chances are nil because of White's total control of the kingside lines. There is nothing to be done about Bxg5 and Qh5. Black resigned after *33 Bxg5 Nf6   34 Rxb8 Rxb8 35 Rg2.*

The d5 Chain

Technically there is no difference between the dynamics of a pawn chain with links on d5 and e4 and a chain with links at e5 and d4, but any experienced player knows they are of quite distinct characters. The d5 chain involves White in strategic play on the queenside most of the time. The e5 chain, considered in the next chapter, is an attacking formation. White is almost forced into kingside aggression in that situation.

Besides driving a cramping wedge into the opponent's camp, the effect of the attack on the base of the enemy pawn chain is to provide opportunities to open up files at least halfway. The advantages of this are demonstrated by Botvinnik–Kholmov, Moscow 1947:

1 c4 Nf6   2 Nc3 e6   3 d4 Bb4   4 e3 0-0   5 Bd3 d6
6 Ne2 e5   7 0-0 Nc6   8 d5 Nb8   9 a3 Bxc3?!
10 Nxc3 a5   11 e4 Ne8   12 Be3 f6   13 Qd2 Rf7
14 b4 Nd7

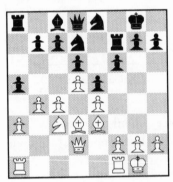

Position after 14 . . . Nd7

Black has made at least one minor and one major error in the opening. He gave up his king bishop without compensation—and unlike the Korchnoi–Barcza game just cited, it is not a "bad" bishop. Worse, Black adopted a passive, defensive attitude on the kingside rather than the dynamic 12 . . . g6 followed by . . . Ng7 and . . . f5.

With *15 c5* White carries forward a threat of 16 c6!; e.g., 16 . . . bxc6   17 dxc6 Nb6   18 Nb5 or 16 . . . Nf8

17 cxb7 Bxb7   18 Rfc1 with pressure against Black's newly revealed queenside weaknesses. Black offered to close up that side of the board with *15 . . . b6* hoping for 16 c6?.

But White cannot forfeit such an opportunity to open up "his" side of the chain. He continued *16 cxb6!*. Open lines are more important than constriction because constriction alone cannot win a game. Whether Black plays 16 ... cxb6 17 Nb5 and defends the c-file or, as in the game, plays *16 . . . Nxb6*, the initiative is solidly on White's side. The game continued *17 bxa5! Rxa5   18 Nb5 Ra8   19 Qc2.*

Position after 19 Qc2

White threatens to make a decisive breakthrough with a4-a5 or Rfc1 followed by Nxc7!. This was enough to elicit *19 . . . Na4*, after which White made steady progress with *20 Rfb1 g6   21 Na7! c5   22 Nxc8 Qxc8   23 Bb5*. Even with his c-pawn "repaired" Black must lose material because of White's use of open lines to exploit the position of the stranded knight on a4. The game ended abruptly with *23 . . . Rfa7   24 Bc6 f5   25 f3 f4* (a bit late) *26 Bf2 g5   27 Rb3 g4   28 fxg4*

Qxg4 29 *Bxa8 Rxa8* 30 *Rab1* Resigns because Rb8 will win a piece.

Another point may be obvious but is often overlooked: There is no essential difference between White's playing c5xd6 and Black's playing . . . c6xd5. In both cases the c-file is opened and the rest of the chain is left intact.

What this means to Black is that he must be in a position to contest the c-file and other queenside lines in order to consider . . . c6. Otherwise he will have done White a favor by dispensing with White's need for c5xd6. This idea crops up in many modern opening positions, such as this:

1 d4 Nf6   2 c4 g6   3 Nc3 Bg7   4 e4 d6   5 f3 0-0
6 Be3 e5   7 d5 c6   8 Bd3 cxd5   9 cxd5 Nbd7
10 Nge2 Nc5   11 0-0 Nh5

Position after 11 . . . Nh5

Black's play is not without logic. He prepares . . . f5 and obtains room on the queenside to anticipate White's expected attack. But Black might have taken greater measures of antic-ipation such as 11 . . . a5 or 11 . . . Bd7 and 12 . . . Rc8. In the diagram White can obtain an initiative with *12 b4!* long be-fore Black's kingside play appears.

After *12 . . . Nxd3 13 Qxd3 f5 14 Rac1 Rf7 15 Rc2!*, it is clear that White is making progress. Black can reduce the momentum of White's play with 15 . . . Rc7 16 Rfc1 Bd7; e.g., 17 Nb5 Rxc2 18 Rxc2 Bxb5 19 Qxb5 Qe7 20 Qa5 fxe4 21 fxe4 Qh4. White still has the upper hand, but Black is much more secure on both sides of the chain.

In Bagirov–Bednarski, from the 1962 world student team championship, Black rejected queenside defense with 15 . . . Rc7. He also rejected kingside liquidation with 15 . . . Nf4 16 Nxf4 exf4 17 Bd4! fxe4 18 Nxe4. He choose instead to begin the familiar kingside pawn march against the distant base, but with the queenside already semiopen his play was doomed: *15 . . . f4 16 Bf2 g5 17 h3 Nf6 18 Rfc1 Ne8.*

The next stage of the game illustrates another point about chains. The target on the kingside is White's king. This ob-ject of attack can simply get out of the way of Black pieces by moving Kf1-e1-d2. But Black's queenside pawns lack the mo-bility of the White king. The inevitable penetration came with *19 Nb5 a6 20 Nc7! Rxc7 21 Rxc7 Nxc7 22 Bb6 Qf8 23 Bxc7*, and White evacuated his king with *23 . . . Bd7 24 Qa3! Bf6* (to protect the d-pawn from Qa5-b6) *25 Qa5 Be7 26 Qb6 Bc8 27 Kf1! h5 28 Ke1 g4 29 hxg4 hxg4 30 Kd2.*

After *30 . . . Qh6 31 Bd8! Bf8 32 Qc7* Black faced this position:

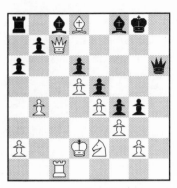

Position after 32 Qc7

And he realized his attack was hopeless after *32 . . . Qh2 33 Be7* because 33 . . . Qxg2   34 Bxf8 gxf3 loses the queen to 35 Rg1. Black had to transpose into a lost endgame that came about after *33 . . . Qh7   34 Bxf8 Qxc7   35 Rxc7 Kxf8 36 fxg4 Bxg4   37 Rxb7 Rc8   38 Nc3 Rc4   39 Rb6 Ke7 40 a3 f3   41 gxf3.* Black resigned because of variations such as 41 . . . Bxf3 42 Kd3 Rd4+   43 Ke3 Rc4   44 Rc6!—the triumph of the open file Black lost control of.

This and *Supplemental Game #2* show how careful Black must be about the open queenside lines. The kingside is the opposite side of the coin. Black's problem is not whether to play . . . f5 but whether to continue . . . fxe4 or . . . f4. An open f-file greatly eases the natural crampedness of Black's game—the d5 chain simply gives White a greater share of the board. But . . . f4 and . . . g5 transfer the attack to a point that is more difficult to defend than e4 is for White.

Historically the most important game on this theme is Taimanov–Najdorf from the 1953 Candidates tournament: *1 d4 Nf6   2 c4 g6   3 Nc3 Bg7   4 e4 d6   5 Nf3 0-0*

6 Be2 e5   7 0-0 Nc6   8 d5 Ne7   9 Ne1 Nd7   10 Be3 f5 11 f3. At the time it was played White's queenside play was rated higher than Black's mating attack. But long after this game Bent Larsen remarked, "White was mated too many times, so everyone started to play 11 exf5." We'll consider the exf5 plan shortly. But to certify the strength of Black's attack, see what happens after *11 . . . f4   12 Bf2 g5   13 Nd3.*

Position after 13 Nd3

Black's knight has served its function on d7, that of delaying c4-c5, as long as it could. If Black tries to delay the White plan further with 13 . . . b6 he encourages b2-b4, which may open the queenside even more after the inevitable c4-c5.

It should be noted that an immediate attack with Black's *pieces* rather than his pawns is faster but less accurate. Two years after this game David Bronstein tried 13 . . . Rf6?!   14 c5 Rh6 but noticed after 15 cxd6 cxd6 16 Nb5 that White is ready to play 17 Rc1 with thoughts of Nc7 or Rxc8 already. Bronstein prevented Nc7 with 16 . . . Nf8   17 Be1 a6, but White found that opening the queenside was easy after 18 Na3 (intending Nc4-b6) b5 19 Nc2 Nd7 20 a4! bxa4 21 Rxa4 Nf6 22 Nf2 Bd7 23 Ba5. Black resigned shortly after 23 ... Qe8 24 Rb4 Qh5 25 h3 Qf7 26 Na3 Nh5 27 Rb7 Bc8 28 Rc7 because of the penetration of White's pieces.

In the original 1953 game Black continued from the diagram: *13 ... Nf6! 14 c5 Ng6 15 Rc1 Rf7!* to counter the Nb5-c7 threat.

Position after 15 ... Rf7!

Another game from the same tournament saw White try *16 Qb3* unsuccessfully (16 ... g4 17 fxg4 Nxg4 18 Bxg4 Bxg4 19 Qxb7 f3! 20 Be3 Nf4 21 Bxf4 exf4 22 gxf3 Bh3 with a quick mate). Instead, Taimanov chose *16 Rc2* as in the Bagirov–Bednarski game, but Black has made much more progress in this game since it was White, not Black, who took time to open the c-file. Black's pieces now swept over the kingside with a pawn sacrifice: *16 . . . Bf8   17 cxd6   cxd6   18 Qd2   g4   19 Rfc1   g3!   20 hxg3 fxg3   21 Bxg3   Nh5   22 Bh2   Be7*. Black's attack with . . . Bg5 . . . Nh4, and . . . Rg7 is decisive since the White king cannot escape to the closed center without making great concessions. White tried *23 Nb1*, hoping for some relief through 24 Rxc8 Rxc8   25 Rxc8 Qxc8   26 Qb4, but Black just played *23 . . . Bd7*.

The game ended with *24 Qe1   Bg5   25 Nd2   Be3+ 26 Kh1   Qg5   27 Bf1   Raf8   28 Rd1   b5   29 a4   a6 30 axb5   axb5   31 Rc7   Rg7   32 Nb3   Nh4   33 Rc2   Bh3 34 Qe2   Nxg2!   35 Bxg2   Bxg2+   36 Qxg2   Qh4 37 Qxg7+* (Black plays 37 . . . Ng3+ if the queen moves away) *Kxg7   38 Rg2+   Kh8   39 Ne1   Nf4   40 Rg3   Bf2   41 Rg4 Qh3* and White resigned.

Counterstrategies: g2-g4 and . . . c5

On the opposite wings of the chain a player on the defensive can take the steam out of his opponet's march with certain flanking thrusts. On the White kingside the challenging idea of g2-g4 serves this purpose. On the face of it g2-g4 seems suicidal, but it prevents . . . g4 and takes vital squares away from Black. If g2-g4 can be played safely, the Black kingside march is stopped.

In the same King's Indian variation we've just considered White can try out this idea with 10 f3 and 11 g4 instead of 10 Be3 and 11 f3.

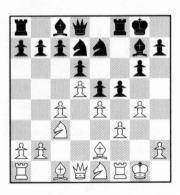

Position after 11 g4

White can keep the kingside lines closed or under his control now. For instance, on 11 . . . f4 he plays 12 h4! preparing to answer . . . h5 with g4-g5 and . . . g5 with h4-h5. The diagram also shows how quickly a middlegame plan can be altered by a pawn move. Now it makes sense for Black to strike on the queenside with 11 . . . Nf6 and 12 . . . c6; e.g., 12 Ng2 c6   13 Rb1 cxd5   14 cxd5 Bd7 15 Bd2 Rc8   16 a4 Qb6+   17 Be3 Qb4!, as in a 1966 Soviet game.

The 11 g4 idea was introduced by Pal Benko in 1958, but, oddly enough, it was considered unsound because of *11 . . . h5   12 g5* (12   gxh5?? f4 turns control of an open kingside over to Black again) *h4*, which isolates White's g-pawn. A good sense of chess values tells us that the several moves Black will have to invest in order to win the g-pawn are wasteful because of the relentlessness of White's unchecked queenside attack.

But it was not until the 1965 Larsen–Tal match that this was verified by *13 Nd3 f4   14 Kh1 Kf7   15 c5!.*

Now on 15 . . . Nxc5   16 Nxc5 bxc5 White has all the action with 17 Qb3 Ke8   18 Rd1 threatening d5-d6 or Nb5. The game continued *15 . . . Rh8   16 Qb3 b6* (otherwise 17 c6!) *17 cxd6 cxd6   18 Qa3 Nc5   19 Nxc5 bxc5*. Black can still try to win the g-pawn with . . . Rh5, but White would finish off the game on the queenside anyway.

The conclusion was *20 b4! cxb4   21 Qxb4 Bh3   22 Rg1 Rb8   23 Nb5 Nc8   24 Ba3 Bf8   25 Qc4 Be7   26 Qc7! Qxc7   27 Nxc7   Rh5   28 Bf1   Bxf1   29 Rgxf1!   Rxg5 30 Ne6 Rh5   31 Rac1 Kf6   32 Rc7 Rh8   33 Rfc1 g5 34 h3 Rg8   35 R7c6 Kf7   36 Kg2 Kf6   37 Kf1 Rh8 38 Ke2 Rg8   39 Kd3 Rh8   40 Rc7 Nb6   41 R1c6 Rhc8* and Black resigned because of *42 Bxd6*. See also *Supplemental Game #3*.

The queenside version of this is . . . c5 by Black, turning the chain into what is called a full Benoni formation. (A Benoni formation occurs when White has a pawn on d5 and Black has one on c5.) In the full Benoni the c4-c5 plan has been eliminated. White can open up the position with dxc6 en passant if . . . c5 is played at a late stage in the opening (or if Black plays . . . c6). But after . . . c5 has been secured, what of White's middlegame plans?

The natural replacement is b2-b4, intending to open up the b-file. Black's choices are revealed in this sample position:

1 d4 Nf6   2 c4 g6   3   Nc3 Bg7   4 e4 d6   5 Nf3 0-0   6 Be2 e5   7 0-0 Nc6   8 d5 Ne7   9 Nd2 c5 10 Rb1! Ne8   11 b4

Position after 11 b4

Black must decide among three formations. After 11 . . . cxb4 White will recapture and prepare for c4-c5. Black's knight on e8 is better suited for something different, such as playing 11 . . . b6   12 bxc5 dxc5. The knight can then go to d6 as a blockade, but White can still drum up play with a4-a5.

There is another possibility, *11 . . . b6   12 bxc5 bxc5*, and it is illustrated by Commons–Zuckerman, Chicago 1974. Black tried to compete along the open file and leave the king-side temporarily untouched. This turned out badly because White with his superior terrain can shift his pieces back and forth between the two wings much more easily than Black on the cramped side of the chain.

The game proceeded: *13 Qa4 f5   14 Nb3* (threatening Na5-c6!) *a5   15 f3 Nf6   16 Bd2 Bd7   17 Qa3 Qc7 18 Nc1 Rfb8   19 Rxb8+ Rxb8   20 Nd3 Rb4   21 Nf2* (21 Nxb4? cxb4 wins material) *fxe4?!   22 Nfxe4 Nxe4 23 fxe4 Nc8.*

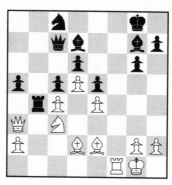

Position after 23 . . . Nc8

Black managed to plug up the queenside's only open line with a rook, but this is temporary since Black's rook must give ground after Nd1. White took advantage of the deserted kingside with *24 Nd1! Ra4 25 Qf3! Qd8 26 Nc3 Rb4 27 Nb5! Rb2 28 Qf7+ Kh8 29 Bxa5!.* Black will be mated after *29 . . . Qxa5 30 Qxd7,* so he held on for another 15 moves with *29 . . . Qe8 30 Nc7 Qxf7.* Black loses a pawn and that is enough to decide the endgame after *31 Rxf7 Rxe2 32 Rxd7 Bf6 33 Rf7 Be7 34 Ne6! h5 35 Bd8.* For an example of *. . . c5/dxc6* see *Supplemental Game #4.*

White Fights on the Kingside: exf5

"The attacking party must never forget that he on his side has a base to defend," Nimzovich reminded his readers. Besides the radical g2-g4 or *. . . c5* ideas, there is another counterstrategy of surrendering the base of the chain in order to obtain freedom or to attack enemy weaknesses that have so far been concealed.

The most common example of this occurs in the d5 chain when White meets . . . f5 at some point with exf5. Three reactions stand out (1) Black recaptures on f5 with a piece, conceding White an outpost on e4; (2) Black recaptures with a pawn on f5 and White tries to fix the enemy center with f2-f4; and (3) Black recaptures with a pawn and White attacks the new enemy f-pawn with Ng3, Bd3, and even g2-g4.

"As every Russian schoolboy knows," Mikhail Botvinnik used to say, "one always captures with a pawn [on f5] in such positions." True, Black can use the vacant f5 square for a minor piece outpost, but White's outpost is generally more influential on the course of events. And if White can seize control of Black's outpost square as well as his own, the game is strategically decided.

This sounds like an overstatement but is borne out by examples such as Toth–Gasztonyi, played in 1967 in Hungary:

1 d4 c5   2 d5 e5   3 c4 d6   4 e4 f5?   5 exf5 Bxf5
6 Ne2 Nf6   7 Nbc3 Be7

Position after 7 . . . Be7

The battle is joined over the e4 and f5 squares. Black seems to have temporary mastery over at least one of them, but it is only temporary: *8 Ng3 Bg6 9 Bd3! Bxd3 10 Qxd3 0-0 11 0-0 Nbd7 12 Nce4.*

To compete for control of the two outposts Black has exchanged his good bishop, the one not blocked by his own pawns. Because of this e6 is threatened by Ng5-e6 and f5 is weak. The threats force Black into a dispersal of strength which invites White to open the game further: *12 . . . Ne8 13 Bd2 Bh4 14 Rae1 a6 15 f4.*

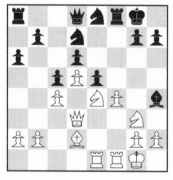

Position after 15 f4

Black has too many weaknesses (d6 and g5 as well as e6 and f5), and he soon acquires one more: *15 . . . Qe7 16 Ng5! Bxg5 17 fxg5 g6* (gaining f5 but surrendering f6) *18 Rxf8+ Nxf8 19 Ne4 Nd7 20 Rf1 b5 21 b3 b4 22 h4 Ng7 23 Nf6+ Kh8 24 Qh3! Nf5 25 h5 Nf8* (25 . . . Nxf6 *26 gxf6 and 27 g4*) *26 hxg6 Nd4 27 Nxh7 Nxh7 28 Rf7* Resigns. (See also *Supplemental Game #5.*)

Recapturing with a pawn makes more strategic sense and keeps dynamic possibilities open for Black. But f2-f4! offers up a dilemma to him. He must eventually decide between . . . e4, which fixes his center pawns and concedes d4 to White, and allowing an exchange of pawns that isolates Black's f-pawn.

The choice is excellently illustrated by this pair of examples from "Pawns in Action," a booklet by Sokolsky. It comes about through *1 d4 Nf6   2 c4 g6   3 Nc3 Bg7   4 e4 d6   5 Nf3 0-0   6 Be2 e5   7 0-0 Nbd7 8 d5 Nc5   9 Qc2 a5   10 Ne1 Nfd7   11 Be3 f5   12 exf5 gxf5   13 f4*.

Position after 13 f4

When this position occurred in a 1950 Soviet championship game (Flohr–Suetin) Black kept his pawns united with *13 . . . e4?*, but within five moves White had transformed an equal position into a substantial advantage by occupying his center outposts: *14 Qd2! Nf6   15 Nc2 Qe8   16 Nb5 Qf7 17 Bd4! Ne8   18 Ne3!*.

These occupied squares make possible a direct attack on the Black king with pieces (Rc1-c3-g3) or with pawns by g2-g4 (which also undermines the enemy e-pawn). Because of the new center situation it is White who looks optimistically toward the kingside. After *18 . . . Kh8 19 Rac1 Bd7 20 Rc3! Rd8 21 Kh1 Na6 22 Nc2 Bxd4 23 Nbxd4 Nf6 24 Rg3 Rg8* (24 . . . b6 25 Ne3 Ne8 26 Ndxf5 Bxf5 27 Qd4+ Qf6 28 Nxf5) *25 Rxg8+ Rxg8 26 Ne3!*, and the Black pawns began to fall. Black cannot fight a two-front war. Take note of White's magnificent knights.

Going back to the position after *13 f4*, we can see that *13 . . . exf4!* was correct despite the isolation of Black's f-pawn. This works because after *14 Bxf4 Ne4!* Black has excellent piece play: *15 Nxe4 fxe4 16 g3* (16 Qxe4 Bxb2 17 Rb1 Nc5! also favors Black. White wants to blockade with Ng2-e3.) *16 . . . Qf6! 17 Rb1 Qd4+ 18 Kh1 Nc5 19 b3 Bh3! 20 Rd1 Qc3! 21 Qxc3 Bxc3 22 Ng2 a4 23 Rc1 Bg7 24 b4 Nd3! 25 Bxd3 exd3 26 c5 Bb2! 27 Rcd1 Bg4 28 Rxd3 Be2*. This occurred in Filip–Matanovic, Munich 1958, and Black won easily.

There are times when . . . e4 is superior and also times when . . . exf4 is not enough for equality. An example of the former was the remarkable strategy of Bronstein–Petrosian, Amsterdam 1956:

1 c4 g6 2 Nc3 Bg7 3 Nf3 d6 4 d4 Nf6 5 e4 0-0 6 Be2 e5 7 0-0 Nbd7 8 Re1 c6 9 d5 c5 10 a3 Ne8 11 Bg5 f6 12 Bd2 f5 13 Ng5 Nc7 14 exf5 gxf5 15 f4 e4

Position after 15 . . . e4

When he is ready White can choose whether to advance his b-pawn or g-pawn to the fourth rank. (A fine example of the g2-g4 strategy with colors reversed is given as *Supplemental Game* #6.) But White has to defuse Black's irritating plan of 16 . . . Bd4+ 17 Kh1 h6 18 Nh3 Nf6 followed by . . . Qe8-g6 and attacking play on the g-file.

To handle this apparently slight threat White played 16 *Be3* permitting 16 . . . *h6* 17 *Nh3 Bxc3!*. Black need no longer fear b2-b4, and he won't have trouble from White's two bishops. With a pawn on c3 White will find it impossible to seize control of the long diagonal leading to h8.

Black built up a squadron of kingside pieces to restrain White's g2-g4 plan and to insure counterplay against White's king. This resulted in a draw after 18 *bxc3 Nf6* 19 *a4 Kh8!* 20 *Nf2 Rg8* 21 *Kh1 Qe8* 22 *Rg1 Qg6* 23 *Qd2 Bd7* 24 *g3 Rae8* 25 *a5 Re7* 26 *Rab1 Bc8* 27 *Rg2 Reg7* 28 *Rbg1 Nce8* 29 *h3 h5*. White cannot play g3-g4 without risking mate.

And, to emphasize the problems facing Black after . . . exf4, there is the Polugaevsky–Geller game of Portoroz 1973:

1 d4 Nf6 2 c4 g6 3 Nc3 Bg7 4 e4 d6 5 f3
0-0 6 Be3 e5 7 d5 c6 8 Bd3 cxd5 9 cxd5 Nh5
10 Nge2 f5 11 exf5! gxf5 12 0-0 Kh8 13 f4 Nd7
14 Rc1 a6 15 Bb1!

Position after 15 Bb1!

Here the center has been simplified with an open c-file.
On 15 . . . e4?? White can continue as in a previous example by placing a bishop on d4, exchanging it off, and then
occupying d4 and e3 with knights. Black correctly chose
15 . . . exf4 16 Nxf4 Nxf4 . 17 Bxf4 Ne5, but his problems
weren't over.

Whenever a player sacrifices pawn health for piece activity he must remember that a loss of the initiative or a badly
placed piece can sink his game. Once Black's pieces have been
neutralized his f-pawn is dead. White gained the upper hand
now with *18 Kh1 Bd7 19 b3 Rc8?* (better to use the e-file
with *19 . . . Qe7* followed by *. . . Rae8* and *. . . Ng4* or *. . . Ng6*)
20 Ne2! Rxc1 21 Bxc1 Qb6 22 h3.

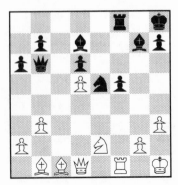

Position after 22 h3

Now we see that Black's weaknesses at e6 and f5 are more vulnerable than before because Black's counterchances on the kingside have disappeared. Following *22 . . . Ng6 23 Ng3!* Black realized that he could not hold onto the f-pawn because of *23 . . . f4 24 Bxg6 fxg3 25 Rxf8+ Bxf8 26 Bb2+* and *27 Qh5* winning. So he made a sacrifice with *23 . . . Bb5* and resigned soon after *24 Rxf5 Rxf5 25 Nxf5 Be5 26 Be3 Qc7 27 Bd4 Bd7 28 Ne3 Qa5 29 Nc4 Qc7 30 Bxg6 hxg6 31 Bxe5+ dxe5 32 Qe2.*

The third strategic plan arising from exf5 is the attack on Black's new f-pawn with Bd3 and Ng3 or g2-g4. White usually puts his own f-pawn on the third rank to discourage . . . e4; but he wants to encourage . . . f4 which concedes the outpost square e4.

A game that explains this strategy better than words is Spassky–Tal from the 1956 Soviet championship:

1 d4 Nf6   2 c4 g6   3 Nc3 Bg7   4 e4 d6   5 f3 e5
6 d5 Nh5   7 Be3 f5   8 Qd2 Na6   9 0-0-0 Nf6

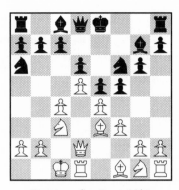

Position after 9 . . . Nf6

Black might have tried 9 . . . f4   10 Bf2 Bf6 with the idea of eliminating his bad bishop with 11 . . . Bh4   (12 g3 is bad since it would weaken White's kingside pawns). But White could avoid the exchange with 11 Nge2 Bh4   12 Bg1! and then proceed with his traditional queenside attack. He doesn't have to worry about getting mated on the kingside, and his king is actually safer on a semiopen queenside because he controls the lines there.

In the diagram, White began his middlegame plan with *10 exf5 gxf5* (10 . . . Bxf5? favors White as usual after 11 Nge2,   12 Ng3, and 13 Bd3) *11 Bd3 0-0   12 Nge2 Qe7 13 Rde1!*

"Already in these few moves Black has suffered a strategic defeat," Simagin noted. Black's f-pawn is vulnerable and . . . f4 is not only a positional error but a tactical one as well (14 Ng3 f4?   15 Bxf4). For a case in which Black was permitted to play . . . f4 see *Supplemental Game #7*. Note also that Black hasn't enough control of the center play to use the finesse of the Pilnik–Geller game cited on page 148—that of . . . e4/fxe4/ . . . f4.

Black's *13 . . . c5?* ignores the clear signs that White has rejected a c4-c5 plan in favor of a kingside strategy involving the Black f-pawn. Black was in bad shape after *14 Ng3 Ne8 15 Nh5! Nac7   16 g4!*

Position after 16 g4!

This decides the game because of the vulnerability of Black's king and his center. Again, 16 . . . f4 cannot be played (17 Bxf4) and neither can Black open up the g-file (16 . . . fxg4   17 fxg4 Bxg4   18 Nxg7 Nxg7   19 Rhg1; e.g., 19 . . . h5   20 Bh6 Rf7   21 Ne4 or 21 Bg6). The game continued: *16 . . . Kh8   17 Rhg1 Qf7   18 Nxg7 Nxg7   19 f4!.*

Black couldn't afford the murderous opening of the center (19 . . . exf4   20 Bxf4 Nce8   21 Nb5 or 20 . . . Rd8 21 gxf5 Bxf5   22 Rxg7 Kxg7   23 Bxf5 Qxf5   24 Re7+). He tried *19 . . . e4,* but we know that this formation dooms Black's e-pawn after g4. White wins at least a pawn, and he won the ending after some minor excitement beginning with *20 Bc2 b5!?   21 cxb5 Rb8   22 gxf5 Bxf5   23 Bxe4 Bxe4 24 Nxe4 Qxd5   25 Qxd5 Nxd5   26 Nxd6 Rbd8   27 Bxc5 Nxf4   28 Bd4 Ng6   29 Re7!.*

Complications on the f-File

Of course, these strategies for White don't always work. Favorable conditions (elimination of a bad bishop, lead in development, etc.) may not exist. But Black has an easier time freeing his pieces if White fails to pick *any* strategy.

One ideal situation for Black is to clear e5 of pawns. If this can be accomplished cleanly—such as if White plays f2-f4 and Black replies . . . exf4—Black may have an ideal outpost at e4. An example of the outpost—achieved through different means—is Alatorzev–Levenfish, Tiflis 1937:

1 d4   Nf6   2 c4   e6   3 g3   Bb4+   4 Bd2   Bxd2+
5 Nxd2   Nc6   6 Ngf3   d6   7 Bg2   e5!   8 d5   Ne7
9 0-0 0-0   10 e4 Nd7   11 Ne1 f5

Position after 11 . . . f5

The opening is a fine example of chain-building. Black eliminated his black-squared bishop and then created a pawn formation that would make the bishop exchange favorable.

In the diagram, White shouldn't think long before playing 12 exf5! to secure e4, even though Black has an equal game after 12 ... Nxf5   13 Ne4 Nc5   14 Nd3 b6 and ... Nd4 because of the bad White bishop. But White blindly followed the c4-c5 strategy with *12 Nd3?*, a move that allowed *12 ... f4!* with dangerous kingside play. Then White compounded his error with *13 gxf4? exf4   14 Nf3?* as he overlooked the sound sacrifice 14 c5 Nxc5   15 Nxc5 dxc5   16 Qb3 which would have given him a reasonable position.

All that has happened is a slight weakening of the White kingside and the clearing of e5, but that e5 is a tremendous observation point. Black proceeded to occupy the square with pieces, and although White succeeded in exchanging them off, Black secured a won endgame after *14 ... Ng6!   15 Rc1 Qe7   16 Re1 Nde5   17 Nfxe5 Nxe5   18 f3* (Black threatened 18 ... f3) *b6   19 Nxe5 Qxe5   20 Qd2 Bd7   21 Qc3 Rfe8   22 Qxe5 Rxe5   23 a3 a5*.

Position after 23 ... a5

White has a very bad bishop, but he would not lose this game if it were not for the activity of Black's pieces on the center outpost square. White never had time for c4-c5. Even now 24 b4 would give Black the initiative on both sides with

24 . . . axb4   25 axb4 Ra4   26 Rb1 Rg5, and most of all the pawn formation clears the path for a majestic king march to c3 via f7, f6, e5, and d4.

The final stage of the game is easy to understand: *24 b3 Kf7 25 Kf2 Kf6   26 Ke2 Rh5   27 Rh1 Ke5!   28 Kd3 h6 29 h3* (29 h4 eases Black's penetration after 29 . . . Rh8 and 30 . . . g5) *29 . . . Rg5!   30 Rh2 Rg3   31 h4 Rg8   32 Ke2 g5   33 hxg5 hxg5   34 Kf2 g4!   35 Rh5+ Kd4!   36 Rd1+ Kc3   37 Rh7 gxf3 38 Bf1* (38 Bxf3 Rxf3+!) *Kc2   39 Rd3 Bh3!* winning a piece and soon ending the game.

When White plays f2-f4 before there has been an exf5 exchange, Black need not fear the isolation of his f-pawn. He can—and in many cases he must—free e5 with . . . exf4. The tension cannot be maintained for long, but Black should be able to find good places for his pieces after the pawns are swept away.

A case in point is Najdorf–Ivkov, Bled 1961:

1 d4 Nf6   2 c4 c5   3 d5 g6   4 Nc3 Bg7   5 e4 d6 6 Nf3   0-0   7 Be2 e5   8 0-0 Ng4   9 Ne1 Nh6 10 Nd3 Nd7   11 f4

Position after 11 f4

In the opening both players took two moves to relocate their king knights so that they could advance their f-pawns. White should have spent this time in preparation for b2-b4, but now he threatens 12 f5, an expansion that would squash Black on the kingside. Therefore, *11 . . . f5!* is needed.

The various possible pawn exchanges make this a fascinating problem position. Black will obtain e5 for his pieces unless White isolates his own f-pawn (12 g3? exf4 13 gxf4), and both players will free f4 and f5 for pieces. But the tension cannot remain long because Black threatens . . . exf4 and . . . Bxc3, winning the e-pawn.

White could have maintained a slight superiority with 12 exf5; e.g., 12 ... gxf5 13 Bd2 or 12 ... Nxf5 13 Ne4, but his *12 fxe5?* was dubious because of *12 . . . Nxe5 13 Nxe5 Bxe5!*. Perhaps White overlooked that 14 Bxh6 gives Black an edge after 14 . . . Qh4 which threatens mate.

Now White has a big problem because Black will have a lead in development if White plays 14 exf5 Bxf5 (Black's re-captures develop pieces), and Black will have a superb attacking formation with . . . f4 if White doesn't. There followed *14 Bf4? Bd4+ 15 Kh1 g5! 16 Bd2 f4 17 Rb1 Be5*.

Position after 17 . . . Be5

As the diagram indicates, Black has all the play, and he will continue ... g4 and ... Qh4 with an easy win if White cannot distract him. The ensuing complications were just as fatal: *18 Qc1 Ng4 19 Bxg4 Bxg4 20 Qc2 Qe8 21 Nb5 Be2! 22 Rf2 f3 23 Bc3 Bxc3 24 Nxc3 fxg2+ 25 Kxg2 Rxf2+ 26 Kxf2 Bxc4 27 Kg2 Qh5 28 Qf2 Rf8 29 Qg3 Rf4 30 h3 h6 31 Re1 Qf7 32 b3 Bf1+! 33 Kg1 Rf3 34 Qxd6 Bxh3 35 Qxh6 Rf1+ 36 Kh2 Qf4+ 37 Kxh3 g4+* White resigns.

Black's ... c6xd5

We've seen that opening the c-file favors the player who can occupy it first and maintain control. That is not always White. Nor is it White alone who can play aggressively on the queenside. A fine illustration of a queenside attack by Black comes about after *1 d4 Nf6 2 c4 g6 3 g3 Bg7 4 Bg2 d6 5 Nf3 0-0 6 0-0 Nbd7 7 Nc3 e5 8 e4 c6 9 h3 Re8 10 d5? cxd5.*

Position after 10 ... cxd5

So far we've only considered a White recapture with his c-pawn here. Ideally White would like to recapture with pieces to keep the Black d-pawn subject to attack along an open file. But 11 Nxd5 doesn't work because of 11 . . . Nxe4. Nor can White obtain an advantage with 11 exd5. The pawn formation would resemble the aftermath of a Marco Hop (see Chapter 3) but with the important difference in the Black e-pawn position—solid and dynamic on e5 rather than passive and weak on e7. Black could mobilize his kingside with 11 . . . Nh5 and 12 . . . f5 and have a good game.

White played *11 cxd5* in Cafferty–Basman, Bristol 1968, but Black began a queenside initiative before White was ready. After *11 . . . b5!* Black threatens 12 . . . b4 and is eager to exchange a wing pawn for a center pawn after 12 Nxb5 Nxe4 13 Re1 Qb6 followed by . . . f5!

The Black initiative took shape after *12 a3 Nb6! 13 Re1 Bd7 14 Bf1 Qb8* (so that 15 Bxb5 Bxb5 16 Nxb5 can be met by 16 . . . Nbxd5 17 Nxd6 Qxd6 18 exd5 Qxd5) *15 Qb3 a6 16 Be3 Rc8 17 Nd2 Be8!*.

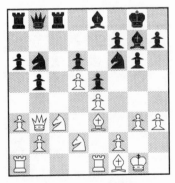

Position after 17 . . . Be8!

Black has one good outpost at c4, and he is ready to occupy another at c5 with . . . Nfd7-c5. Since White has no kingside play he panicked into a queenside counterattack with *18 Bxb6? Qxb6 19 a4.* This gave Black momentum on both sides of the board: *19 . . . Rab8 20 axb5 axb5 21 Ra2 h5! 22 Nf3 Bh6 23 Bd3 Bd7 24 Kg2 Kg7 25 Qd1 Qd8 26 Qe2 Rc5 27 Rea1 Qc8.*

Black's triumphant use of the open c-file was made possible by *28 Ng1 h4 29 g4 b4 30 Nd1 b3 31 Ra5 Rc2!.* White would then lose a piece after *32 Bxc2 bxc2,* and he would lose his queen after *32 Qf3 Nxg4 33 hxg4 Bxg4.* White sought complications with *32 Ba6* but resigned after *32 . . . Qc7 33 Qd3 Rb4!* (intending . . . Rd4) *34 Nf3 Nxe4 35 Bb5 Nxf2! 36 Nxf2 Qb6.*

Supplemental Games

(1) White closes up the queenside to attack Black's base at b7 with pieces. Sololsky–Livschitz, Minsk 1956: 1 b4 e5 2 Bb2 f6 3 b5 d5 4 e3 Be6 5 d4 e4 6 Nd2 c6 7 a4 a6? (An error similar to Rivera–Suttles. Better is 7 . . . Bd6 8 c4 Ne7 awaiting events on the kingside.) 8 Ne2 Bd6 9 c4 Nd7 10 c5! (Now if the Black bishop retreats to e7 White can continue 11 Nf4 Bf7 12 Qg4 with good kingside prospects.) 10 . . . Bb8 11 b6! Ne7 12 Nb3! 0-0 13 Na5 Qc8 (White has a sizable advantage despite being on the side of the chain with fewer squares. Unless Black can engineer a significant breakthrough on the kingside, his queen rook, king bishop, and queen will be tied to the defense of the base pawn.) 14 Qd2 f5 15 g3 g5 16 h4! (This is a fine move that gives Black a worrisome choice of closing up the board with 16 . . . g4 or speculating on 16 . . . f4. Sokolsky gives this winning variation—16 . . . g4 17 Nc1! Nf6 18 Ncb3 Ng6 19 Nxb7! Qxb7 20 Na5 Qd7 21 Bc3 Rf7 22 Rb1 Qe8 23 b7 Ra7 24 Rb6 Bc7 25 Qb2! Bxb6 26 Qxb6 and the b-pawn wins.) 16 . . . f4 17 hxg5 fxg3 18 fxg3 Rf3 19 0-0-0 Nf8 (or 19 . . . Bxg3 20 Nxg3 Rxg3 21 Qh2) 20 Nf4 Nf5 21 Nxe6 Nxe6 22 Bh3 Nxe3 23 Qh2 h6 24 Rdg1 Qe8 25 Bxe6+ Qxe6 26 Qxh6 Qxh6 27 gxh6 Bxg3 28 Nxb7 Kh8 29 Na5 Rc8 30 Kb1 Nf5 31 Rh5 Ne7 32 Rg5 Bf4 33 Rg7 Nf5 34 b7! Re8 35 Rf7 Nxh6 36 Rxf4! Rxf4 37 Nxc6 e3 38 b8(Q) Rxb8 39 Nxb8 e2 40 Re1 Resigns. An amazing game.

(2) Black cooperates in the liquidation of the queenside. Geller–Zaitsev, Moscow 1970: 1 Nf3 Nf6 2 c4 g6 3 Nc3 Bg7 4 e4 d6 5 d4 0-0 6 Be2 e5 7 0-0 Nc6 8 d5 Ne7 9 Nd2 Nd7 10 b4 f5 11 c5! Nf6 (Black can win a pawn temporarily with 11 . . . dxc5 12 bxc5 Nxc5 13 Ba3 b6 14 Bxc5 bxc5 but his queenside is in ruins and White will recapture on c5 eventually with a big edge.) 12 f3 a5? (Suicidal. Only when Black can keep the queenside under control can he try to open the a-file this way.) 13 bxa5 dxc5 14 Nc4 Bd7 15 Rb1 (Black's b-pawn, c-pawn, and e-pawn are weak enough to cost him the game.) 15 . . . Nc8 16 Be3! fxe4 17 fxe4 Nd6 18 Qd3 Qe7 19 Bxc5 Rab8 20 Nxd6 cxd6 21 Ba7! Ra8 22 Rxb7 Qe8 23 Bb6 Bc8 and Black resigned. He could continue, but would only be postponing the inevitable after 24 Rc7 and 25 Nb5.

(3) White's g2-g4 nips the Black kingside attack in the bud.
Gurgenidze–Soos, Tiflis 1965: 1 e4 c5 2 Nf3 Nc6 3 Bb5
g6 4 c3 Bg7 5 0-0 e5 6 d3 Nge7 7 Be3 d6 8 d4
cxd4 9 cxd4 0-0 10 d5 Nb8 11 Nfd2! f5 12 f3! Nd7
13 g4! (White's farsighted last three moves enable him to
defuse the kingside.) 13 ... Nf6 14 h3 h5 15 g5 Nh7
16 h4 Rf7 17 Kg2 fxe4? (Premature. Black should do battle
on the queenside with ... a6, ... b5, and ... Rc8, keeping ...
fxe4 as an option.) 18 fxe4 Bg4 19 Be2 Rxf1 20 Nxf1
Bxe2 21 Qxe2 Qd7 22 Nc3 a6 (Notice how useless Black's
kingside pieces are due to the pawn structure.) 23 Nd2 Rf8
24 Rf1 Nc8 25 Rc1 Rf7 26 Nd1 Bf8 27 Nf2 Qd8
28 Qc4 Nb6 29 Qc2 Kg7 30 a4! Be7? 31 a5 Nd7
32 Qc7! Qf8 (Desperation. The endgame was also hopeless.)
33 Qxd7 Bxg5 34 Qh3 Bxe3 35 Qxe3 Qd8 36 Nf3
Qxa5 37 Nh3 Qb4 38 Nhg5 Qxb2+ 39 Kg3 Nxg5
40 Nxg5 Re7 41 Ne6+ Kh7 42 Rc8 Resigns.

(4) White opens up the center with dxc6 en passant.
Korchnoi–R. Byrne, Leningrad 1973: 1 d4 Nf6 2 c4 g6
3 Nc3 Bg7 4 e4 d6 5 Nf3 0-0 6 Be2 e5 7 0-0 Nc6
8 d5 Ne7 9 Bd2 c5 10 dxc6 bxc6 (10 ... Nxc6 leads to
a very bad version of Boleslavsky's formation with a Maroczy
Bind!) 11 Bg5 (White intends c4-c5 to isolate Black's
c-pawn. Black cannot afford 11 ... c5 12 Bxf6 Bxf6
13 Nb5 or 11 ... h6 12 Bxf6 Bxf6 13 Qd2 Kg7
14 Rfd1 Qb6 15 Na4 because of the weak d-pawn.) 11
... Be6?! 12 c5! Ne8 (White obtains a positionally won
game whether Black chooses 12 ... dxc5 13 Nxe5 Qb8
14 Nd3! or 12 ... d5 13 Nxe5 d4 14 Na4 Nxe4
15 Nxc6!) 13 cxd6 Nxd6 14 Qa4 f6 15 Be3 Qc7

16 Rac1 Rfb8   17 Rfd1 Bf8   18 Rd2 Nec8   19 Nd5! Qf7
20 Qxc6 Nxe4   21 Nxf6+ (The "primitive" move, 21 Nc7,
wins faster, White said afterwards.)   21 ... Nxf6   22 Ng5
Bd7   23 Qa6 Qe7   (23 ... Qg7   24 Bc4+ picks up the
queen, e.g.   24 ... Kh8   25 Nf7+ Kg8   26 Nxe5+ Kh8
27 Nf7+ Kg8   28 Bh6.)   24 Bc5 Qg7   25 Qc4+ Kh8
26 Nf7+ Kg8   27 Nxe5+ Kh8   28 Bxf8 Resigns (because
of   28   ...   Qxf8   29 Nxd7   Nxd7   30 Rxd7   Nb6
31 Qd4+).

(5) With colors reversed, Black obtains a "substitute center," as Nimzovich put it, on e5. Cobo–Suetin, Havana 1968:
1 e4 c5   2 Nc3 e6   3 g3 Nc6   4 Bg2 Nf6   5 d3 Be7
6 f4 d5   7 Nh3 d4   8 Ne2 e5   9 Nf2 h5!?   10 Ng1 Ng4
11 Nxg4 Bxg4   12 Bf3! (to eliminate the bad bishop)   12
... exf4   13 Bxf4?? (After 13 gxf4 Bh4+ 15 Kf1 White
has excellent chances despite his king position because he retains control of e5.)   13 ... g5!   14 Bd2 Ne5   15 Qe2
Qb6   16 0-0-0?! Rc8   17 b3? (Black threatened ... c4 but
this doesn't stop it. Note that 17 Bxg4 hxg4 would leave
White's kingside entangled.)   17 ... c4! 18 dxc4 Rxc4 19
Kb1 (19 bxc4 Ba3 mate) Rxc2!   20 Bxg4 hxg4   21 Ba5 d3!
22 Bxb6 dxe2   23 Re1 Nd3   24 Nxe2 Rb2+   25 Ka1
axb6 White resigns.

(6) With colors reversed, Black realizes the ... g5 plan after e4-e5. Bednarski–Korchnoi, Bucharest 1966: 1 e4 e6
2 d3 c5   3 g3 Nc6   4 Bg2 g6   5 Ne2 Bg7   6 0-0 Nge7
7 Nbc3   d6   8 Be3 Nd4   9 Qd2 0-0 10 Nd1?! d5!
11 Nc1 e5!   12 c3 Ne6   13 Bh6 Bxh6   14 Qxh6 d4!
15 c4 Bd7   16 f4 exf4!   17 gxf4 f5 (Black has a better game
than White usually obtains in a King's Indian or Benoni De-

fense because he has exchanged off his bad bishop and has better developed knights.) 18 e5? Bc6 19 Qh4 Bxg2 20 Kxg2 g5!! (Usually it takes further prepartion with . . . Qc7, . . . Kh8 and . . . Rg8 before this is effective. Now Black wins at least a pawn.) 21 fxg5 Ng6 22 Qg3 f4 23 Qg4 Nxg5! 24 h4 Nf7 25 h5 Nxe5 26 Qe6+ Kg7 27 Rh1 (White banked on 27 hxg6, overlooking 27 . . . Qg5+ 28 Kh1 hxg6 or 28 Kf2 Qg3+ 29 Ke2 Rae8, overloading the files against the enemy king.) 27 . . . Qg5+ 28 Kf1 f3 29 Rg1 Qg2+!! 30 Rxg2 fxg2+ 31 Kg1 Nf3+ 32 Kxg2 Nf4+ 33 Kxf3 Nxe6+ White resigns.

(7) White attacks the enemy f-pawn with Bd3 in order to provoke . . . f4. Gheorghiu–Minic, Bucharest 1966: 1 d4 Nf6 2 c4 g6 3 Nc3 Bg7 4 e4 d6 5 f3 0-0 6 Be3 e5 7 d5 Nh5 8 Qd2 f5 9 0-0-0 Nd7 10 Bd3 Ndf6 11 exf5! gxf5 12 Nge2 Kh8 13 h3! (preparing to win e4 with 14 g4) 13 . . . f4?! 14 Bf2 Bd7 15 Kb1 Qe8 16 Rhe1 Qf7 17 Bc2 Rg8 (Black's position is lacking in counterplay since his kingside pawns are fixed and because no queenside action is likely to succeed without . . . c7-c5, a move that would lose the d-pawn after an en passant capture.) 18 Rg1 Bf8 19 g4! fxg3 20 Nxg3 Nxg3 (Black can't block the kingside with 20 . . . Nf4 because of 21 Be3 Bh6 22 Nce2.) 21 Bxg3 Be7 22 f4! (A relatively rare case when f3-f4 works—because Black cannot occupy e5 with minor pieces. Note that 22 . . . Nh5, more appropriate on the previous move, would permit 23 fxe5 Nxg3 24 e5! with a strong attack.) 22 . . . exf4 23 Qxf4 Rg7 24 Bf2! Nh5 25 Qh6 Bf5 26 Ne4 Bxe4 27 Bxe4 Rf8 28 Bd4 Nf6 29 Bf5! Rfg8 30 Rge1 Rg6 31 Bxg6 Rxg6 32 Qe3 and Black resigned after 32 . . . Bf8.

THE e5 CHAIN

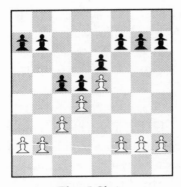

The e5 Chain

IF THERE WERE NO SUCH THING AS CHECKMATE THE PATTERNS of middle-game play would be identical in the e5 and d5 chains. But the presence of kings is clearly felt: in the e5 chain the player with his e-pawn advanced to the fifth rank can quickly develop a whirlwind attack.

This is only partly because Black, in the above diagram, cannot post a knight, that excellent kingside defender, on its most natural square, f6. White's strategic attack on the base of the chain with f4-f5 not only gains space but also denudes the Black king. Even without attacking the base White can develop a mating attack effortlessly on the side of the board where he enjoys a huge spatial advantage.

We can isolate four basic cases of the chain: (1) Black opens up the c-file with . . . cxd4/cxd4; (2) Black plays . . . f6 and permits exf6; (3) White exchanges off his d-pawn for the enemy c-pawn, clearing d4 but retaining the attacking wedge at e5; and (4) White exchanges off his d-pawn and e-pawn.

The first case is easiest to understand. If Black makes something out of *his* c-file, White's attention is drawn away from the kingside. If Black fails to distract White, he is likely to be mated.

This is shown by the following:

Ornstein–Friedgood, Nice 1974:

1 e4 e6 2 d4 d5 3 Nd2 Nf6 4 e5 Nfd7 5 Bd3 c5
6 c3 Nc6 7 Ne2 cxd4 8 cxd4 Nb6 9 f4 Bd7
10 Nf3 Rc8 11 0-0 Be7

Position after 11 . . . Be7

Clearly, White plans f4-f5 and Black intends to use his open file. Black might have played it safer with . . . Qc7, . . . 0-0-0, . . . Kb8, and . . . Rc8 which takes his king out of danger. As it is, he intends . . . Nb4 and . . . Qc7. This doesn't succeed immediately because after 11 . . . Nb4 12 Bb1 (White must preserve this, his good bishop) Qc7 White can stop . . . Nc2 with 13 Nc3.

White decided to use his king rook to watch c2 and prepare a kingside advance. Tactically, however, *12 Rf2* ran into *12 . . . Nb4 13 Bb1 Qc7*, and now 14 Nc3 Na4! 15 Nxa4 Qxc1 could not be permitted. Black completely dominated the file with *14 a3 Nc2 15 Ra2 Ba4! 16 Qd3 Qc4! 17 Qxc4 Rxc4*

Position after 17 . . . Rxc4

White had to lose his weakened d-pawn (18 Nd2 Rc7 19 b3 Nxd4! 20 bxa4 Nxe2+), and there was no doubt as to the outcome of the ending after *18 Nc3 Nxd4 19 Nxd4 Rxd4 20 Be3 Bc5! 21 b4 Rc4! 22 bxc5 Rxc3 23 cxb6 Rxe3*

Black has no reason to hurry . . . cxd4; he should retain the possibility of . . . c4 and . . . b5-b4, the well-known shift of the attack to a different base. And with pawns arranged as in the diagram for the e5 chain, White cannot develop his queen knight normally at c3. (See *Supplemental Game #1* for a case in which . . . cxd4 would have been much better than . . . c4.)

Most of all Black should not open a file unless he can use it and maintain it. The greatest calamity is to lose *your* file to the enemy, as in Steinitz–Halpern, New York 1894:

1 e4 e6   2 d4 d5   3 Nd2 Nf6   4 e5 Nfd7   5 f4 c5
6 c3 Nc6   7 Ngf3 cxd4   8 cxd4 Bb4?   9 a3 Ba5
10 Bd3 f5   11 b4 Bb6 12 Nb3 Qe7

Position after 12 . . . Qe7

Black's reasoning must have gone something like this: My king bishop is my good bishop, but where can I develop it? On e7 it is somewhat passive. Other squares are forbidden by White pawns. How about developing the bishop to b6, ex-changing pawns, and using the bishop to attack White's cen-ter?

But White has profited from this maneuver by taking the initiative on the queenside. The rest of Black's pieces suffer the fate common to poorly thought out strategies. They have few good squares. Black's attempt to develop them gave White the time for a decisive use of the open file: *13 Bd2! Nf8 14 b5 Nd8 15 Bb4 Qf7 16 a4! h6?* (16 . . . a5 was a must) *17 a5 Bc7 18 Rc1*.

Position after 18 Rc1

In this position Black, who never had control of the file, is about to lose a piece on it. He won a few moves' time with diversions such as *18 . . . b6 19 a6 Ng6 20 g3!* but lost the game soon after *20 . . . Qd7 21 Qc2!*

Attack on the Chain's Front: . . . f6

Nimzovich argued that the base was the proper target in a chain. "If we wish to sap a building," he wrote, "we should not begin with its architectural ornaments, but we should blow up its foundations, for then the destruction of the ornaments with all the rest automatically follows."

But a player can attack the base and front of a chain simultaneously. In the d5 chains we saw how Black can maximize his chances with . . . f5 and . . . c6 in some instances. However, with e5 there is an added problem because of Black's king. On . . . f6/exf6 Black must either weaken his kingside by recapturing with a pawn or leave his e-pawn backward and weak by recapturing with a piece on f6.

The difficulties are highlighted by the following example with colors reversed:

Bondarevsky–Botvinnik, Moscow 1941:

1 d4 d5 2 Nf3 c6 3 e3 Bg4 4 c4 e6 5 Nc3 Nd7
6 Bd3 Ngf6 7 0-0 Be7 8 b3 0-0 9 Bb2 e5!
10 Be2 e4 11 Nd2 Bxe2 12 Qxe2 Bb4 13 a3 Bxc3
14 Bxc3 Re8 15 f3

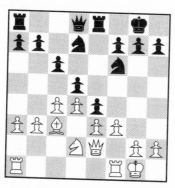

Position after 15 f3

White has played passively to encourage . . . e4 so that he could later undermine the front of the new chain with f2-f3. Right now he doesn't fear . . . exf3 because he can recapture with his g-pawn and continue Kh1 and Rae1, but later Black will be able to make that exchange more power-fully when his rooks are poised against the enemy e-pawn. This is why 15 f4, giving Black a one-time option of taking en passant, is better—although it makes the bad bishop worse.

After *15 . . . Nf8   16 Rf2 Qd7   17 Raf1* the failing of White's logical, consistent, but inaccurate play was revealed by *17 . . . exf3*. White can't recapture with a pawn because of 18 . . . Ng6 (threatening . . . Nf4) 19 Qd3 Qe6, which wins a pawn since Black plays . . . Nf4 when a rook moves to the e-file. This means that *18 Rxf3* was required, which led to the following position after *18 . . . Re6!   19 Qd3 Rae8   20 Nb1 Ng6.*

Position after 20 . . . Ng6

White has a bad game. He should protect his e-pawn with the passive Bd2. Black's use of the outpost on e4 and his pres-sure against the e-pawn wouldn't be immediately successful then, as it was after *21 Be1?: 21 . . . dxc4!   22 Qxc4* (22 bxc4 loses to 22 . . . Ne5) *Rxe3   23 Rxe3 Rxe3   24 Bf2 Nd5*

25 Nd2 Ngf4 26 h3 Rc3 27 Qa4 Ne2+ 28 Kh2 Rxh3+
and White resigned in view of 29 . . . Ndf4.

The opposite case is suggested by Westerinen–Korchnoi,
Majorca 1968:

1 e4 e6   2 d4 d5   3 Nc3 Bb4   4 e5 Ne7   5 Bd2 b6
6 Nf3 Qd7   7 Nb5 Bxd2+   8 Qxd2 a6   9 Na3 a5
10 Nb5 Ba6   11 a4 Nbc6   12 Bd3 h6   13 c3 0-0
14 Bb1?!

Position after 14 Bb1?!

White's intentions are advertised by his last move, which
threatens Qc2. Black has already weakened his kingside with
. . . h6. He cannot afford further loosening with . . . g6. But
what about *14 . . . f6?*

This move is essential because of Black's lack of immediate
counterplay on the queenside. It would appear that White has
a big advantage since he has eliminated his bad bishop and
forced Black to make another weakening pawn advance, but
Black's move turns the kingside from a White stronghold to a
Black one. There are no terrors after 15 Qd3 fxe5!

16 Qh7+ Kf7. White played *15 exf6 Rxf6   16 Qc2*, still hoping for the attack despite *16 . . . Ng6   17 0-0 Raf8*.

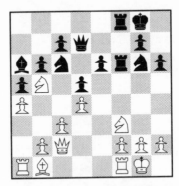

Position after 17 . . . Raf8

Here it is obvious that White is in no position to exploit the backward e-pawn. On the other hand Black has outposts at f5, e4, and f4, and after *18 Re1!* he had *18 . . . Bxb5! 19 axb5 Nce7   20 Qd3 Rxf3*. Black's attack, actually a counterattack, won swiftly: *21 gxf3 Nh4   22 Qh7+ Kf7   23 Kh1 Nxf3   24 Rg1!?* (best was *24 Re3*) *Nxg1!   25 Bg6+ Nxg6 26 Rxg1 Ne7   27 Rxg7+ Ke8   28 Kg2 e5!* White resigns.

The Wedge Formation

One of the most popular pawn configurations for attacking players is one in which one side has given up his d-pawn for the enemy c-pawn and arranged a center with his e-pawn on the fifth rank adjoining enemy pawns on d5 and e6.

This comes most frequently from e5 chain formations when

the base of the chain at d4 is exchanged off; e.g., 1 e4 e6 2 d4 d5 3 e5 c5 4 dxc5 or 4 Nf3 cxd4. It can also come out of other formations. In the Slav, for example, after Black has played . . . e5 *à la* Tichigorin he can create the Wedge by pushing his e-pawn to the fourth rank.

The advantages of the Wedge formation include the ideal outpost on d4 and the cramping effect on the enemy kingside. If White has a Wedge pawn at e5 Black cannot defend his king position with a knight on f6.

The disadvantages from White's point of view are that his e-pawn is weakened by the exchange of d-pawn and that Black can open up the f-file whenever he wants to with . . . f6. Black also has good outpost squares such as e4 and c4.

A good example of White's attacking chances is a Colle System won by Geza Maroczy in 1929:

1 d4 Nf6 2 Nf3 e6 3 e3 Be7 4 Bd3 d5 5 Nbd2 c5 6 c3 Nc6 7 0-0 a6 8 Qe2 0-0 9 dxc5! Bxc5 10 e4 Re8? 11 e5! Nd7 12 Nb3 Be7 13 Bf4 Nf8 14 Rad1 b5 15 Nfd4 Qd7 16 Bg3

Position after 16 Bg3

White's pieces are nicely posted for kingside aggression. This aggression does not require any pawn action, although f4-f5 is always available. On the other hand, Black needs some pawn action to equalize, but . . . f6 opens the kingside and. . . b4 may prematurely weaken the queenside.

In this game Black chose a typical method of blocking White's attacking line b1-h7. He played *16 . . . f5*, a kingside version of . . . c5 in the d5 chain, and just as in the situation in the d5 chain, this move permits White to open a knight file by force: *17 f4! Bd8   18 Bf2 Rb8   19 g4! g6   20 h4 Na5   21 Nxa5 Bxa5   22 a3.*

All that White needs to win now is to prevent . . . b4 as he prepares to open up the kingside. The inevitability of success in this strategic plan led Black to an error that shortened the game. He exchanged off his black-squared bishop thinking that White would be left with a "bad" queen bishop: *22 . . . Bb6   23 Kg2 Bxd4?   24 Bxd4 Re7   25 h5 Rg7   26 Kf2 Qe7   27 Rh1 Kf7   28 Rdg1 Ke8   29 Ke3! Kd8   30 Kd2 Qf7   31 Bc5!.*

Position after 31 Bc5!

Black suffers from another problem of the Wedge formation, a weakness on black squares that have been exposed by ... cxd4. The best he can do is bid for active play with 31 ... d4!, opening up a line for his poor queen bishop. But in the game Black prepared for ... d4 with *31 ... Bb7* and had to resign after *32 gxf5 gxf5 33 Rxg7 Qxg7 34 Rg1 Qf7 35 Qf2! Bc6 36 Qg3 Rb7 37 Qg8! Ke8 38 Bxf8* because *38 ... Qxf8 39 Qe6+* costs a piece.

The positional inferiority of Black in a Wedge endgame is frequently brought out in master games. Good examples are *Supplemental Game #3* and the following, which arose out of Tarrasch–Teichmann, San Sebastian 1912:

1 e4 e6   2 d4 d5   3 Nc3 Nf6   4 Bg5 Be7   5 e5
Nfd7   6 Bxe7 Qxe7   7 Qd2 0-0   8 f4 c5   9 Nf3
Nc6   10 g3?   a6?   11 Bg2   b5   12 0-0   cxd4
13 Nxd4 Nxd4   14 Qxd4 Qc5   15 Qxc5 Nxc5

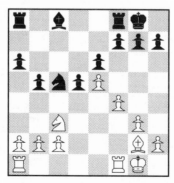

Position after 15 ... Nxc5

Black missed a chance to destroy the chain with 10 . . . f6!; e.g., 11 exf6 Nxf6 12 0-0-0 cxd4 13 Nxd4 and 13 . . . e5! 14 fxe5 Qxe5. No better is 11 Bh3? cxd4 12 Nxd4 Nxd4 13 Qxd4 fxe5 14 fxe5 Nb8! and 15 . . . Nc6. The attack on the chain is a matter of timing despite the rocklike nature of the links.

White won this game with textbook logic. First he occupied the golden outpost: 16 Ne2! Bd7 17 Nd4. Black could have attacked the center with 17 . . . f6, but it is his own center that would be brittle after 18 exf6 gxf6 19 f5!.

To prevent White from winning on the kingside Black should have taken emergency action such as . . . Na4 to provoke b2-b3, after which . . . Nc3, . . . b4, and . . . a5-a4 would give him counterplay. Black had a very bad game after 17 . . . Rac8 18 Kf2 Rc7 19 Ke3 Re8? 20 Rf2 Nb7? 21 Bf1 Na5 22 b3 h6 23 Bd3 Nc6 24 Nxc6! Bxc6 25 Kd4! Bd7 26 g4.

Black is bereft of counterplay needed to take White's attention away from f4-f5, the simplest winning plan. What makes White succeed are the positions of the two kings and the superiority of White's bishop. The rest of the game was flawed but demonstrated White's ease in winning: 26 . . . Bc8 27 h4 g6 28 Rh1 Kg7 29 h5 Rh8 30 Rfh2 Bd7 31 g5! hxg5 32 fxg5 (32 h6+ creating a powerful passed pawn also wins) Rxh5 33 Rxh5 gxh5 34 Rxh5 Kf8 35 Rh8+ Ke7 36 g6? (36 Rh7 Ke8 37 c3 and Be2-h5 wins fastest) 36 . . . fxg6 37 Bxg6 b4 38 Rh7+ Kd8 39 Bd3 Rc3? (39 . . . Rc6 would force White to turn to the queenside for a win) 40 a3 a5 41 Rh8+ Ke7 and Black resigned because of 42 Rb8 cleaning up the queenside.

Counterstrategies

Black is not without counterplay and the primary source is
. . . f6, the most natural pawn action. With just his pieces
Black can accomplish a lot with maneuvers and exchanges.
He can exchange off his queen bishop, for example. He can
try to prevent White's use of d4 as an outpost by concen-
trating his queen knight and king bishop on the square. He
can occupy his own outposts at e4 and c4.

An example of the maneuvering themes is Bondarevsky–
Lilienthal from the 1948 interzonal tournament:

1 e4 e6   2 d4 d5 3 Nc3 Nf6   4 Bg5 Be7   5 e5 Nfd7
6 Bxe7 Qxe7   7 f4 0-0   8 Nf3 c5   9 Bd3 f5!   10
0-0 a6   11 dxc5 Nxc5   12 Ne2 Nc6   13 c3 Bd7
14 Ned4 Rac8   15 Bc2 Ne4

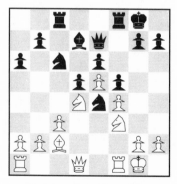

Position after 15 . . . Ne4

Black's outposted knight is at least as useful as White's. His ninth move was played to secure that square and to stop White's threat of 10 Bxh7+ Kxh7 11 Ng5+ and Qh5. Black has a nice game even though . . . f6 is out of the question.

The nature of the pawn structure after . . . f5 suggests that Black can take the initiative on the kingside with . . . g5!, a more effective break than . . . b5-b4. White could have anticipated this attack on the base of the new chain with Qe3, but he continued listlessly with *16 Qe2 Kh8 17 Kh1? Nxd4 18 Nxd4*, and Black answered *18 . . . g5!*.

Black has excellent prospects on the kingside now. If White establishes a new base with 19 g3 Black can extend his attack further with . . . g4 and . . . h5-h4. White actually played *19 Qe3 gxf4 20 Qxf4 Rg8 21 Bd1*, and Black rid himself of his bad bishop with *21 . . . Bb5!*.

Position after 21 . . . Bb5

It is clear in the diagram that White can ruin his opponent's pawns with 22 Nxb5 axb5, but Black's queenside remains powerful with its threats of 23 . . . b4 and 23 . . . Rc4! (e.g., 23 a3 Rc4 24 Be2 Ng3+ or 24 Qe3 Qg7). White's e-pawn and his vulnerable g-file are key elements in the game now.

White played *22 Nxb5? axb5* and his game rapidly deteriorated with *23 Be2 b4 24 c4* (White cannot permit a Black rook to reach c2) *dxc4 25 g4*, and after *25 . . . Qh4 26 Rac1 c3 27 bxc3 Rxc3 28 Rxc3 bxc3 29 Qe3 c2 30 Kg2* Black could have won immediately with *30 . . . Rxg4+! 31 Bxg4 Qxg4+ 32 Kh1 Qd1!*. He eventually won by the more mundane method of taking the isolated e-pawn and g-pawn.

The . . . f6 Plan

The most natural and generally the most successful counter-strategy for Black is to eliminate White's pawn center with . . . f6. This idea contests squares on the side of the board to which White should be paying the most attention. But there is an inherent weakness to this strategy, and it was Nimzovich, naturally, who popularized it in his game with Salwe at Karlsbad 1911 (*Supplemental Game #5*). He showed that by exchanging off both his center pawns (dxc5 and exf6) he could replace them with minor pieces. Unless Black can recapture on his c5 and f6 with pawns, he will surrender ideal outposts to White on d4 and e5.

"The actual occupation of the center by a pawn or pawns does not necessarily mean its control," Nimzovich wrote. But the surrender of the center—that is, the surrender by pawns—can actually mean reestablishing control with heavier material. A more recent example of Nimzovich's idea is Gurgenidze–Fuchs, Tiflis 1969:

1 e4 e6   2 Nf3 d5   3 Nc3 Nf6   4 e5 Nfd7   5 d4 c5
6 Bb5 Nc6   7 0-0 a6   8 Bxc6 bxc6   9 Na4 Be7
10 c3 0-0   11 b3 cxd4?   12 cxd4 Nb6   13 Nxb6
Qxb6   14 Bg5! Bxg5   15 Nxg5 f6

Position after 15 . . . f6

Examining this and the following diagram shows
how a strategy of attacking the base of the enemy chain
can boomerang. Black missed good chances earlier
with . . . f6 (e.g., 11 . . . f6   12 Bf4 Qe8 and . . . Qg6
or 14 . . . f6   15 exf6 gxf6   16 Bh6 Rf7). His further
exchanges of pawns occurred in a manner that allowed
White to eliminate his bad bishop and dominate the
center.

The second diagram was reached via *16 Nf3 fxe5?
17 Nxe5 c5   18 dxc5 Qxc5   19 Rc1 Qd6   20 Qd4! Bd7
21 Rfe1 Rac8   22 h3 Rxc1   23 Rxc1 Rc8   24 Rxc8+ Bxc8
25 b4!* A beautiful position!

Position after 25 b4!

White was content to make a queen out of his queenside majority, and he could do that easily as long as he maintained the blockade on d4 and e5: *25 ... Qc7 26 f4 Qc1+ 27 Kh2 g5 28 fxg5 Qxg5 29 a4 h5 30 h4!*, and the passed queenside pawn won shortly.

Supplemental Games

(1) When opening a file is better than shifting the attack on the base of a chain. Barczay–Pytel, Lublin 1969: 1 e4 e6 2 d4 d5 3 Nd2 Nc6 4 Ngf3 Nf6 5 e5 Nd7 6 g3 b6 7 Bb5 Ncb8 (Black prepares to attack the base with . . . c5 and to exchange off his bad bishop with . . . Ba6) 8 Qe2 c5 9 c3 a6 10 Bd3 Nc6 11 a3 c4? (There is some logic to this attempt to exploit White's hole at b3 and shift the attack on the chain, but 11 . . . cxd4 12 cxd4 b5 is much more efficient.) 12 Bc2 b5 13 Nf1 Nb6? (Continuing the attack on the new base. Black could cut his losses with 13 . . . f6 14 exf6 Nxf6 to a merely inferior game. Now it becomes lost because of the delay in getting his attack rolling.) 14 h4! Bd7 15 Ng5 g6 (Another fast win follows 15 ... h6 16 Qh5 Qe7 17 Nxf7! and 18 Bg6.) 16 h5! Be7 17 hxg6 Bxg5 18 Rxh7 Rxh7 19 gxh7 Bf6 20 Bg5! Resigns.

(2) **Black's attack along the c-file.** Vasiukov–Suetin, Erevan 1954: 1 e4 e6 2 d4 d5 3 e5 c5 4 c3 Nc6 5 Nf3 Qb6 6 Be2 cxd4 7 cxd4 Nge7 8 Na3 Nf5 9 Nc2 Bb4+ 10 Kf1! Be7! (White correctly avoids exchanges that loosen Black's constriction, and Black retreats his bishop to anticipate a2-a3 and b2-b4.) 11 h4 h5 12 g3 Bd7 13 Kg2 Rc8 14 Bd2 (This bishop will not serve well on c3. White should try to trade it off with 14 Rb1 and 15 Bg5.) 14 ... a5 15 Bc3 Nb4 16 Ne3 Nxe3+ 17 fxe3 Bb5! 18 a3 Bxe2 19 Qxe2 Nc6 20 Rhf1 Qa6! (The bottled-up c-file cannot be maintained by White in an ending after 21 Qxa6 bxa6. Black could then play . . . a4, . . . Na7-b5 and operate without opposition on the queenside.) 21 Qf2 Qd3 22 Ne1 Qg6 (A nice queen maneuver to reposition the piece on g4 or e4. White now tries the endgame despite Black's . . . b5-b4 plan.) 23 Qc2 Qxc2+ 24 Nxc2 b5 25 Rfc1 Kd7 26 Ne1 b4 27 axb4 axb4 28 Bd2 Ra8 29 Nd3 Rhb8 30 b3 Ra3! (White cannot contest the a-file nor protect his b-pawn without giving Black a passed a-pawn now.) 31 Rcb1 Rba8 32 Rxa3 bxa3 33 Kf3 Na7 34 Ke2 Nb5 35 Nc1 Rc8 36 Kd3 f6! 37 exf6 gxf6 38 Na2 e5 39 Rc1 Rg8 40 Rg1 Rg4 41 Nc3 Nxc3 42 Kxc3 Bd6 43 Be1 exd4+ 44 exd4 f5! 45 Bf2 f4 46 gxf4 Rxg1 47 Bxg1 Bxf4 48 Bf2 (to stop . . . Bg3) 48 . . . Bc1!, and White resigns before . . . a2.

(3) The Wedge in the endgame. Tal–Stahlberg, Stockholm 1960: 1 e4 e6 2 d4 d5 3 Nc3 Nf6 4 e5 Nfd7 5 f4 c5 6 Nf3 Nc6 7 Be3 cxd4 8 Nxd4 Bc5?! (heading for an inferior endgame in which Black will have a bad bishop and White will enjoy iron control of d4) 9 Qd2 Nxd4 10 Bxd4 Bxd4 11 Qxd4 Qb6?! 12 Nb5! Qxd4 13 Nxd4 Nb6 14 Bd3 Bd7 15 0-0-0 0-0-0 16 Rhf1 g6 17 Be2 Kb8 18 Rd3 (White prepares to probe for kingside weaknesses.) 18 ... h5 19 Rh3 Bc6 20 Rff3 Rc8 21 b3 Bd7 22 Kd2 Rcd8 23 Rh4 Nc8 24 Rfh3! (White now forces open a file with g2-g4.) 24 ... Rhg8 25 g4 hxg4 26 Rxg4 Rh8 27 Rgh4 Rxh4 28 Rxh4 Rf8 29 Rh7 (To White's other advantages he now adds the superior rook.) 29 ... Ne7 30 Nf3 Nc6 31 Ng5 Nd8 32 h4 Bc6 33 Ke3 Kc8 34 Bd3 Be8 35 Kd4 b6 36 Ke3 Rg8 37 Nf3 Kd7 38 Nh2 Kc6 39 Ng4 Kc5 40 c3 a5 41 a3 b5 42 b4+ Kb6 43 Nf6! Rf8 44 Kf3 axb4 45 axb4 d4 (else Kg4-g5-h6-g7!) 46 cxd4 Nc6 47 Nxe8 Rxe8 48 Rxf7 Nxd4+ 49 Kg4 Resigns.

(4) When to trade the "good" bishop. Sax–Groszpeter, Hungarian Super Championship 1991: 1 e4 c6 2 d4 d5 3 e5 Bf5 4 c3 (Until recently, the recommended move here was 4 Bd3?! Bxd3 5 Qxd3 after which Black has solved most of his opening problems) e6 5 Be2 Nd7 6 Nf3 h6 7 0-0 Qc7 8 Nh4 Be4 9 Nd2 g5? 10 Nhf3 Bf5 11 Ne1! 0-0-0 12 Bd3! (Now that Black has severely weakened himself on squares such as h5, f6 and f7, White wants to play f2-f4-f5 as well as attack the enemy king) Ne7 13 Qe2 Kb8 14 b4! Rg8 15 Nb3 Nb6 16 a4 g4 17 Nc5 h5? 18 Ba6! Nc4 (not 18 ... bxa6 19 Nxa6+) 19 Bxb7 and

20 Na6+ won. Black was beaten on the queenside but he was also much worse on the other wing.

(5) Liquidation of the e5 chain. Nimzovich–Salwe, Karlsbad 1911: 1 e4 e6   2 d4 d5   3 e5 c5   4 c3 Nc6   5 Nf3 Qb6   6 Bd3 Bd7? (6 . . . cxd4 followed by 7 . . . Bd7 presents White with problems defending the d-pawn.) 7 dxc5! Bxc5   8 0-0 f6   9 b4! Be7   10 Bf4 fxe5   11 Nxe5 Nxe5   12 Bxe5 Nf6 (White uses as outposts the squares formerly occupied by his pawns. He can pressure the kingside along the d4-h8 diagonal as well as the d3-h7 one.) 13 Nd2 0-0   14 Nf3 Bd6   15 Qe2   Rac8   16 Bd4   Qc7   17 Ne5!   Be8   18 Rae1 Bxe5   19 Bxe5 Qc6   20 Bd4 Bd7 (Black's e-pawn clearly became a weakness after . . . f6.) 21   Qc2 Rf7   22 Re3 b6   23 Rg3 Kh8   24 Bxh7! e5! (White wins easily after 24 . . . Nxh7   25 Qg6 Kg8   26 Bxg7! Nf8   27 Qh6.)   25 Bg6 Re7   26 Re1 Qd6   27 Be3 d4 (Black's center pawns finally speak.) 28 Bg5 Rxc3   29 Rxc3 dxc3   30 Qxc3 Kg8   31 a3 Kf8   32 Bh4 Be8   33 Bf5 Qd4   34 Qxd4 exd4   35 Rxe7 Kxe7   36 Bd3 Kd6   37 Bxf6 gxf6   38 Kf1 Bc6   39 h4 Resigns.

THE KING'S
INDIAN COMPLEX

The King's Indian Complex

EACH MEMBER OF THE FAMILY OF FORMATIONS THAT STEMS FROM the above diagram has such distinct qualities that any exchanges or advances must be weighed with extreme care. The most obvious moves are often positional blunders. For example, dxe5 by White may win control of the d-file, but ease Black's cramped quarters. On the other hand, . . . exd4 may simply expose Black's d-pawn to decisive pressure along the half-open d-file.

An experienced player may readily recognize this structure as the spine of the King's Indian and Old Indian Defenses. The difference between the two is the placement of Black's king bishop—on g7 or e7. A master may notice further that the formation also appears in the Ruy Lopez and can occur even in the Sicilian Defense with colors reversed.

We've already mentioned in the d5 chain (Chapter 4) what kinds of issues arise from d4-d5 in the diagram above. The other options are (1) c4-c5 by White, a plan that liquidates the center in a few moves; (2) dxe5 by White; and (3) . . . exd4 by Black.

The c4-c5 Plan

This is an explosive idea since a center of six pawns is likely to be reduced to four or two within a few moves of c4-c5. After c5/ . . . dxc5/dxc5 the center becomes stable and will transpose into the next section. But White can also play c5/ . . . dxc5/dxe5!?.

Position after 11 . . . b5?!

This is Donner–Euwe, match 1955, and came from *1 Nf3 Nf6 2 c4 g6 3 g3 Bg7 4 Bg2 0-0 5 d4 d6 6 0-0 Nbd7 7 Qc2 e5 8 Rd1 Re8 9 Nc3 c6 10 e4 Qc7 11 h3 b5?!.* Black's last move seeks to strip away some of White's pawn control of the center (since 12 cxb5 cxb5 13 Nxb5 loses the queen).

Here *12 c5* was ideally suited for the position. On 12 . . . exd4 White takes time for 13 cxd6! Qxd6 14 Nxd4 with a powerful game in the newly opened center. Black preferred to accept the pawn sacrifice with *12 . . . dxc5 13 dxe5! Nxe5 14 Nxe5 Qxe5*.

Now 15 Bf4! would have presented White with a large positional edge: 15 . . . Qh5 16 e5 Nd5 17 Nxd5 cxd5 18 g4, or 15 . . . Qe7 16 Bd6 and 17 Bxc5, or finally 15 . . . Qe6 16 Rd6 Qc4 17 Bf1 Qb4 18 Rxc6 threatening 19 a3 Qa5 20 Bc7.

The only thing wrong is that White tried to win by using his kingside majority—and lost: *15 f4? Qh5 16 e5 Bxh3!!* (forced, but sound; e.g., 17 Bxc6 b4! 18 Bxa8 bxc3 19 Bg2 Bf5 20 Qb3 Ng4!) *17 exf6 Bxf6 18 Ne4* (to anticipate . . . Bf5) *Rxe4! 19 Bxe4 Re8* (threatening 20 . . . Rxe4 and 21 . . . Bd4+) *20 Be3 Bf5 21 Qxc5* (White also should lose after 21 Bxf5 Rxe3 22 Qf2 Bd4 23 Rxd4 cxd4 24 Bc8 Re2 25 g4 Rxf2 26 gxh5 Rxf4) *21 . . . Rxe4 22 Rd2 Qf3* White resigns.

There is a second theme of c4-c5, which is more positionally oriented. The exchange of White's c-pawn for Black's d-pawn creates opposing pawn majorities. Black's queenside mass can be subjected to a kind of minority attack before c4-c5 or after it, so that Black's will have a weak isolated c-pawn.

This may sound obscure, but it is made clearer by the following diagram from Lilienthal–Boleslavsky, Moscow 1941:

1 d4 Nf6   2 c4 d6   3 Nc3 e5   4 Nf3 Nbd7   5 g3 g6
6 Bg2   Bg7   7 0-0   0-0   8 e4   Re8   9 Be3   Ng4
10 Bg5 f6   11 Bc1 c6   12 b3 Nh6   13 Bb2 Qc7
14 Rc1 Nf8

Position after 14 . . . Nf8

White began his middlegame strategy with *15 b4! Nf7 16 b5*, a disguised version of the minority attack that is examined in Chapter 7 in a different formation. After the game continued *16 . . . Bg4   17 h3 Bd7   18 bxc6*, Black could not afford to give up pawn control of d5 with 18 . . . Bxc6 19 Nd5; so he played *19 . . . bxc6* and then *19 c5!* revealed his plan. On 19 . . . exd4 he can interpolate 20 cxd6 before recapturing d4. Thus, White obtained a fine position with *19 . . . dxc5   20 dxe5! fxe5   21 Na4 Ne6   22 Nxc5 Nxc5 23 Rxc5*.

Position after 23 Rxc5

Black's c-pawn can be considered lost unless Black obtains active counterplay to draw attention from it. In the 1941 game Black had just enough activity with *23 . . . Rab8   24 Qa1 Rb5!   25 Rc2 Reb8* to draw.

As we said earlier, it is vital to understand structures rather than openings because different formations pop up in a variety of opening systems. A 1 e4 player might consider this c4-c5 strategy irrelevant to his interests, but he would be proved wrong by this diagram.

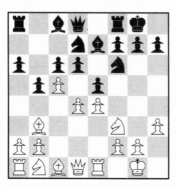

Position after 12 c5!?

This comes from a once-popular variation of the Ruy Lopez: 1 e4 e5 2 Nf3 Nc6 3 Bb5 a6 4 Ba4 Nf6 5 0-0 Be7 6 Re1 b5 7 Bb3 d6 8 c3 0-0 9 h3 Nb8 10 d4 Nbd7 11 c4 c6! 12 c5!?

Two important tactical points of c4-c5 are evident in this example. Black cannot play 12 . . . exd4 because of 13 cxd6 and 14 e5 winning a piece, and he should avoid 12 . . . dxc5 because of 13 dxe5 creating a hostile kingside majority. This majority might also be weak (as in *Supplemental Game #1*), but from the diagram White's majority translates into a powerful attack after 12 . . . dxc5 13 dxe5: Averbakh–Furman, Moscow 1961: 13 . . . Ne8 14 e6! fxe6 15 Bxe6+ Kh8 16 Nc3 Nc7 17 Bf5 c4 18 Bf4 Ne6 19 Bg3 Nec5 20 Nd4 Qb6 21 e5! Rd8 22 Bxh7! Kxh7 23 Qh5+ Kg8 24 Nf5 Bf8 25 Qg6 Kh8 26 Ne4 Ne6 27 Nf6! Nxf6 28 exf6 Ra7 29 Re4 Nf4 30 Rxf4 Bxf5 31 Rxf5 Rd5 32 Rxd5 Resigns.

Going back to the diagram we can see that Black's best move is 12 . . . Qc7!, which preserves some control over the center squares e5 and d6. After the likely continuation 13 cxd6 Bxd6 14 Bg5 we have transposed into a form of Tchigorin's . . . e5 plan of the Slav (Chapter 2)!

Remembering the strategic thinking behind Tchigorin's plan, it should be clear that Black needs counterplay on the black squares after . . . exd4. In one early disaster (Tal–Unzicker, Stockholm 1960–61) Black played 14 . . . c5? which weakens his d5, opens up a file that passes to White's control, and is totally out of character with the formation. The game ended 15 dxc5! Bxc5 16 Nc3 Bb7 17 Rc1 Qb6 18 Re2! Rfe8 19 Nd5! Bxd5 20 Bxd5 Rd8 21 Rec2 Be7 22 Rc6 Qa5 23 Bd2 b4 24 Bxf7+! Kxf7 25 Qb3+ Resigns.

White Plays dxe5

The center formation that occurs after dxe5 by White can be identified, oddly enough, with a Soviet player who rarely played 1 d4. This was V. Rauzer, who popularized another formation (in the Dragon—see Chapter 3). Examine the following position:

Position after 13 . . . axb5

This came about from a normal Ruy Lopez after *1 e4 e5 2 Nf3 Nc6 3 Bb5 a6 4 Ba4 Nf6 5 0-0 Be7 6 Re1 b5 7 Bb3 d6 8 c3 Na5 9 Bc2 c5 10 d4 Qc7 11 Nbd2 Nc6 12 a4 Rb8 13 axb5 axb5*

For many years the accepted plan for White was d4-d5 followed by a kingside attack involving either g2-g4 and Nf1-g3-f5 or Nh2 and f2-f4. But Rauzer discovered in the 1930s that White had an advantage in the center with *14 dxc5! dxc5*— even though he might lose control of the d-file.

White's advantage is simple: he can protect both d4 and d5 with pawns. Black has lost pawn control of d5. Therefore, White will try to occupy d5 (or f5) with minor pieces. Black will have to find forceful play on the queenside. In the inaugural game of Rauzer's 14 dxc5 plan (vs. Ryumin, Leningrad 1936) White obtained a strong initiative after *15 Nf1 Be6 16 Ne3 0-0 17 Ng5 Rfd8 18 Qf3 Rd6* (18 ... h6!) *19 Nf5! Bxf5 20 exf5!*. White's control of the white squares, especially e4, gave him the freedom to mount a pawn march on the kingside: *20 ... h6 21 Ne4 Nxe4 22 Bxe4 Bf6 23 Be3 Ne7 24 b4 c4 25 g3 Rd7 26 Ra7 Qd8 27 Rxd7 Qxd7 28 h4 Kh8 29 g4! Ng8* (29 ... Bxh4 *30 Qh3* and g5) *30 g5 Be7 31 Rd1 Qc7 32 f6 Bxf6 33 gxf6 Nxf6 34 Bc2 Rd8 35 Bxh6 Rxd1+ 36 Bxd1 e4 37 Bf4 Qd8 38 Qe2* Resigns. Notice how useless the open file was to Black.

A more drastic version of this is indicated by *1 e4 c5 2 Nf3 d6 3 Bb5+ Bd7 4 Bxd7+ Qxd7 5 0-0 Nc6 6 c3*

Position after 6 c3

This time it is a Sicilian Defense, but the same basic formation can be derived following *6 ... e5?* This is an error, and we might ask what formation Black should head for. The answer is one in which the exchange of white-squared bishops favors him. That means an e5 chain, and Black can obtain one after 6 ... Nf6 7 Qe2 e6! 8 d4 cxd4 9 cxd4 d5! 10 e5 Ne4. White has the bad bishop.

But after 6 ... e5 Black ends up with a pawn-bound bishop after 7 d4 Nf6 8 dxe5 dxe5. This is what Rauzer obtained in the center in the previous example. The game continued 9 Qe2 Rd8 10 Bg5! Be7 11 Bxf6 Bxf6 12 Na3!

Position after 12 Na3

We can see that White will occupy d5 very easily with Nc4-e3-d5 or some similar maneuver. Again, Black may get the d-file, but his lack of pawn control of one square counts more. (For a full game see *Supplemental Game #2.*)

The reason we bring up the Rauzer idea here is that dxe5 in the Indian complex leads directly into the same formation with colors reversed. Frequently you may see a player with the White pieces in a King's Indian Defense play dxe5 and lose. Why? Because he is giving Black the same center that it took Rauzer time to engineer with colors reversed.

But dxe5 is deceptive. It appears to give White a valuable open file and the chance to exploit a hole at d6. But this hole isn't the weakness it's cracked up to be. Occupying it with a rook, for instance, is painless to Black. Meanwhile Black can whip up a whirlwind attack, as in the following:

Hernandez–Berliner, Southern Champ. 1949:

1 d4 Nf6 2 Nf3 g6 3 c4 Bg7 4 Nc3 0-0 5 e4 d6
6 Bd3 Nbd7 7 0-0 e5 8 dxe5? dxe5 9 Qe2 c6
10 b3 Qc7 11 Ba3 Rd8 12 Rad1

Position after 12 Rad1

Black appears to be on the defensive; yet he has a decisive attack within six moves. He begins with *12 . . . Bf8!* to encourage an exchange of bishops that will allow him to plant a knight on d4; e.g., 13 Bxf8 Nxf8 followed by . . . Ne6.

White preserved his bishop with *13 Bb2*, but enemy pieces took control of the board: *13 . . . Nh5 14 g3 Nc5 15 Bc2? Bg4! 16 Kg2 Ne6! 17 Qe3* (or 17 Qe1 Bxf3+ and 18 . . . Nd4+) *17 . . . Bc5 18 Qc1* and now *18 . . . Nhf4+!*

19 gxf4 Nxf4+ 20 Kg3 Bxf3 21 Kxf3 Rxd1 22 Qxd1 Rd8 23 Nd5 (23 Qe1 Qc8 and 24 . . . Qh3+) 23 . . . cxd5 24 cxd5 Qe7 25 Qd2 Qg5 26 Bxe5 Qh5+ forced resignation. (See also *Supplemental Game #3* for exploitation of this key f8-a3 diagonal.)

Counterstrategies: c4-c5

The White side of the positions deriving from dxe5 is not without opportunities. The most fruitful plan is to play c4-c5 which (1) strengthens control of d6, (2) permits a piece to be stationed at c4, and (3) closes Black's good a7-g1 diagonal while opening up White's a2-g8.

This c4-c5 counterstrategy makes special sense when there are further weaknesses in the enemy structure. Geller–Boleslavsky, Moscow, 1952, illustrated this after *1 c4 Nf6 2 Nc3 g6 3 e4 d6 4 d4 Bg7 5 f3 0-0 6 Be3 e5 7 Nge2 Nbd7 8 Qd2 c6 9 0-0-0 Qa5 10 Kb1 a6 11 Nc1 Re8 12 Nb3 Qc7*

Position after 12 . . . Qc7

The added feature of this formation is Black's hole at b6. Black can live with a hole on d6 but curiously not with another one on b6: *13 dxe5! dxe5 14 c5! Nf8 15 Qd6*. The real danger to Black is the loss of a queenside pawn after White occupies d5 and d6 with knights.

Black could put up a better fight with *15 . . . Qxd6 16 Rxd6 Be6 17 Na5 Rb8*, but he incurred a lasting White momentum following *15 . . . Ne6 16 Bc4 Bf8 17 Qxc7 Nxc7 18 Na5 Rb8 19 Na4 Be6 20 Bxe6 Nxe6 21 Nc4*.

White will not only threaten the b-pawn but also the e-pawn and d7 with his rooks and knights. It is no surpise that Black was lost after *21 . . . Nc7 22 Nab6 Ne6 23 b4 Nf4 24 Rd2 Rbd8 25 Rhd1 Rxd2 26 Rxd2 Bg7 27 Na5 Rb8 28 Bxf4 exf4 29 Nd7! Rd8 30 Nxf6+ Bxf6 31 Rxd8+ Bxd8 32 Nxb7*. See also *Supplemental Game #4*.

An excellent demonstration of the use of three counterstrategy ideas—the a3-f8 diagonal, the d6 square, and c4-c5—was Portisch–Sax, Budapest 1975. It arose out of *1 c4 g6 2 e4 Bg7 3 d4 d6 4 Nc3 Nd7 5 Nf3 e5 6 Be2 Ne7 7 dxe5! dxe5 8 b3 c6 9 0-0 Qa5*.

Position after 9 . . . Qa5

Black didn't want to give up his center trump—having pawn control of both d4 and d5—with the solid 9 . . . c5. Instead, to stop Ba3 he provokes White into a secondary plan of b2-b4 and c4-c5. (He wouldn't live long after 9 . . . 0-0 10 Ba3 Re8 11 Qd2; e.g., 11 . . . Nf8 12 Qxd8 or 11 . . . Qa5 12 Bxe7 Rxe7 13 Nd5 or 11 . . . Qb6 12 Na4 Qd8 13 Rfd1 followed by Bd6 and c4-c5.)

White shifted plans with *10 Rb1!* (10 . . . Qxc3 11 Bd2), and Black's refusal to play . . . c5 gave White a powerful game: *10 . . . Nf6 11 b4 Qc7 12 c5 0-0 13 Be3 h6 14 b5 Be6 15 bxc6*. To prevent White from sinking a knight on b5 or d5 Black had to recapture with a pawn, *15 . . . bxc6*.

Black faced a dismal endgame after *16 Qd6*, but he should have kept the pawn structure stable with 16 . . . Ne8. He played *16 . . . Qxd6?* and was sunk: *17 cxd6 Nc8 18 Rfd1 Rd8 19 Bc5 Nd7 20 Ba3 Ncb6 21 Nd2* (heading for c5, the golden square cleared of pawns) *f5 22 Nb3 fxe4 23 Nxe4 Na4 24 Rbc1 Bd5 25 f3 Bf8 26 Na5! Bxa2 27 Nxc6 Re8 28 Ne7+ Kf7 29 Bb5 Nab6 30 Rc7 Red8 31 Nc6* Resigns.

Every time you move a pawn you also make weaknesses, and c4-c5 is no different. By sticking his pawns on b4 and c5 White may be sentencing them to a pounding by Black's minor pieces.

A fine example of this in the ending was Gross–Kalme from the 1955 U.S. junior championship. White combined the unfortunate dxe5 and e2-e4 plans again:

1 d4 Nf6　2 c4 g6　3 Nc3 Bg7　4 Nf3 d6　5 Bf4 0-0　6 h3 Nfd7　7 e3 e5　8 Bh2 c6　9 Be2 Qe7　10 dxe5 dxe5　11 0-0 Rd8　12 Qc2 Nf8　13 Rad1 Bf5!　14 e4? Bd7　15 Rd2 Bh6　16 Rdd1 f6　17 b4

Na6   18 c5? Nc7   19 Bc4+   Be6   20 Qb3   Bxc4
21 Qxc4+   Qe6   22 Qxeb+ Nfxe6   23 Rxd8+   Rxd8
24 Rd1 Rxd1+   25 Nxd1

Position after 25 Nxd1

Earlier White could have capitalized on a Black slip with
an exchange sacrifice, 16 Bxe5! Bxd2   17 Qxd2, to break
the center up. Now his bishop is quite inferior. But the real
difference between the two sides is explained by 25 . . . a5!,
destroying the overextended queenside.

On 26 a3 Black simply plays 26 . . . axb4   27 axb4 Na6
and takes the b-pawn. White tried to complicate with *26 bxa5
Nxc5   27 Nd4* since the e-pawn was lost anyway. Black won
with *27 . . . exd4! 28   Bxc7 Nxe4   29 Bb6 c5   30 f3 Nc3!
31 Nb2 Bf8* and the entrance of the Black king to support his
c-pawn's advance. (See also *Supplemental Game #5.*)

The Boleslavsky Wall: . . . exd4

Kmoch dubbed the formation derived by . . . exd4 in the diagram on page 197 the Boleslavsky Wall, after the Soviet grand-

master who did as much as anyone to popularize the King's Indian Defense during the late 1940s. The opening was still viewed with suspicion because it appeared that if Black had to exchange his e-pawn for the enemy d-pawn he would have no protection for his own d-pawn.

But Boleslavsky demonstrated something that was known by a few masters in the previous century and long since forgotten—that Black can find many tactical resources in such a formation to keep White occupied. A remarkable strategic dinosaur of the last century, Paulsen–Anderssen, Leipzig 1877, shows this:

1 e4 e5   2 Nc3 Bc5   3 Nf3 Nc6?   4 Nxe5! Nxe5   5 d4 Bd6   6 dxe5 Bxe5   7 Be2 c6   8 0-0 Nf6   9 Bf3 h6   10 Be3 d6   11 Bd4 Be6   12 b3 0-0   13 Qd3 Qe7   14 Rael? Rfd8   15 Nd1 Nd7   16 c4 Qf6! 17 Bc3 a5!   18 Be2 g5   19 f3 Nf8   20 Bd2 Ng6 21 g3

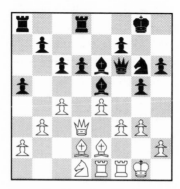

Position after 21 g3

After forcing his opponent to surrender the center on the fourth move White has shown a stark misunderstanding of how to deal with this formation. He blocked his f-pawn at move nine and was restrained from moving it later by Black's quickly developing power on the black squares. Thus White had no center threats of e4-e5 or f4-f5 and he could not prevent Black from occupying e5.

White put his queen rook on a useless square and then played b2-b3, giving Black the opportunity to open up the queenside with ... a4. Black's play has been astonishingly modern by comparison. (Ironically Paulsen, who handled the White pieces, is regarded today as a far-thinking iconoclast, whereas Anderssen, who played Black, is usually remembered as a one-dimensional romantic.)

When Boleslavsky and David Bronstein popularized Black's formation after World War II they used all of these themes— the threat of ... a4, pressure against the e-pawn, use of the black squares on the long diagonal. Anderseen could have anticipated another modern idea here with 21 ... h5 followed by ... Kg7 and ... h4 to use the black squares for a mating attack.

But Black chose another thematic idea with *21 ... d5!?*. With the advantage of a hundred years' hindsight we see that 22 exd5 cxd5   23 c5 is the best strategic response (although the White c-pawn may fall). But White permitted the center to be liquidated, and the difference between the activity of the two players' pieces was no longer obscured by the center: *22 cxd5 cxd5   23 Be3 dxe4   24 Qxe4 Bd5   25 Qg5 Qg7 26 Nf2 Be6   27 Qa4 Bd4* followed by ... g4 gave Black a mating attack.

White Strategies: c4-c5, e4-e5, etc.

White has two levers—c4-c5 and e4-e5—and an attack against a weak enemy d-pawn to blend into his middlegame plan. It is a true blend since there are few maneuvers available to White that promote e4-e5 and prevent taking aim at the d-pawn.

The e4-e5 idea is primarily a tactical attempt to break the center completely open for the White minor pieces. With best play e4-e5 cannot be achieved without creating a crippled, isolated White e-pawn on the fifth rank. But small errors by Black, as in Reti–Spielmann, Marienbad 1925, make e4-e5 possible:

1 c4 e5   2 Nf3 d6   3 d4 exd4   4 Nxd4 Nf6   5 Nc3
Be7   6 g3 0-0   7 Bg2 c6   8 0-0 Re8   9 b3 a5
10 Bb2 Na6   11 e4 Nc5   12 Qc2 Bf8   13 Rad1
Bd7   14 Nde2 Nh5?   15 h3 Qg5

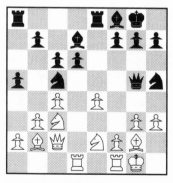

Position after 15 ... Qg5

White would find it hard to exploit the Black d-pawn as long as Black protected it with his king bishop. He might think of a queenside advance with a2-a3 and b3-b4, but Black's kingside action suggests a sharper reaction by White. That meant 16 f4! Qe7 17 g4 Nf6 18 e5!.

Black has a problem of limited space that is common to the Indian complex. His king knight cannot retreat. If d7 were free he could stand better by exchanging pawns and dropping his knight to the vacant square. But now he must play 18 . . . dxe5 19 fxe5 Qxe5 and face the consequences of 20 Ne4 Qc7 21 Nxf6+ gxf6 22 Nf4 which threatens Nh5.

The Black kingside cost him the game quickly: 22 . . . Re5 23 Nh5 Rxh5 24 gxh5 Ne6 25 Bxf6 Bh6 26 Qd3 Be8 27 Kh1 Ng7 28 Rg1 Qf4 29 Rdf1 Qe3 30 Qxe3 Bxe3 31 Be4! Resigns.

The story is quite different in Reshevsky–Bronstein, Zurich 1953. White's c-pawn was under fire, and after . . . a5-a4-a3 he had to weaken his queenside black squares to reach this position:

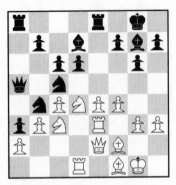

Position after 22 . . . Bd7

Black has excellent control of queenside squares, but that portion of the board remains closed while White readies a kingside attack. A good plan for White would be 23 g4 followed by Bg3 and f4-f5. *It is difficult to do anything quickly in the basic Boleslavsky Wall.*

But White forced the issue with *23 e5? dxe5 24 fxe5*. There is no way he could have exploited the newly opened d-file and half-open f-file right now. And Black had no difficulty in contesting the open lines: *24 . . . Rad8 25 g4 Ne6! 26 Bh4 Nxd4 27 Rxd4 Qc5 28 Rde4 Bh6! 29 Kh1 Be6* (*30 Bxd8 Rxd8 31 Rf3 Rd2!*).

Even though White was able to liquidate his bad pawn— *30 g5 Bg7 31 Rf4 Bf5 32 Ne4 Bxe4+ 33 Rfxe4 Na6 34 e6 fxe6 35 Rxe6 Rf8 36 Re7 Bd4 37 R3e6 Qf5 38 Re8 Nc5 39 Rxd8 Nxe6 40 Rxf8+ Kxf8*.

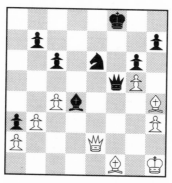

Position after 40 . . . Kxf8

Here, the inherent advantage of operating from an originally cramped but now liberated position bears fruit. Black's pieces occupy squares formerly forbidden to them by White's pawns. His king is still protected by interior lines of his own pawns. White's defenses are stretched thin, however.

White played *41 Bg3*, sacrificing a pawn to get his bishop into play. But White's endgame chances went downhill after *41 . . . Qxg5 42 Qxe6 Qxg3* (43 Qc8+ Ke7 44 Qxb7+ would have given Black a mate after 44 . . . Kd8 since 45 Qa8+ Kc7 46 Qa5+ Bb6 stops the White checks).

A useful move for White is b2-b4 because it takes away the c5 square from Black's use and prepares for b4-b5, a line-opening queenside motif. Even if the move b2-b4 doesn't forward any specific middlegame plan it may be important because it restricts Black. The nature of the Boleslavsky Wall is that Black will be crushed if his pieces do not obtain early activity.

A demonstration of this theme with b2-b4 is Korchnoi–Ivkov, Hastings 1955–56:

1 d4 Nf6   2 c4 d6   3 Nc3 e5   4 Nf3 Nbd7   5 g3 c6
6 e4 g6   7 Bg2 Bg7   8 0-0 0-0   9 h3 Re8   10 Be3
a5   11 Qc2   a4   12 Rfd1   Qa5   13 Rab1!   exd4
14 Nxd4 Nc5

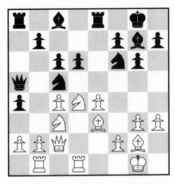

Position after 14 . . . Nc5

Here *15 b4! axb3   16 axb3* is strong even though it opens up the a-file for Black. The truth is that Black's queen and queen knight will be kicked back by b3-b4 and that White can take the open a-file away from Black with a subsequent Ra1 if Black is cramped enough.

Black chose to stop b3-b4 mechanically with *16 . . . Qb4*. This is very double edged because it means that Black will have greater difficulty extricating his pieces if b3-b4 is indeed played. White found a way of doing it: *17 Bf4! Bf8   18 Bd2* (threatening a discovered attack on the queen) *Qb6   19 Be3* (ditto) *Qb4   20 Qd2!*

Now Black must give up the queenside blockade because of the threat of Nc2!. Black continued *20 . . . Qb6* and had to lose material after *21 b4* either with *21 . . . Ncd7   22 Ne6* or, as in the game, with *21 . . . Ncxe4   22 Nxe4 Nxe4   23 Qd3!*.

It's true that Black could have saved his material with *19 . . . Qc7   20 b4 Ncd7*, but after *21 f4* White would have a tremendous game and could choose either to attack the king, the queenside, or the d-pawn.

Black Counterstrategies: . . . d6-d5, . . . f7-f5, etc.

Black's middlegame plans and attitudes are similar to those in the Maroczy Bind. He needs a central break or he will eventually be crushed. Since in the Boleslavsky Wall Black does not have the Maroczy theme of . . . b7-b5, his choice is somewhat narrower. Under certain conditions the advance of the c-pawn by Black is OK, although it conceded a tremendous hole on d5; the main interest focuses on ... f7-f5 and ... d6-d5.

The former is more loosening than in the comparable Maroczy formation because after ... f7-f5 Black has neither e-pawn nor f-pawn available for kingside defense. Its chief virtue, at least in the practice of masters during the last thirty years, has been as a secondary threat. When ... d6-d5 cannot be played, Black may have ... f7-f5.

This was the case in Kan–Boleslavsky, Moscow 1952:

1 d4 Nf6   2 c4 g6   3 Nf3 Bg7   4 g3 0-0   5 Bg2 d6
6 0-0 Nbd7   7 Qc2 e5   8 Rd1 Re8   9 Nc3 c6
10 e4 exd4   11 Nxd4 Qe7   12 h3 Nc5   13 f3

Position after 13 f3

White's last move is superior to Re1 because the rook move would permit 13 . . . d5!; e.g., 14 cxd5 Nxd5 15 Nxd5 cxd5 16 e5 Ne4!. But White marred this by answering the natural 13 . . . a5 with 14 g4?. This is an overreaction to Black's quiet play and is greatly inferior to 14 b3 with a likely continuation of 14 . . . Nfd7 15 Bb2 a4 16 Rab1.

There followed 14 . . . Nfd7! 15 Rb1 Ne5 16 b3 and now 16 . . . f5!. White may have thought this idea was defused by 14 g4, but the weakening of White's kingside that resulted only made it more powerful. After 17 exf5 gxf5 White avoided both the risky 18 Nxf5 Bxf5 19 Qxf5 (19 gxf5 Ned3!) Rf8 20 Qg5 Qxg5 21 Bxg5 Nxf3+ and the safe 18 Bf4. He played the consistent 18 gxf5 and was lost thus: 18 . . . Ned3! 19 Rxd3 Nxd3 20 Qxd3 Qe1+ 21 Bf1 (21 Kh2 Qe5+ and 22 . . . Qxd4) 21 . . . Qg3+ 22 Kh1 Re1 23 Be3 Qxh3+ 24 Kg1 Qg3+ 25 Kh1 Qh4+ 26 Kg2 Rxe3 27 Qxe3 Bxd4 28 Qe8+ Kg7 29 f6+ Bxf6 30 Qe4 Qg5+ White resigns.

The strength of . . . d6-d5 is no less in an Indian formation than in the Maroczy formation. White's solid formation has subtle weaknesses in it that are revealed once the center pawns are swept away. White must either stop . . . d6-d5, exploit the opened center with better developed pieces, or create a favorable center with the remaining pawns with some such device as exd5 and c4-c5.

A vivid illustration of this powerful break occurs after a normal King's Indian opening such as 1 d4 Nf6 2 c4 g6 3 g3 Bg7 4 Bg2 0-0 5 Nf3 d6 6 Nc3 Nbd7 7 0-0 e5 · 8 e4 exd4 9 Nxd4 Re8

Position after 9 . . . Re8

Here *10 f3?* is a logical but inaccurate move. White has to defend his e-pawn during most of a typical Boleslavsky Wall. He doesn't want to use his king rook because of some tactical problems (. . . Nc5 and . . . Nfd7-e5-d3) and because it may be more useful on the f-file after f4-f5. But here 10 f3 is bad because after *10 . . . c6!* White cannot stop Black's . . . d6-d5; e.g., 11 Nde2 Nb6 12 b3 d5 or 11 Nb3 Nb6 12 Qe2 Be6 13 Nd2 d5 14 e5 Nfd7 15 cxd5 cxd5 16 f4 Nc5 and . . . d4.

What are White's options if he cannot stop . . . d5? One is to exploit the newly opened position with 11 Be3 d5 12 cxd5 cxd5 13 Ndb5, for example. This may be enough to keep a balance. If White ignores the problem completely with 11 Re1? d5 12 exd5, he can be surprised, as in Liebert–Kuzmin, Zinnowitz 1971: 12 . . . Rxe1+ 13 Qxe1 Nb6! (threatening 14 . . . Nfxd5 or 14 . . . Nxc4) 14 Nc2 Nxc4 15 dxc6 bxc6 16 Kh1 Nd5! 17 Bf1 Ne5 18 Qd1 Qb6! 19 Bg2 Bf5 20 Nxd5 cxd5 21 g4 Bd3 22 Ne3 Bc4 23 Nxd5? Rd8 24 f4 Bxd5 25 Bxd5 Qc6

26 Qf3 Rxd5! White resigns in lieu of 27 fxe5 Rd1+ 28 Kg2 Rg1+ 29 Kf2 Rf1+.

A third option is the retention of some pawns in the center. This often is done with exd5 and c4-c5. In Jones–Dueball, Nice 1974, White played *11 Kh1 Nb6 12 b3 d5 13 exd5 cxd5* and *14 c5*.

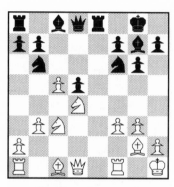

Position after 14 c5

White's c4-c5 is sharp and unbalancing. Either White's c-pawn or Black's d-pawn will be weak and perhaps both. White will keep his outpost square on d4. But here the problem of the c-pawn is too great, and White played *14 . . . Nbd7 15 Na4 Qe7 16 c6* rather than tie up his pieces with Ba3. As it turned out the isolated Black d-pawn was more than made up for by his excellent pieces: *16 . . . bxc6 17 Nxc6 Qd6 18 Nd4 Ba6 19 Rf2 Rac8 20 Bf1 Bxf1 21 Rxf1 Ne5 22 Bb2 Qa6! 23 Rc1 Rxc1 24 Bxc1 Nd3 25 Bd2 Nd7 26 Nc2? Re1!! 27 Bxe1 (27 Rxe1 Nf2+) Nb2 28 Bc3 Nxd1 29 Rxd1 Qe2* White resigns.

But when exd5 and c4-c5 both work Black's pieces look silly. *Supplemental Game* #6 and the following show this:

Kavalek–Garcia-Orus, Haag 1967:

1 c4 Nf6   2 Nc3 d6   3 d4 e5   4 Nf3 Nbd7   5 e4 g6
6 g3 Bg7   7 Bg2 0-0   8 0-0 c6   9 Rb1 Re8   10 h3
exd4   11 Nxd4

Position after 11 Nxd4

Black can continue conservatively with 11 . . . Nc5 and 12
. . . a5, but he rushes into *11 . . . Nb6?   12 b3 d5* thinking
that . . . d5 is always good. White's *13 exd5 cxd5   14 c5!*
throws Black's pieces into disarray. On 14 . . . Nbd7   15 b4
White can maintain his c-pawn and continue with Ndb5-d6.
His center play would confer a big advantage.

Black retained the tempo of the game with *14 . . . Ne4!?
15 Nxe4 dxe4* attacking the White knight on d4. But
16 Nb5 was still strong. Black continued *16 . . . Nd5
17 Bb2 Bxb2   18 Rxb2 Qf6* to compensate for his problems
in the center with strength along the long black diagonal. But
White played *19 Rd2!.*

Position after 19 Rd2!

White now has won a game (19 ... Nc3   20 Qa1! pins and wins the knight). There followed *19 ... Qa6   20 Nd6 Nc3   21 Qa1!   e3   22 Qxc3   exd2   23 Nxe8   Qxf1+ 24 Bxf1* Resigns. Bad pawns, bad pieces, bad game.

A third strategy, apart from ... f5 and ... d5, is the exploitation of White's pawns, especially his c-pawn. An illustration of this is *Supplemental Game #7*.

Supplemental Games

(1) c4-c5 in the basic Indian complex position. Portisch–Aaron, Varna 1962: 1 d4 Nf6   2 c4 g6   3 Nf3 Bg7   4 g3 0-0   5 Bg2 d6   6 0-0 Nbd7   7 Nc3 e5   8 e4 c6   9 h3 h6 (For the next few moves White makes developing moves but fails to come up with a plan. A good one would the Rb1 and b2-b4-b5.) 10 Be3 Kh7   11 Qc2 Qe7   12 Rad1 Nh5 13 Rfe1 Rg8   14 Kh2 Nf8   15 c5! (This is correct but badly followed up. White must open the d-file, after 15 ... dxc5, with 16 dxc5 followed by Nd2-c4-d6)   15 ... dxc5 16 dxe5?? Nd7   17 Qd2 Nxe5   18 Nxe5 Bxe5   19 f4

Bc7   20 Bf3 (White compensation for the sacrificed pawn appears adequate but . . .) Nxg3! 21 Kxg3 g5   22 Kh2 gxf4   23 Bf2   Qe6! 24 Bg4   Rxg4   25 hxg4   Qxg4 26 Kh1 Qh3+   27 Kg1 Be6 White resigns.

(2) Rauzer's formation arising out of a Sicilian Defense. Kurajica–N. Littlewood, Bognor Regis 1967: 1 e4 c5   2 Nf3 d6 3 c3 e5? 4 Bb5+ Bd7 5 Bxd7+ Nxd7 6 0-0 Ngf6 7 d4! (This will lead to the favorable formation after dxe5. Note that 7 . . . Nxe4   8 dxe5 dxe5   9 Qa4 Nd6   10 Nxe5 must favor White.) 7 . . . Be7   8 dxe5 dxe5   9 Qe2 h6 10 Nbd2 Qc7   11 Nc4 b5? (Now the queenside squares become weak and subject to exploitation by a2-a4.) 12 Ne3 Qc6 13 Nd5! Bd6 (or 13 . . . Nxd5   14 exd5 Qxd5   15 Qxb5 with advantage to White) 14 Rd1 c4   15 Nh4 g6   16 Qf3 Be7   17 Nxe7 Kxe7   18 b3! (When this formation occurs in the Ruy Lopez the move b2-b3 often serves to attack Black's queenside pawns. Here the idea is Ba3.) 18 . . . Nc5   19 Ba3 Rac8   20 Qg3 Qc7   21 bxc4 (There was a faster win with 21 Bxc5+   Qxc5   22 Rd5! Nxd5   23 Qxe5+) bxc4 22 Rab1 Rhd8   23 Qe3 Rxd1+   24 Rxd1 Qc6   25 Qxh6 Qxe4   26 Nf3   Qc2   27 Re1   Qxc3   28 Rxe5+   Kd7 29 Qf4 Qxa3   30 Qxf6 Nd3   31 Qxf7+ Kc6   32 Nd4+ Resigns

(3) White obtains the Rauzer formation in an unusual fashion and exploits the a2-g8 diagonal. Botvinnik–Szilagyi, Amsterdam 1966:   1 g3 d5   2 Nf3 c6   3 Bg2 Bg4   4 d3 Nd7   5 h3 Bxf3   6 Bxf3 e5   7 Nd2 Ngf6   8 e4 dxe4? (This leads to pawn symmetry in the center. White's development gives him the first chance to upset the balance.) 9 dxe4 Bc5   10 0-0 Qe7   11 c3 0-0   12 b4! Bb6   13 a4 Rfd8

(The thematic idea of 13 . . . a5, which confronts White's queenside expansion, walks into Nc4 and Ba3.) 14 Qc2 Rac8 15 Be2 c5? (This completes the Rauzer formation and virtually decides the game. Black's attack on the queenside should come from . . . a5, not from . . . c5, which gives up control of d5 and all hopes of blocking the diagonal White now seizes.) 16 b5 Ne8 17 Nc4 Nd6 18 Bg5! (This forces a weakening of the a2-g8 diagonal because the alternatives 18 . . . Nf6 19 Ne3 and Nd5 or 18 . . . Qxg5 19 Nxd6 c4 20 Kg2! are unpalatable.) 18 . . . f6 19 Be3 Nxc4 20 Bxc4+ Kh8 21 a5 Bc7 22 Rfd1 Nf8 23 Qa2! Rxd1+ 24 Rxd1 Rd8 25 Rxd8 Bxd8 26 a6! b6 27 Kg2 Qd7 28 Qe2 Ng6 29 Bb3 Ne7 30 Qc4 h6 31 Qf7 Kh7 32 Bc4 Qd6 33 h4 Qd1 34 Qe8 f5? (Black was lost in any case. He cannot cover his kingside white squares indefinitely.) 35 exf5 Nxf5 36 Bg8+ Kh8 and Black resigned before White could play 37 Bf7+ and 38 Qg8 mate.

(4) A useful c4-c5 in the Rauzer formation. Tarrasch–Vogel, Nuremberg 1910: 1 e4 e5 2 Nf3 Nc6 3 Bb5 d6 4 d4 Bd7 5 Nc3 Nf6 6 0-0 Be7 7 Re1 exd4 8 Nxd4 Nxd4 9 Qxd4 Bxb5 10 Nxb5 0-0 11 Bg5 Ng4 12 Bxe7 Qxe7 13 c4 a6 14 Nc3 Qe5 (This queen move competes for center squares now the exclusive domain of the White queen. After queens are exchanged on e5 White should hold the advantage regardless of how Black retakes.) 15 Qxe5 dxe5 16 Nd5 c6?! (The weakness of d6 becomes critical for the rest of the game. 16 . . . Nf6! was playable and preferable, since 17 Nxc7 Rac8 regains material equality.) 17 Ne7+ Kh8 18 Nf5 Rad8 19 Rad1 g6 20 Nd6 Rd7 21 c5! (Now White can win by exploiting the weak enemy b-, f-, and e-pawns. Note that 21 . . . Rfd8 fails to 22 Nxf7+.) 21 . . . Kg8

22 Nc4 (On 22 ... Re7 White would double rooks on the d-file.) 22 ... Rfd8   23 Rxd7 Rxd7   24 f3 Nh6   25 Nxe5 Rd2   26 Nc4 Rc2   27 b3 Rxa2   28 Rd1! a5   29 Rd8+ Kg7   30 Ra8 a4   31 Rxa4 Rxa4   32 bxa4 Ng8   33 Nd6 Kf6   34 Nxb7 Ke5   35 a5 Ne7   36 Nd6 Kd4   37 a6 Resigns.

(5) Exploiting c4-c5 in the Rauzer formation. Golombek–Fuderer, Munich 1954: 1 d4 Nf6   2 c4 d6 3 Nc3 e5   4 Nf3 Nbd7   5 e4 g6   6 Be2 Bg7   7 0-0 0-0 8 Re1   c6   9 dxe5? dxe5   10 b3   Qa5   11 Bd2   Qc7 12 b4 Rd8   13 Qc1 Nf8! (The knight takes aim at d4 via e6.)   14 Bh6 Bg4   15 Bxg7 Kxg7   16 Qb2 Bxf3 (All in keeping with Black's plan to occupy d4—a plan White aided with Bh6xg7)   17 Bxf3 Rd4   18 c5 Ne6   19 Rad1 Rad8 20 Rxd4 Rxd4 (The rook helps in the attack on the b4-pawn.) 21 Ne2 Rd7   22 Ng3 h5   23 h4 Nd4   24 Bd1 Qd8 25 Nf1 Ng4   26 f3 Nh6   27 Qf2 a5!   28 a3 Nb5! 29 Bb3 axb4   30 axb4 Rd4 (The queenside pawns fall one at a time. White now tries a doomed kingside attack.) 31 Qg3 Qe7   32 Ne3 Rxb4   33 Bc4 Nd4   34 Kh1 Qxc5 35 Bd3 b5   36 Kh2 Kh7   37 Kh3 Ne6   38 Bf1 Rb3 39 Qf2 Qd4   40 g3 c5 and White resigns.

(6) The double-edged consequences of ... d6-d5 in the Boleslavsky Wall. Gligoric–Tringov, The Hague 1966: 1 d4 Nf6   2 c4 g6   3 Nc3 Bg7   4 e4 d6   5 Nf3 0-0   6 Be2 e5   7 Be3 exd4   8 Nxd4 Re8   9 f3 c6   10 Qd2 d5 11 exd5 cxd5   12 0-0 Nc6? (Even though White has a preponderance of material in an open center, Black should immediately liquidate with 12 ... dxc4.)   13 c5! (White seeks an advantage with Rad1 and Ndb5-d6. A tactical trick like 13 ... Rxe3 14 Qxe3 Ng4 15 fxg4 Bxd4 fails to 15 Nxc6!. Black decides to go after the pawn.) 13 ... Bd7 14 Rad1 Qe7 15 Bf2 Qxc5?! 16 Ne6! Qd6 17 Nxg7 Kxg7 18 Nb5 (White has plenty of compensation for his pawn in view of the weak enemy dark squares and his excellent minor pieces.) 18 ... Qe5 19 Rfe1 a6 20 Bf1 Qh5 21 Nd4! (Better than regaining a pawn. White uses the d4 outpost beautifully for the rest of the game.) 21 ... h6 22 Nxc6 Bxc6 23 Bd4 Re6 24 Rxe6 fxe6 25 Re1 Re8 26 Re5 g5 27 f4 Kg8 28 Be2 (to stop ... Ng4) 28 ... Qg6 29 Bd3 Ne4 30 Bxe4 dxe4 31 fxg5 Rd8 32 Qe3 h5 33 h3 Rd5 34 Rxd5 Bxd5 35 Qf4 Qf7 36 Qe5 Kh7 37 Qh8+ Kg6 38 Qh6+ Kf5 39 g6! Qxg6 40 Qf8+ Kg5 41 Be3+ Resigns.

(7) Black grabs queenside space with ... b5-b4?! Chekhov–Fishbein, Moscow 1989: 1 d4 Nf6 2 c4 c5 3 d5 b5 4 Nf3 (Rather than accept the Benko Gambit pawn, White wants to retake on c4 with a minor piece after 4 ... bxc4) b4!? 5 Bg5 d6 6 Nbd2 g6 7 e4 Bg7 8 Bd3 0-0 9 h3 a5 10 0-0 a4!? (To attack the ultimate dark-square target with 11 ... a3) 11 a3! Qa5! 12 e5 dxe5 13 Nxe5 e6 14 Re1 Ra7 15 Qf3 Nfd7 (Now 16 Nxd7 gives up any chance for serious White advantage) 16 Ng4 Bxb2 17 Ne4 f5! 18 Nh6+ Kg7 19 Qe2? (Better was 19 Nd6 first) Bxa1 20 Rxa1 fxe4 21 Qxe4 e5 22 Ng4 Rf5?! 23 Qe3! Rf7 24 f4! e4 25 Qxe4 Qc7 26 Qe2? (Missing a last chance of 26 Qe8) Qd6 27 Re1 Nf6! 28 Bh6+ Kg8 29 Nxf6+ Qxf6 30 Qe8+ Rf8 White forfeits.

THE QUEEN'S GAMBIT FAMILY
AND ITS RELATIVES

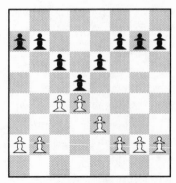

Typical Queen's Gambit

FOR NEARLY TWENTY YEARS IN THE EARLY PART OF THIS CENTURY the formation above threatened to monopolize the middlegame. In the 1927 world championship match the Queen's Gambit Declined occurred in thirty-two of the thirty-four games. Too much emphasis on any one opening or structure becomes boring, and the arrival of the Indian systems was a welcome change. But the controversies over the Queen's Gambit (and Nimzo-Indian Defense) formations—the Isolani, the hanging pawns, the Orthodox Exchange—haven't been re-solved. Although the diagramed formation ultimately leads to a simpler structure, the strategies remain difficult to evaluate.

A. THE ISOLANI

When you talk about the isolated pawn you are usually speak-ing of a d-pawn. Why? In most openings it is easy to play e2-e4, d2-d4, and c2-c4, but often risky to play f2-f4. This means that exchanges on d5, leaving a single center pawn, your d-pawn, are more likely to occur than exchanges on e5 that result in an isolated e-pawn.

Nimzovich and others called it the Isolani although nobody has ever explained why the Latin singular ("isolanus") isn't correct. In any event it was Nimzovich who first spelled out the basic issue of the Isolani. The d-pawn is either a "static weakness" or a "dynamic strength." Left alone it will advance ("the lust to expand") and cramp the enemy center. Block-aded it will be both a target and a bottleneck.

For years the consensus held that it was more of a weakness than a strength. But chess theory is constantly evolving, and clear cases in which the Isolani is favorable are appearing regularly. In another match, the Karpov–Korchnoi *de facto* world championship of 1974, Black accepted an isolated d-pawn in seven games, equalized every time, and never lost. (In those games the Isolani came not from the Q.G.D. but from the French Defense: 1 e4 e6 2 d4 d5 3 Nd2 c5 4 exd5 exd5 5 Nf3 Nc6 6 Bb5 Bd6 7 0-0 cxd4 8 Nb3 and Nbxd4.)

In the diagram above White can liquidate his d-pawn with d4-d5. If Black's e-pawn were on the seventh rank we would see d4-d5 clearly as the "lust to expand." After d4-d5, the squares e6 and c6 are under pawn attack, reducing Black's scope. The disorienting effect of the advance can be shown by Ostojic–Vaganian, Vrnjacka Banja 1971:

1 e4 e6 2 d4 d5 3 Nd2 c5 4 Ngf3 Nc6 5 exd5 exd5 6 Bb5 Bd6 7 dxc5?! Qe7+! 8 Be2? Bxc5 9 0-0 Nf6 10 Nb3 Bb6 11 Bg5 0-0 12 Qd2

Position after 12 Qd2

In the opening Black was eager to sacrifice his d-pawn for active pieces or exchange it for another pawn; e.g., 9 Nb3 Bb6 10 Qxd5 Nf6 11 Qd1 Bf5 and 12 . . . Rd8 or now in the previous diagram 13 Bxf6 Qxf6 14 Qxd5 Qxb2. Black has a fine game in any event after *12 . . . Qe6!* in the diagram. He has an outpost, e4, that is as useful as White's d4.

After *13 Bd3 Ne4 14 Qc1 Qg6!* Black's d-pawn had given him an early middlegame momentum. White was pushed backward with *15 Bf4 Bh3 16 Ne1* (16 Bg3 Nxg3!) *Rfe8 17 Kh1 Bf5 18 Be3 d4!* Once "expanded" the d-pawn keeps Black's initiative rolling. White's c-pawn is now a weakness and the White king may be vulnerable from c6-h1.

The game drew to a rout of the White pieces after *19 Bf4 Nb4 20 a3 Nxd3 21 Nxd3 Nf6 22 Qd2 Be4! 23 Bg3 Nh5 24 Rae1 Qc6!*

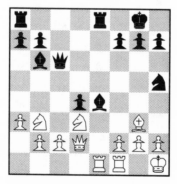

Position after 24 . . . Qc6!

Then with *25 f3 Bxd3*, whichever way White captures on d3 he is faced with the occupation of e3—a direct consequence of Black's pressure along the c6-h1 line. White resigned after

*26 cxd3 Nxg3+   27 hxg3 Re3!   28 Nc1 Rc8   29 Ne2 Qg6
30 Rd1   Rce8   31 Rf2   Bc7   32 Kg1   h5!   33 f4   Qg4
34 Kf1 h4   35 gxh4 Qxh4   36 Ng1 Bxf4   37 Qa5 Bg3.*

When blockaded the Isolani is a different animal. Then it just gets in the way of an attack on the blockading piece. The greatest weakness of an isolated pawn is often the square *in front of it*. The use of this square permits operations against other pawns, as exemplified by Bogolyubov–Rosenthal, St. Petersburg 1914:

**1 d4 d5   2 Nf3 c5   3 c4 e6   4 cxd5 exd5   5 Nc3
Nc6   6 g3 Nf6   7 Bg2 Be6   8 0-0 h6   9 b3 Rc8
10 Bb2 cxd4**

Position after 10 . . . cxd4

White should make sure of a knight blockade on the d4 square; therefore *11 Nb5!* is correct. After 11 . . . d3 he can repulse Black's temporary initiative with *12 Qxd3 Nb4 13 Qd1 Qb6   14 Nbd4.*

In the game Black found nothing better than *11 . . . Qa5 12 Nbxd4 Nxd4   13 Nxd4 Be7*, after which White cashed in the positional advantage of his d4 square with *14 Nxe6 fxe6 15 Qd3! 0-0   16 e4!*. Black had to accept either a weak e-pawn with *16 . . . dxe4* or a weak d-pawn with *16 . . . Rfd8 17 exd5 exd5   18 Rfe1.*

Black chose the former and lost a textbook ending: *16 . . . dxe4   17 Bxe4 Nxe4   18 Qxe4 Qd5   19 Qg4 Bf6 20 Bxf6 Rxf6   21 Rad1 Qf5   22 Qd4! Qc5   23 Qxc5 Rxc5   24 Rc1   Rff5   25 Rfd1   Rxc1   26 Rxc1   Rf7 27 Rc8+ Rf8   28 Rxf8+ Kxf8   29 Kg2 Ke7   30 Kf3 Kd6   31 Ke4 b6   32 f4 g6   33 h3 h5   34 Kd4 Kd7* (zugzwang: White wins control of the e5 outpost) *35 Ke5 Ke7   36 b4 b5   37 g4 hxg4   38 hxg4 Kf7   39 Kd4!* Resigns.

Control of the square immediately in front of the Isolani is enough to decide a game. With just a pawn at e6—to capture the d-pawn when it advances—the defender against an Isolani is taking inadequate insurance. When the d-pawn eventually does advance, pawns will be swept from the center and the player with more direct threats will prosper.

A fine case of this was a brilliancy by Tigran Petrosian, a player hardly known for explosive middlegames (vs. Balashov, U.S.S.R. 1974):

1 c4 Nf6   2 Nc3 e6   3 d4 Bb4   4 e3 c5   5 Bd3 d5 6 Nf3 0-0   7 0-0 dxc4   8 Bxc4 Nc6   9 Bd3 cxd4 10 exd4 Be7   11 Re1 b6   12 a3! Bb7   13 Bc2 Rc8 14 Qd3 Re8?

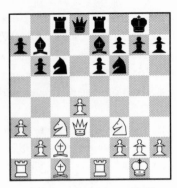

Position after 14 . . . Re8?

White began an attacking plan with his ninth move that should be as familiar to 1 d4 players as how to mate a bare king with bishop and knight. He positions his king bishop and queen to threaten mate on h7 in coordination with Bg5xf6. His king knight goes to e5. After Black defends his kingside with . . . g6, White can play Bh6 followed by Bb3 and Qh3. If he accomplishes all this without interruption it is inevitable he will be threatening sacrifices on e6, f7, or g6.

Note White's 12th move. It stopped Black from blockading d5 with his best piece (. . . Nb4-d5). Black's moves have been natural, but he should have taken time for 14 . . . g6. The negligence of 14 . . . Re8 was revealed in *15 d5!!*.

It doesn't seem logical that White, apparently less well developed than Black, should dissolve the center, but the exchanges will also remove Black's best kingside defender. To take the place of the king knight Black will have to make pawn advances: *15 . . . exd5 16 Bg5! Ne4* (White threatened 17 Bxf6, and Black couldn't defend against it with 16 . . . g6

17 Rxe7!) *17 Nxe4 dxe4 18 Qxe4 g6 19 Qh4 Qc7 20 Bb3!*.

This new diagonal is seized and Bxe7 followed by Ng5 is threatened. Black's game collapsed with *20 . . . h5 21 Qe4* (threatens Qxg6+) *Kg7 22 Bxf7! Kxf7 23 Bh6* (threatens a check at c4, d5, or e6) *Qd6* (*23 . . . Nd8 24 Ng5+!*) *24 Qc4+ Kf6 25 Rad1 Nd4 26 Qxd4+ Qxd4 27 Rxd4 Rc5 28 h4!* and Black resigned in expectation of Bg5+ and Rd7. (See also *Supplemental Game #1*.)

Dissolution of the Isolani is therefore not just the disappearance of a weakness but the conversion of potential energy into power. It requires a great deal of exact timing, however. Sometimes d4-d5 leads to deadly symmetry . . . or worse. The possibilities are made distinct by this opening:

1 d4 Nf6   2 c4 e6   3 Nc3 Bb4   4 e3 0-0   5 Ne2 d5
6 a3 Be7   7 cxd5 exd5   8 Ng3 c5   9 dxc5 Bxc5

Position after 9 . . . Bxc5

In the last game of the 1937 world championship Max Euwe played 10 b4? here, thinking that 10 . . . Bb6   11 Na4 and 12 Bb2 would give him a fine game. But he had not taken 10 . . . d4! into consideration. On 11 exd4 Bxd4 Black has too much too soon. And 11 Na4 dxe3! threatens 12 . . . exf2+ and 13 . . . Bg4+ whether White plays 12 Qxd8 or 12 Nxc5. Euwe played 11 bxc5 dxc3   12 Qc2 (12 Qxd8 Rxd8   13 Ne2 Ne4 also favors Black) 12 . . . Qa5   13 Rb1 Bd7   14 Rb3 Ba4   15 Qxc3 Qd8 and had to concede the game and his title in 28 moves more.

A more exact method of dealing with the d-pawn is *10 Be2 Nc6* (10 . . . d4   11 Na4) *11 0-0*. Black could still play 11 . . . d4, but after 12 Na4 Be7   13 b4 dxe3   14 Bxe3 White has a slight pull. In the game Lilienthal–Larsen, Moscow 1962, Black made the error of first defending the d-pawn, *11 . . . Be6*, and then advancing it, *12 b4 d4?*

White's response of *13 Na4 Be7   14 e4!* (and not 14 b5 Na5   15 exd4 Bb3 or 15 Qxd4 Qxd4   16 exd4 Nb3) kept the d-pawn as a target and gave White chances of mobilizing his majority with f2-f4. Larsen tried to force the issue with *14 . . . a5?* and was crushed: *15 b5 Ne5   16 Bb2 d3 17 Bxe5 dxe2   18 Qxe2 Rc8   19 Rfd1 Qe8   20 Qb2! Kh8 21 Nb6 Rc5   22 a4 Bd8   23 Nd5 Bxd5   24 exd5 Qd7 25 Qa3 Resigns.*

When is the Isolani favorable? Nimzovich said it depends on where the pieces are—a statement true of all formations. When White controls the c-file or is able to play d4-d5, the Isolani is good. When the endgame is approaching or when the Isolani can be converted into the "hanging pawns," it isn't. This leaves out the case of the basic kingside attack by White as illustrated by the following.

Position after 14 Re3

This is Keene–Miles, Hastings 1975–76, and arose after *1 Nf3 Nf6 2 c4 c5 3 Nc3 Nc6 4 e3 e6 5 d4 d5 6 cxd5 Nxd5 7 Bd3 cxd4 8 exd4 Be7 9 0-0 0-0 10 Re1 Nf6 11 Bg5 Nb4 12 Bb1 b6 13 Ne5 Bb7 14 Re3!*.

So far, both sides have made routine moves, and White already threatens 15 Bxf6 Bxf6 16 Bxh7+ and Qh5+ with a mating attack. After *14 . . . g6 15 Rg3* Black made what may seem a minor error, *15 . . . Rc8* instead of *15 . . .* Nc6 16 Bh6 Qxd4! 17 Qxd4 Nxd4 18 Bxf8 Kxf8 with equal chances, and yet was destroyed immediately: *16 Bh6 Re8 17 a3 Nc6 18 Nxg6! hxg6 19 Bxg6 fxg6 20 Qb1!! Ne5* (else *21 Qxg6+*) *21 dxe5 Ne4 22 Nxe4 Kh7 23 Nf6+ Bxf6 24 Qxg6+ Kh8 25 Bg7+ Bxg7 26 Qxg7* mate.

As a final example for comparison there is Regedzinsky–Rubinstein, Lodz 1917, which shows the evils of exchanges:

1 d4 d5 2 Nf3 Nf6 3 c4 e6 4 Bg5 Nbd7 5 Nc3 Be7 6 e3 0-0 7 Bd3? dxc4 8 Bxc4 a6 9 0-0 b5

10 Bd3 Bb7   11 Qe2 c5   12 Rad1 cxd4   13 exd4
Nb6

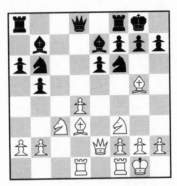

Position after 13 . . . Nb6

White made a typical error that cost him a tempo when he
developed his king bishop. He should delay Bd3 in favor of
moves such as Rc1 or Qc2 so that he can play Bxc4 in one mo-
tion after . . . dxc4. Black used this extra time to convert the
Slav formation into the Isolani. The position, need we say it,
calls for Bb1, Ne5, and Qd3.

But White's choice, 14 Ne4??, reveals a gross misconcep-
tion of the position. That move forces the exchange of three
of the minor pieces that White needs to compensate for his
endgame weakness. The attack was dead after 14 . . . Nxe4
15 Bxe7 Qxe7   16 Bxe4 Rfd8   17 Rd3 Bxe4   18 Qxe4
Rac8   19 Rfd1 Nd5   20 R3d2 Nf6   21 Qe3 Qb7. Black
forced queens off the board with 22 h3 h6   23 Re2 Qd5
24 b3 Qd6   25 Rc1 Nd5   26 Qd2 Qf4!.

Position after 26 . . . Qf4!

In this position White cannot play 27 Qxf4 Nxf4 28 Rxc8 Nxe2 or 28 Rec2 Ne2+. He tried *27 Rc2 Qxd2 28 Rexd2*, but the threat of further exchanges cost him a pawn after *28 . . . Rxc2 29 Rxc2 Nb4 30 Rb2 Rc8 31 Kf1 Rc1+ 32 Ke2 Ra1*. The pawn was enough to win, but White's desperation cost him his last piece with *33 Kd2 Rxa2 34 Rxa2 Nxa2 35 Ne5 Nb4 36 Nd7 f6 37 g3 Kf7 38 Nb6? Ke7 39 Kc3 a5* White resigns (. . . Kd8-c7).

B. THE HANGING PAWNS

The hanging pawns hang because they are vulnerable and unsupported. When one of them responds to attack by advancing, the other becomes backward and weak. Together on the fourth rank they control several key center squares but are subject to pummeling along the open files.

The Hanging Pawns

Nimzovich noted that the downfall of the hanging pair was partly psychological. They should be advanced eventually, he said, but "in general the defending party proceeds to this a move or two soon, he does not hold tight long enough, perhaps because the consciousness of being 'in the air' is not greatly to the taste of the human psyche." This led to the warning: "Never let yourself be drawn into a dead blockaded position; rather remain 'in the air.' "

The pawns are most vulnerable to blockade when on c3 and d4, usually just after being created. At that moment they can be blocked with pieces on d5 and c4. Once the blockade is established it can become permanent; e.g., Rubinstein– Salwe, Lodz 1908:

1 d4 d5　2 c4 e6　3 Nc3 c5　4 cxd5 exd5　5 Nf3 Nf6　6 g3　Nc6　7 Bg2　cxd4?　8 Nxd4　Qb6 9 Nxc6! bxc6　10 0-0 Be7　11 Na4 Qb5　12 Be3 0-0　13 Rc1 Bg4　14 f3 Be6

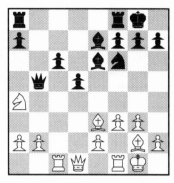

Position after 14 . . . Be6

Black's seventh and eighth moves were designed to break White's control of d4 before it could be maintained with other pieces. White correctly converted the Isolani into the hanging pawns. Black is ready to rectify the holes in the pawns with 15 . . . Nd7 and 16 . . . c5; therefore *15 Bg5!* is required.

White maintained the blockade on c5 and d4 with apparently effortless play: *15 . . . Rfe8   16 Rf2! Nd7   17 Bxe7 Rxe7   18 Qd4! Ree8   19 Bf1 Rec8   20 e3 Qb7   21 Nc5 Nxc5   22 Rxc5 Rc7   23 Rfc2.*

Position after 23 Rfc2

Now Black's pawns are fixed targets and under pressure from White rooks. Eventually White can isolate one of them with b4-b5 or e3-e4. For this reason 23 . . . a5 was called for. But 23 . . . Qb6? cost Black a pawn after 24 b4! a6   25 Ra5! (e.g., 25 . . . Qxd4   26 exd4 Bc8   27 Rxd5). Black conceded after 25 . . . Rb8   26 a3 Ra7   27 Rxc6! Qxc6   28 Qxa7 Ra8   29 Qc5 Qb7   30 Kf2 h5   31 Be2 g6   32 Qd6 Qc8   33 Rc5 Qb7   34 h4 a5   35 Rc7 Qb8   36 b5 a4   37 b6 Ra5   38 b7! because of (38 . . . Kg7   39 Rxf7+).

The pawns are weak only when under direct pressure. When the attack on them develops slowly, the player with the hanging pair can either take time to protect them or, even better, seize the initiative on the kingside. One opening illustration of this begins with 1 d4 d5   2 c4 e6   3 Nc3 Nf6   4 Nf3 c5   5 cxd5 Nxd5   6 e3 Nc6   7 Bc4 cxd4   8 exd4 Nxc3   9 bxc3 Be7   10 0-0 0-0   11 Re1 b6   12 Bd3 Bb7   13 Qc2!.

Position after 13 Qc2!

Until Black attacks the c-pawn White has a free hand. (Note that Black played . . . cxd4 before . . . Nxc3 because if he reverses the order White could keep his pawns united by recapturing on d4 with his new c-pawn.) Now 13 . . . h6 is frowned upon because White could continue Qe2-e4 or Bc2 and Qd3. He should play 13 . . . g6, but after 14 Bh6 Re8 15 Qd2! Rc8 White has the same kind of attack as in the Isolani but without pressure on his center pawn.

Two examples come to mind here. In Botvinnik–Ragozin, training match 1947, White attacked with h4-h5 and swinging his rooks to the kingside. The Russian game went 16 Rab1 Bf6 17 h4 Qd6 (or 17 . . . Bxh4 18 Nxh4 Qxh4 19 Bg5 Qg4 20 Re4) 18 Bf4 Qa3 19 h5 Na5 20 Be5! Qe7 21 Bxf6 Qxf6 22 Ne5 Red8 23 Ng4 Qg7 24 hxg6 hxg6 25 Qg5! Kf8 26 Rb5 Nc6 27 Nf6 Ne7 28 Re3 Ng8 29 Nxg8 Kxg8 30 Qe7 Bc6 31 Rbe5 Rd7 32 Qh4 Qh8 33 Qf4 Qg7 34 Rg3! Bd5 35 Reg5 Rxc3 36 Bxg6! and wins

In Bolbochan–Pachman, Moscow 1956, however, White improved with 16 Rac1!, which took away most of Black's counter-chances on the queenside. White won with a neat combination: 16 . . . Bf6 17 Qf4 Na5? 18 Ne5 Nc6 19 Ng4! Bh4 20 g3 Be7 (White would have played Bg5 if the bishop had retreated to g7 at move 19) 21 Bc4 Rc7 22 Qxf7+! Resigns (22 . . . Kxf7 23 Bxe6 mate).

When the pawns reach the fourth rank their potential for disrupting center play becomes crucial. The other side wants to commit them to advanced squares, while the owner of the pair tries to keep them fluid until the right moment. If d4-d5 is eventually played a new Isolani will be created. This may be temporary, but the immediate threats created by d4-d5 are what frequently count most.

The tension is suggested by a position that occurred twice in the Yugoslavia–U.S.S.R. match in 1958 between Svetozar Gligoric and Paul Keres after:

1 d4 Nf6 2 c4 e6 3 Nc3 Bb4 4 e3 0-0 5 Bd3 c5
6 Nf3 b6 7 0-0 Bb7 8 Bd2 cxd4 9 exd4 d5
10 cxd5 Bxc3 11 bxc3 Qxd5! 12 c4 Qd6 13 Bc3
Nbd7 14 Re1 Rac8 15 h3 Rfd8 16 Re3. (See
Supplemental Game #3 for a similar example.)

Position after 16 Re3

All things being equal, it would have been preferable to recapture on d5 with a pawn (11 . . . exd5). But things are rarely
equal in an early middlegame, and White could have then
played an annoying 12 Bg5 and 13 Ne5.

The first time the position occurred Black defended solidly
with 16 . . . h6, and after 17 Qb3 he continued 17 . . . Bxf3!
18 Rxf3 e5! White could preserve neither his two bishops nor
his center pawns, and the game was agreed drawn after
19 dxe5 Nxe5 20 Bxe5 Qxe5 21 Rb1.

In the rematch Black varied with the speculative 16 . . .
Nh5?. White rose to the occasion with 17 d5!! threatening
18 Bxh7+ Kxh7 19 Ng5+ now that his queen bishop is part
of the attack. Black tried 17 . . . Nc5, but he had to make
kingside holes with 18 Ng5! g6 19 Be2 Ng7 20 Qd4 Qf8

21 Qh4 h5 22 Bg4!. Black didn't get a chance to resign: (*22 . . . hxg4 23 Qh7* mate) *22 . . . f5? 23 Nxe6 Nxe6 24 dxe6 Re8 25 Bxh5 Qh6 26 Qf6 f4?* (the kingside pawns were lost anyway) *27 Qf7* mate.

Fixing the Pair

By fixing we don't mean "repairing" but rather fixing Black's pawns in place—in stationary, blockaded positions. If the pawns cannot be lured forward, they can be fixed by pawn action from the other side. We've already seen one case of this in the first Gligoric–Keres game. Another illustration is Ojanen–Trifunovic, Mar del Plata 1953:

1 d4 Nf6 2 c4 e6 3 Nc3 Bb4 4 e3 0-0 5 Nf3 d5 6 a3 Bxc3+ 7 bxc3 c5 8 cxd5 Nxd5 9 c4 Nf6 10 Qc2?! cxd4 11 exd4 Bd7! 12 Be2

Position after 12 Be2

White didn't want to permit 10 . . . Ne4, and he didn't want to develop his king bishop at d3. This inaccurate development left him vulnerable to a strategic thrust: *12 . . . b5!*. It is based on 13 cxb5 Bxb5   14 Bxb5 Qa5+ and . . . Qxb5 after which White has a bad bishop and a bad d-pawn.

White gamely kept his pawns together with *13 c5*, but the damage to his hanging pawns was done. Black took command of the center: *13 . . . Bc6   14 0-0 Be4!   15 Qc3 Nc6 16 Be3* (16 Bxb5 Bxf3 and . . . Nxd4) *Nd5   17 Qc1 Rb8.* White tried to dissolve his backward d-pawn at the expense of isolating his c-pawn, but Black ignored it: *18 Ne5 Qc7! 19 Nxc6 Qxc6.* White's d5 is the main weakness not his pawns.

White had a very poor game even with *20 f3*. But he overlooked *20 Bd2 Bxg2!* (21 Kxg2 Nf4+) and fell apart: *21 Re1 Ne7   22 Bf4 Rb7   23 Bd6 Bd5   24 Qc3 Rc8   25 Bxe7 Rxe7   26 Reb1 e5!* (the other flanking break) *27 Bxb5 Qg6+ 28 Qg3 Qe4!   29 f3 Qxd4+   30 Qf2 Qxf2+   31 Kxf2 Rxc5   32 Bd3 g6* White resigns. (See *Supplementary Game #2* where Black achieves . . . e5!)

The attack on the pair is especially powerful when it can be coordinated with an attack on other weaknesses. A game that comes easily to mind is Larsen–Radulov, Leningrad 1973:

1 c4 Nf6   2 Nf3 e6   3 b3 Be7   4 Bb2 0-0   5 Nc3 d5   6 e3 b6   7 d4 Bb7   8 Bd3 c5   9 0-0 Nbd7 10 Qe2   Ne4?!   11 cxd5   exd5   12 Rfd1   Nxc3 13 Bxc3 Rc8   14 Rac1 Rc7   15 dxc5! bxc5   16 Qc2

Position after 16 Qc2

The kingside appears to be White's primary target. He provokes Black to advance one of his kingside pawns. As we've seen, . . . h6 encourages White to reverse the positions of his queen and king bishop. But here . . . h6 is better than 16 . . . g6? 17 e4!.

Now it can be seen that White can also work against the hanging pawns. Black's queen is on the same file as a White rook. But 17 . . . Qa8 threatening 18 . . . dxe4 allowed White to go back to his primary target with 18 Qd2! Black is faced with 19 Qh6 or 19 exd5 Bxd5 20 Bxg6 now, and 18 . . . dxe4 19 Qh6 Nf6 20 Ng5 Re8 21 Nxh7! and 18 . . . Rfc8 19 exd5 Bxd5 20 Bxg6 are losing ideas.

Also, 18 . . . d4 cannot be played because of 19 Bxd4! Black made the humble retreat 18 . . . Bf6 19 Qf4 Qd8 and tried to cope with his disintegrating center after 20 Ba5 Nb6 21 b4!

Position after 21 b4!

But there was no real defense (21 . . . c4   21 Bxc4!). The game went *21 . . . Be7   22 exd5 Bd6   23 Qh6 cxb4* (23 . . . f6 holds out longer) *24 Ng5 f5   25 Ne6 Qd7   26 Rxc7* Resigns.

For the case of a badly timed e3-e4 break see *Supplemental Game #4*.

C. THE ORTHODOX EXCHANGE FORMATION

Kmoch named the formation in the diagram below after the exchange systems (cxd5/ . . . exd5) in the orthodox (read "normal") variation of the Q.G.D. It also occurs with colors reversed in the Caro-Kann (1 e4 c6   2 d4 d5   3 exd5 cxd5   4 c3 and . . . e6) and some rarer openings. What distinguishes it most is a solidity that makes it one of the safest formations to play.

The Orthodox Exchange

The board is cut in half by a spine of white and black pawns. The spine is not easily broken and remains solid in most middlegames. If White plays e3-e4 or if Black plays . . . c5 the other side can unfavorably isolate the enemy's d-pawn with a pawn capture. Therefore the two players pay most of their attention to the wings. White usually needs pawn action (such as b4-b5). Black can work on the king-side without moving pawns. If both kings are castled king-side Black has a task similar to a d5 chain: he must conjure up a mating attack before White breaks through on the queenside.

The Minority Attack

Position after 13 b4

The minority attack with b4-b5 seems antipositional. When Wilhelm Steinitz advanced his b-pawn against F. J. Lee at London 1899 he was criticized in the tournament book:

Black has a capital development—the open e-file, a majority of pawns on the Queen's side, without even a sign of an attack by White. *The plan of attacking on the left wing practically four pawns with two should not succeed.* (Emphasis added.)

Why should White advance his queenside pawns when it is likely to create a passed pawn for Black? The tournament book recommended 13 . . . b6 in the diagram to meet b4-b5 with . . . c5 with a good passed c-pawn. Today we know that . . . b6 is a common error that weakens the c-pawn and permits White to pile up on the queenside with Rfd1, Rac1, Nf4, Qb3, and b4-b5!.

This is similar to what happened in a recent example. Reshevsky–Myagmasuren, Sousse 1967:

1 d4 e6   2 c4 d5   3 Nc3 Nf6   4 cxd5 exd5   5 Bg5
Be7   6 e3 0-0   7 Bd3 c6   8 Qc2 Nbd7   9 Nf3 Re8
10 0-0   Nf8   11 Bxf6! Bxf6   12 b4! Bg4   13 Nd2
Rc8   14 Bf5   Bxf5   15 Qxf5   g6   16 Qd3   Qd6
17 Rfb1   Bg7   18 a4 Nd7   19 Ra2   Re6   20 Rc2
Rce8   21 Nb3 Nf6   22 h3

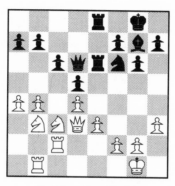

Position after 22 h3

Notice how White eliminates a Black knight at move 11.
White's bishop was not particularly bad, but a Black knight on
e4 would be at least equal to it. If White then captured the
Black knight on e4 Black would then recapture with a pawn,
creating our old friend, the Wedge.

White threatens 23 b5!, and Black is much too slow in
making anything out of the kingside. He needs . . . f5-f4, for
instance. If White gets b4-b5 in and Black cannot play . . . c5,
either a weak c-pawn or a weaker d-pawn await Black; e.g., 22
. . . Nh5 (22 . . . Qxb4   23 Nc5) 23 b5 R6e7 24 bxc6 Qxc6
25 Nb5 or 24 . . . bxc6   25 Qa6 and Na5.

Black tried 22 ... b6 with the old idea of meeting b4-b5 with ... c5, but after *23 Nc1 Bh6   24 N1e2 Nh5   25 b5!* Black couldn't push his c-pawn without losing his d-pawn. He had to accept the isolation of his d-pawn with *25 ... Qd7 26 bxc6 Rxc6   27 Qb5*.

Position after 27 Qb5

Black was lost because of the threat of 28 Nxd5 (27 ... Nf6 28 Nxd5! Rxc2   29 Nxf6+). He tried to use the open file with *27 ... Rec8   28 Rbc1 R8c7*, but *29 g4!* was a killer: 29 ... a6 (29 ... Nf6 or ... Ng7   30 Nxd5!) *30 Qxa6 Nf6 31 Nxd5! Nxg4* (31 ... Qxd5   32 Rxc6 wins the same way) *32 Rxc6 Qxd5   33 Qa8+* Resigns.

Black's defenses on the queenside are very few. His best chance of success in the middlegame is a piece attack on the kingside. Even with White's king esconced on the opposite side of the board Black has good chances on his left. This is "his" side of the board.

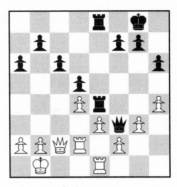

Black to move

The diagram shows a position from Kasparian–Aronin, 20th U.S.S.R. championship. Both sides have heavy pieces to attack an enemy majority, but neither the Black b-pawn nor the White f-pawn will give way. The game, in fact, was soon drawn. But Black discovered after the game that he could have begun his own minority attack—not to weaken White's pawns but to create a passed pawn of his own—with *27 . . . h5!!*. White can do little about . . . f6 and . . . g5 except play hxg5 and try to obtain a queenside break before Black's h-pawn queens.

When the White king has castled short Black's attack is very natural and straightforward. Füster–Simagin, Budapest 1948, is evidence of this:

1 d4 Nf6 2 Nf3 d5 3 c4 e6 4 Nc3 c6 5 cxd5
exd5 6 Qc2 Be7 7 Bg5 0-0 8 e3 Re8 9 Bd3
Nbd7 10 0-0 Nf8 11 Rab1 a5 12 Rfc1? h6

13 Bf4? Nh5!   14 Be5 Bg4   15 Nd2 Bd6   16 Bxd6 Qxd6   17 Na4 Ng6

Position after 17 . . . Ng6

White's queenside play lacks b2-b4. After . . . a5 he doesn't want to prepare the minority attack with a2-a3 because of the open a-file Black receives after b2-b4/ . . . axb4. But this should be a minor consideration. The simple fact is that White's queenside will not be powerful enough to balance the threats to his king without b2-b4.

His *18 Qc5* was OK, but after *18 . . . Qf6   19 Nb6 Rad8* he grabbed the a-pawn with *20 Qxa5?* when the defensive *20 Bxg6 fxg6   21 Nf1* was called for. Winning a pawn is not the same thing as breaking open a side of the board for your pieces. Black's initiative, with three minor pieces, two rooks, and a queen, never let up: *20 . . . Nh4!   21 Bf1 Qg5 22 Kh1 Nf6!* (threatening *23 . . . Bf5 24 Ra1 Ne4*) *23 g3 Nf3   24 Bg2 Qh5   25 Nxf3 Bxf3   26 Qe1 Rd6!   27 Kg1 Bxg2   28 Kxg2 Ng4   29 h3 Nxf2!   30 Qxf2* (*30 Kxf2*

Rf6+   31 Kg1 Rf3) 30 . . . Rf6 31 Qg1 Qe2+   32 Kh1 Rf2!
White resigns.

The "burn the positional bridges" defense on the queenside
is . . . b5. It surrenders c5 and a5 to White pieces in the hopes
of occupying c4 and a4. It stops b4-b5 once and for all and attempts to fix the enemy b-pawn as a target.

Fairhurst–Smyslov, Hastings 1954, shows the strategy well:

1 d4 Nf6   2 c4 e6   3 Nc3 Bb4   4 e3 0-0   5 Ne2
d5   6 a3 Be7   7 Ng3 b6   8 cxd5 exd5   9 Be2 Bb7
10 Nf5 Re8   11 Nxe7+ Qxe7   12 0-0 Nbd7   13 b4
c6   14 Bd2 a6!

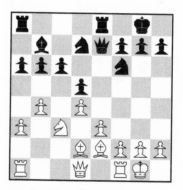

Position after 14 . . . a6!

Black's last move stops b4-b5 for the time being and leaves
. . . b5 as an option. Even though Black has no black-squared
bishop to attack the enemy b-pawn he has knights to occupy
c4 and a4. The presence of White's two bishops suggests that
he should open up the center with e3-e4. Even with identical

sets of minor pieces on the board it is usually in White's interest to play e3-e4 after . . . b5. This is because he can exploit the Black pawn weaknesses much better with an open center—even if it means accepting an isolated d-pawn. A model illustration of this is *Supplemental Game #6*.

The game continued from the diagram with *15 Qb3 b5! 16 Rae1 Nb6 17 Bc1 a5! 18 f3?*. White should open the e-file without trying to establish a pawn center at e4 and d4. The immediate 18 Bd3 and e3-e4 is better. The problems for the White center became apparent after *18 . . . axb4 19 axb4 Bc8! 20 Bd3 Be6 21 Qb1 Nc4 22 e4 Qa7!*

Position after 22 . . . Qa7!

Now Black doesn't need to penetrate on the queenside because the White d-pawn is dead. Black buried his opponent quickly: *23 Ne2 dxe4 24 fxe4 Bg4 25 Bxc4 bxc4 26 Ng3 Qxd4+ 27 Be3 Qd3 28 Qb2 Nxe4 29 Nxe4 Rxe4 30 Qf2 f6 31 Bc5 Be2 32 Ra1 Rae8 33 Rfe1 c3 34 Qf5 c2 35 h4 Qd5 36 Qf2 h5 37 Rac1 Bd1 38 Rxe4 Rxe4 39 Ra1 Qe5!* White resigns.

White's e3-e4 Plan

When the enemy is underdeveloped or when he has incurred queenside weaknesses that are not easily subjected to frontal attack, White can begin thinking of e3-e4. In cases such as *Supplemental Game #8* there is an interesting plan involving f2-f3 and e3-f4 so as to establish a center of pawns at d4 and e4 and then advance them further with d4-d5? or e4-e5.

Perhaps the most famous example of this was Botvinnik–Keres, Moscow 1952:

> 1 d4 Nf6   2 c4 e6   3 Nc3 d5   4 cxd5 exd5   5 Bg5 Be7   6 e3 0-0   7 Bd3 Nbd7   8 Qc2 Re8   9 Nge2 Nf8   10 0-0 c6   11 Rab1 Bd6?

Position after 11 . . . Bd6?

The only thing unusual about the opening is the White knight on e2 rather than f3. White prepares for the time-honored b2-b4. Black's last move threatens 12 . . . Bxh2+ and 13 . . . Ng4+ but is inferior to 11 . . . Nh5 and 11 . . . Ng4 which trades off the obnoxious White queen bishop.

White responded to the threat with *12 Kh1* and then continued *12 . . . Ng6   13 f3!*. He drops the minority attack altogether because now e3-e4 will have added force with its threat of e4-e5. It's true that White will have lost a tempo with Rab1, but Black will have to move his king bishop again and that makes up for it. In fact *13 . . . Be7   14 Rbe1* left White a move ahead of normal lines. White obtained an excellent game after *14 . . . Nd7* (*14 . . . c5   15 dxc5 Bxc5   16 Bxf6*) *15 Bxe7 Rxe7   16 Ng3 Nf6   17 Qf2 Be6   18 Nf5 Bxf5   19 Bxf5 Qb6   20 e4*.

Position after 20 e4

White has not only e4-e5 but if Black doesn't capture on e4 he also has f4-f5. After *20 . . . dxe4   21 fxe4 Rd8   22 e5 Nd5   23 Ne4 Nf8   24 Nd6 Qc7   25 Be4 Ne6   26 Qh4! g6   27 Bxd5 cxd5   28 Rc1 Qd7   29 Rc3 Rf8   30 Nf5! Rfe8* (not *30 . . . gxf5   31 Rg3+* or *30 . . . Ree8   31 Nh6+ Kh8   32 Qf6+ Ng7   33 Nxf7+*) *31 Nh6+! Kf8   32 Qf6 Ng7   33 Rcf3 Rc8* (else *34 Qxf7+*) *34 Nxf7 Re6   35 Qg5 Nf5   37 Nh6 Qg7   37 g4* Resigns.

Supplemental Games

(1) The d4-d5 break from the Isolani. Gligoric–Pomar, Nice 1974: 1 d4 Nf6 2 c4 e6 3 Nc3 Bb4 4 e3 0-0 5 Bd3 d5 6 Nf3 c5 7 0-0 dxc4 8 Bxc4 Nc6 9 Bd3 Bd7 10 a3 cxd4?! (Here 10 ... Bxc3 11 bxc3 Qc7 with a subsequent ... e5 appears best.) 11 exd4 Be7 12 Re1 Rc8 13 Bb1 Re8 14 Qd3 g6 15 Ba2! (Having accomplished its mission of forcing a kingside weakness, the bishop aims indirectly at f7.) a6 16 Bh6 Qa5? (16 ... Bf8!) 17 d5! exd5 18 Nxd5 Bf5 19 Rxe7!! (Now 19 ... Bxd3 20 Nxf6+ Kh8 21 Rxf7 is mate) 19 ... Rxe7 20 Nxf6+ Kh8 21 Qd2 Be6 22 Nd5 Qxd2 23 Bxd2 (White's material edge makes it an easy endgame.) Bxd5 24 Bc3+ Kg8 25 Bxd5 Rd7 26 Bxc6 bxc6 27 Ne5 Rdd8 28 Kf1 h5 29 Re1 Rd5? 30 Nxc6 Resigns (because of 30 ... Rxc6 31 Re8+).

(2) Blockading the hanging pawns and preparing for ... e5. Peters–Rogoff, Oberlin 1975: 1 e4 c6 2 d4 d5 3 exd5 cxd5 4 c4 Nf6 5 Nc3 e6 6 Nf3 Bb4 7 Bd3 0-0 8 0-0 dxc4 9 Bxc4 Nbd7 10 a3 Bxc3! 11 bxc3 Qc7 12 Qd3 b6 13 Re1 Bb7 14 Ba2 Rac8 15 Bb2? (15 Bd2 makes much more sense) Bd5! 16 Nd2 Bxa2 17 Rxa2 Rfd8 18 Qe2 e5! 19 Nf3 exd4 20 Nxd4 (The isolani is sickly after 20 cxd4 but better off than White's c-pawn now.) Re8 21 Qd1 Rxe1+ 22 Qxe1 Re8 23 Qd1 Ne5 24 h3 Nd3 (This incursion, made possible by 20 Nxd4, decides the game.) 25 Nf3 Qc4 26 Qb1 Ne4 27 Ba1 Nc1! White resigns (because of 28 Rc2 Ne2+ 29 Kh2 Qc7+ 30 g3 N4xg3).

(3) The hanging pawns advance through tactical means.
Anand–Timman, Moscow 1992: 1 e4 c6 2 d4 d5
3 exd5 cxd5 4 c4 Nf6 5 Nc3 e6 6 Nf3 Be7 7 cxd5
Nxd5 8 Bc4 0-0 9 0-0 Nc6 10 Re1 Nxc3 (Now was
the time because 10 ... b6 would allow 11 Nxd5! exd5
12 Bb5 with advantage) 11 bxc3 b6 12 Bd3 Bb7
13 h4 Qd5 14 Rb1 Rac8 15 Rb5 Qd6 16 d5?!
(Based on 16 ... exd5 17 Rxd5 Qxd5?? 18 Bxh7+—
but 16 ... Nd8! 17 dxe6 Nxe6 favors Black) Ba6?
17 dxc6 Rfd8 18 Qa4 Qxd3 19 Qxa6 Rxc6 20 Be3!
(And wins, e.g. 20 ... Rxc3 21 Ne5 Ra3 22 Qb7 Qxb5
23 Qxe7 or 21 ... Qe4 22 Bd2) Bf6 21 Bd4 Bxd4
22 cxd4 Rc3 23 a4! Ra3 24 Qxa7 Qxb5 25 Qe7!
Resigns.

**(4) Fixing the hanging pawns fails because of the creation
of a strong passed pawn.** Donner–Darga, Krefeld 1969:
1 d4 d5 2 c4 e6 3 Nc3 Be7 4 Bf4 Nf6 5 e3 0-0
6 Nf3 b6 7 cxd5 Nxd5 8 Nxd5 exd5 9 Bd3 c5
10 dxc5 bxc5 11 0-0 Nc6 12 Ne5 Nxe5 13 Bxe5
Be6 14 Qc2 g6 15 b3 Rc8 (A "pure" middlegame involving the hanging pawns without knights to blockade
them has arisen. White can maintain a slight edge with the
watchful 16 Qb2.) 16 e4? c4! 17 bxc4 dxc4 18 Be2
c3! (Played quickly so that White cannot blockade with
Bc3. Now 19 Bxc3 allows 19 ... Qc7 20 Rac1 Bf6 winning material.) 19 Bd3 Bd6 20 Bxd6 Qxd6 21 f4?
(Drawing chances existed after 21 Rfd1 despite 21 ...
Qa3!) Rfd8 22 Be2? (22 Rad1 Qc5+ 23 Kh1 Bg4
would also lose for White) Qc5+ White resigns (since he
loses a pieces to ... Rd2).

(5) The minority attack with colors reversed. Kamishov–Konstantinopolsky, Moscow 1947: 1 e4 c6 2 d4 d5 3 exd5 cxd5 4 Bd3 Nc6 5 c3 Nf6 6 Bf4 Bg4 7 Nf3 a6 8 Nbd2 e6 9 Qe2 Bh5! (to exchange off Black's bad bishop with . . . Bg6) 10 0-0 Be7 11 Rfe1 0-0 12 h3 Rc8 13 Qe3 Bg6 14 Bxg6 hxg6 15 Ng5 Nh5 16 Ndf3 b5! 17 Bh2 b4 18 g4 Bxg5! 19 Nxg5 Nf6 20 Rac1 Qd7 21 cxb4 (21 Be5 is better. Black already has a slight edge.) Nxb4 22 Qd2 Rxc1 23 Rxc1 Nc6 24 b3? (Having opened the c-file at the expense of his pawns White should play 24 Qc3.) Ne4! 25 Nxe4 dxe4 (Black wins the d-pawn and brings his knight to the weakened kingside.) 26 Qe2 Nxd4 27 Qxa6 (On 27 Qxe4 Black obtains a strong attack with 27 . . . f5 28 Qe3 Qd5 29 Rc3 f4 and . . . e5.) Nf3+ 28 Kg2 Qd2 29 Rc8 Rxc8 30 Qxc8+ Kh7 31 Qc5 Nh4+ 32 Kg3 g5 White resigns. On 33 Qe3 Black checks on d6.

(6) The . . . b5 anti-minority attack fails to e2-e4!. Karpov–Spassky, candidates match 1974: 1 d4 Nf6 2 c4 e6 3 Nf3 d5 4 Nc3 Be7 5 Bg5 h6 6 Bh4 0-0 7 e3 b6 8 Be2 Bb7 9 Bxf6! Bxf6 10 cxd5 exd5 11 0-0 Qd6 12 Rc1 a6 13 a3 Nd7 14 b4 b5!? 15 Ne1! (headed for c5) c6 16 Nd3 Nb6? (16 . . . a5) 17 a4! Bd8 18 Nc5 Bc8 19 a5 Bc7 20 g3 Nc4 21 e4! (White threatens e4-e5 and takes the kingside attack away from Black.) Bh3 22 Re1 dxe4 23 N3xe4 Qg6 (White can win a pawn with 24 Bxc4 but Black would then have attacking chances with . . . f7-f5-f4) 24 Bh5! Qh7 25 Qf3! f5 26 Nc3 g6 27 Qxc6! (a simple combination that wins quickly) gxh5 28 Nd5 (White's threats include 29 Qxc7, 29 Re7 and 29 Nf6+) 28 . . . f4 29 Re7 Qf5 30 Rxc7 Rae8 31 Qxh6 Rf7 32 Rxf7 Kxf7 33 Qxf4 Re2 34 Qc7+ Kf8 35 Nf4 Resigns.

(7) The Orthodox Exchange out of a rare opening. White's f2-f3 drives off a knight but the e-pawn falls before e3-e4. Krogius–Smyslov, Moscow 1967: 1 d4 Nf6 2 c4 e6 3 Nf3 Bb4+ 4 Bd2 a5 5 g3 d6 6 Bg2 Nbd7 7 0-0 e5 8 e3 Bxd2 9 Qxd2 c6 10 Nc3 e4 11 Nh4? Nb6! 12 Nxe4 (12 b3 g5) Nxe4 13 Bxe4 Nxc4 14 Qe2 d5 15 Bd3 Nd6 16 Qh5 Qe7 17 Rfe1 Be6 18 Rac1 g6 19 Qd1 0-0 20 Qc2 Rfc8 21 Ng2 Bf5! 22 Nf4 Bxd3 23 Nxd3 Re8 24 Nf4 Qf6 25 Rf1 Re7 26 Rce1 Rae8 27 b3 Ne4 28 f3 Nd6 29 Ng2 Nf5 30 Qd2 b6 31 Qf2 Qg5 (White could have played g3-g4 on the last move; now it doesn't work and neither does 32 e4.) 32 g4 Nxe3! 33 h4 Nxg2! 34 hxg5 Nxe1 35 Qg3 Re3 36 Qf4 c5 37 Kh1 Re2 38 dxc5 bxc5 (The d-pawn now decides the game.) 39 Qd6 d4 40 Qxc5 d3 41 Qd5 d2 42 Qd7 Nxf3 43 Rxf3 d1(Q)+ White resigns.

(8) White's pawns reach e4 and d4, preparing a devastating advance of the d-pawn. Kasparov–Andersson, Belfort 1988: 1 d4 Nf6 2 c4 e6 3 Nc3 d5 4 cxd5 exd5 5 Bg5 c6 6 Qc2 Be7 7 e3 Nbd7 8 Bd3 0-0 9 Nge2 Re8 10 0-0 Nf8 11 f3 Be6 (A better plan is 11 ... Ng6 12 e4 dxe4 13 fxe4 Be6 and then 14 Rd1 Ng4 15 Bc1 c5!) 12 Rae1 Rc8 13 Kh1 N6d7 14 Bxe7 Rxe7 15 Nf4 Rc7 (Black mistakenly believes that rooks on the two central files will deter the White pawns) 16 Qf2 Nf6 17 e4 dxe4 18 fxe4 Rcd7 19 d5! cxd5 20 Bb5 Rc7 21 exd5 Bd7 22 Be2! (Not 22 d6 Rxe1 23 Rxe1 Rxc3) Rc8 23 Qxa7 b6 24 Qa6 Ne4 25 d6 Nxd6 26 Nfd5 Re5 27 Qxb6 Nf5 28 Qxd8 Rxd8+ 29 Bd3 Rxe1 30 Rxe1 Ng6 31 a4 Nd4 32 a5 Kf8 33 Bxg6 hxg6 34 Rd1 Ne6 35 Nb6 Bc6 36 Rxd8+ Nxd8 37 b4 Ne6 38 b5 Resigns.

8

THE PANOV FORMATION

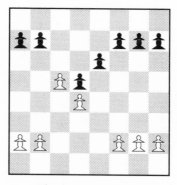

The Panov Formation

THE SEMICLOSED CENTER WITH WHITE PAWNS AT D4 AND C5 AND
Black pawns at d5 and e6 has been popping up in games since
the Queen's Gambit Declined first became popular. But it was
only with the introduction of Vasily Panov's system in the
Caro-Kann Defense (1 e4 c6   2 d4 d5   3 exd5 cxd5   4 c4
and a subsequent c4-c5) that the formation became readily fa-

miliar. And now with its occurrence in recently tested variations of the Alekhine Defense both 1 d4 and 1 e4 players have
to pay attention to it.

The virtues of the formation are clear. White has a passed
c-pawn and pawn control of valuable outpost squares (e5 and
d6). This means that White has excellent use of black squares
in the middlegame and a trump in the ending. His opponent,
however, has the dynamic potential. It is Black who can break
up the center with . . . e5 or . . . b6.

The game in which Panov first played his system (vs.
Mudrov, Moscow Championship 1929) began with *1 e4 c6
2 d4 d5 3 exd5 cxd5 4 c4 Nf6 5 Nc3 Nc6 6 Nf3 Bf5?
7 c5!.* This is the soul of the system. If black had developed
his queen bishop on g4 instead of f5 White would think twice
about setting up his d-pawn as a permanent target in a fixed
center.

Position after 7 c5!

But now White can take iron control of vital black squares:
7 . . . e6 8 Bb5! Nd7 (otherwise 9 Ne5 Qc7 10 Qa4 Rc8

11 Qxa7 wins a pawn) 9 *Bf4 Be7*   10 *h3! 0-0*   11 *0-0 a6*
12 *Ba4 Rc8?*   13 *Qe2 Re8*   14 *Rfe1 Nf8*   15 *Rad1 Ng6*
16 *Bh2 Nh4*.

Position after 16 . . . Nh4

Black's major error in the opening was his failure to put pressure on the black squares (with . . . Bf6 and . . . Bg4xf3). By
move 14 it was too late; e.g., 14 . . . Bf6   15 Bxc6 Rxc6
16 Nxd5. Now with *17 Ne5!* White had a crushing position,
and the best Black could do was cede a pawn with 17 . . . Nxe5
18 Bxe5 Rf8   19 g3 Ng6   20 g4 Nxe5   21 gxf5 Nc6
22 fxe6.

Black actually played *17 . . . Bf8* and was forced to resign
after *18 Nxc6 bxc6*   *19 Qxa6 Qg5*   *20 Bg3 e5*   *21 Bxc6*
Qh6   *22 Bb7 Re6*   *23 Qf1 Bxh3*   *24 Bxh4!*.

Another good illustration of Black's passive defense being
repulsed is *Supplemental Game #1*. This suggest that Black
should strike back with one of three methods: (1) in the center
with . . . e5, (2) on the queenside with . . . b6, or (3) without

immediate pawn action but with . . . Bf6 and . . . Nf5 to attack the d-pawn or with . . . Ne4 and . . . f5 to mate.

For instance, if White rushes to establish the Panov formation he may invite an unstable center in which Black's pieces have excellent scope. This was the case in Mariotti–Pfleger, Olot 1972, which began *1 e4 c6   2 d4 d5 3 exd5 cxd5   4 c4 Nf6   5 c5? e5!   6 dxe5* (6 Nc3!) *Ne4.*

Position after 6 . . . Ne4

Black may be temporarily minus a pawn, but he should be able to recover either the enemy e-pawn or c-pawn—and perhaps take both. White finds it difficult to protect his pawns; e.g., 7 b4 a5!. In the game White played *7 Bd3 Qa5+   8 Bd2 Qxc5   9 Bxe4* to relieve tension but after *9 . . . dxe4 10 Bc3 e3!   11 fxe3 Qxe3+   12 Ne2 Nc6   13 Qd2 Qe4 14 0-0 Bc5+   15 Kh1 0-0* he had a very poor game. He eventually lost the ending.

The . . . e5 break isn't always an equalizer as *Supplemental games #1* and *#2* show. After . . . e5/dxe5 White derives a fine outpost on d4. His big problem is his weak c-pawn, but it may not be any weaker than Black's isolated d-pawn. A case in point is Botvinnik–Konstantinopolsky, Sverdlovsk 1943:

1 e4 c6   2 d4 d5   3 exd5 cxd5   4 c4 Nf6   5 Nc3 e6
6 Nf3   Be7   7 Bg5   0-0   8 Rc1   Nc6   9 c5   Ne4
10 Bxe7 Qxe7   11 Be2 Bd7   12 a3 f5?   13 Bb5!

Position after 13 Bb5!

Black's stonewall formation is a bad choice here. Black doesn't need . . . f5 to support his king knight. He should play 12 . . . f6 followed by . . . Nxc3, . . . Rad8, and . . . e5 with an excellent game. But after exchanging black-squared bishops and weakening e5, Black invites 13 Bb5, a move that undermines e5 further by threatening Bxc6.

Black sought exchanges with *13 . . . Ng5   14 Bxc6 Nxf3+* to prevent White from sinking a knight on e5. However after *15 Qxf3 bxc6   16 Qf4! Rae8   17 0-0* even *17 . . . e5* was unavailing. Black's pawns remain weak, and White uses his

new outpost with *18 Qxe5 Qxe5   19 dxe5 Rxe5   20 f4! Re7*
21 Rfe1 Rfe8   22 Rxe7 Rxe7   23 Kf2.

Position after 23 Kf2

White now has a won ending, and Black could resign after
23 ... Kf7   24 Rd1   Re8   25 Rd2   h6   26 Re2 Rb8
27 Ke3   Rb3   28 Kd4!   Kf6   29 Na2   Rb8   30 b4   g5
31 g3 gxf4   32 gxf4 a6   33 Nc3 Rg8   34 a4 Rg4   35 Rf2
Be6   36 b5! See also *Supplemental Game #3.*

Black's alternative strategies include an attack on the head
of the chain c5 with . . . b6. This can be effective if it exposes
the White d-pawn to a new line of attack. This is what happened when Viktor Korchnoi as Black revived an opening idea
against Toran in the 1956 students' olympiad:

1 e4 Nf6   2 e5 Nd5   3 d4 d6   4 Nf3 g6   5 Be2 Bg7
6 0-0 0-0   7 c4 Nb6   8 exd6 cxd6!   9 Nc3 Nc6
10 Be3 Bg4   11 b3 d5   12 c5 Nc8!

Position after 12 . . . Nc8!

While White has accepted the Panov formation Black marshals his attack on the d-pawn. His knight is headed for f5 where it will join two other minor pieces in the assault on d4. This should have warned White that he must start an active plan such as 13 b4! (13 . . . Nxb4 14 Qb3).

Instead he played *13 h3? Bxf3 14 Bxf3 e6 15 b4 a6 16 b5?* (better is 16 Rb1) *axb5 17 Nxb5 N8e7 18 Bg5 Qa5 19 Bxe7 Nxe7 20 Qd3 Nc6.*

Position after 20 . . . Nc6

It is clear that . . . b6 cannot be prevented. The encirclement of White's d-pawn (and the isolation of his a-pawn) is complete. After *21 a4 b6! 22 cxb6 Qxb6 23 Rfd1 Ra5 24 Qc3 Rfa8 25 Rac1 Nxd4!*, Black won material and eventually the game (26 Nxd4 Rxa4 or 26 Rxd4 Rxb5 27 axb5 Bxd4).

White can treat the . . . b6 strategy in two ways: he can capture on b6 or allow the capture on c5; or he can support his c-pawn with b2-b4. In the former case he will use the opened c-file and the b6 and c5 squares. In the latter he maintains a passed c-pawn.

One example of the former that stands out is Karpov–McKay, Stockholm 1969:

1 e4 Nf6   2 e5 Nd5   3 d4 d6   4 Nf3 g6   5 c4 Nb6
6 exd6 cxd6   7 h3 Bg7   8 Nc3 0-0   9 Be2 Nc6
10 0-0 Bf5   11 Bf4 d5?   12 c5 Nc4   13 b3 N4a5
14 Rc1 b6   15 cxb6 axb6

Position after 15 . . . axb6

This is a case when Black should have avoided . . . d5 and preferred . . . e5. Now White has a simple game with Nb5 followed by doubling rooks along the open file. His isolated d-pawn cannot be attacked easily. Black's collapse was remarkable yet inevitable: *16 Qd2 Nb7 17 Nb5 Rc8 18 Rc3 Qd7 19 Rfc1 f6 20 Bc7!.*

Black had to lose material (20 . . . Rxc7 21 Nxc7 Qxc7 22 Rxc6. He played *20 . . . Ncd8 21 Bxb6 Rxc3 22 Rxc3 e5 23 a4 Nc6 24 b4 e4 25 Nh2* and watched White advance his queenside pawns to victory. (Compare with *Supplemental Game #4.*)

The second counterstrategy for White is often much trickier because after . . . b6/b2-b4 Black can attack the new support with . . . a5. White may not be able to support his pawn on b4 or accept the consequences of a translucent queenside.

A good illustration of this is a 1959 encounter between two Soviet players, Estrin and Liberzon:

**1 e4 c6   2 d4 d5   3 exd5 cxd5   4 c4 Nf6   5 Nc3 e6
6 Nf3 Be7   7 c5   0-0   8 Bd3 b6   9 b4 a5**

Position after 9 . . . a5

Black cannot delay the attack on the White pawns for one move; e.g., 9 ... Bd7? 10 Be3 a5 11 b5! or 10 ... Ng4 11 0-0 a5 12 Na4 and White has coordinated his queenside.

In the diagram we have a critical position for a major opening. White cannot maintain the integrity of his pawns with 10 a3 because then 10 ... axb4 pins his a-pawn to his queen rook. White must play 10 Na4.

In this game Black chose 10 ... Nbd7 and play continued 11 a3 axb4 12 axb4 bxc5 13 bxc5 e5! 14 Nxe5 (or 14 dxe5 Ne4 15 Bc2 Bb7)14 ... Nxe5 15 dxe5 Ne4.

Position after 15 ... Ne4

The position is open, tense, and unbalanced, but Black's chances are superior even after 16 Bxe4 dxe4 17 Qxd8 Rxd8 18 Bb2 Bd7 19 Nc3 Rxa1+ 20 Bxa1 Bc6.

The best try is 16 0-0, although 16 ... Nxc5 17 Bc2 Ba6 favors Black. But White, a world correspondence champion, tried to take the sting out of 16 ... Nxc5 with 16 Bb2? and was lost after 16 ... Qa5+ 17 Kf1 Bd7 18 Bc2 Qb5+ 19 Qe2 Rxa4 20 Bxa4 Nd2+ 21 Ke1 Qxb2 22 Rd1

Bxa4 White resigns. As in the Maroczy Bind, Black can sacrifice pawns sometimes to turn White's favorable pawn formation into a porous ruin.

A third strategy for Black is to upset White's pawns with Black pieces. With colors reversed this often occurs in the Tarrasch Defense to the Queen's Gambit Declined. An early example is Rotlewi–Nimzovich, Karlsbad 1911:

1 d4 d5 2 Nf3 e6 3 c4 c5 4 Nc3 Nc6 5 cxd5 exd5 6 g3 Nf6 7 Bg2 h6 8 0-0 Be6 9 Be3 Ng4 10 Qd2 c4?

Position after 10 . . . c4?

Black has just set up the Panov formation from his side of the board and has a nice game in view if he can play . . . Bb4 and . . . Nf6-e4. The normal reaction by White would be e2-e4, but here this is impossible.

Yet White does have *11 Ne5!*, a powerful move that opens the center. Once White's d-pawn captures on e5 Black's d-pawn is doomed. Nimzovich tried to contain the pressure with *11 . . . Ncxe5   12 dxe5 Nxe3   13 fxe3 (13 Qxe3 d4) Bb4,* but after *14 Rad1 Qg5 15 Bxd5 Rd8 16 Qc1 Qxe5 17 Bxe6 Qxe6 18 Rxd8+ Kxd8 19 Rd1+ Kc8 20 Nd5* the course of the ending was determined. White won in 54 moves. (See also *Supplemental Game #5.*)

Supplemental Games

(1) Passive play and a delayed . . . e5 fail to equalize. Matulovic–Damjanovic, Ljubljana 1959: 1 c4 e6 2 Nf3 Nf6 3 Nc3 c5 4 e3 Be7 5 d4 cxd4 6 exd4 d5 7 c5 Nc6 (On 7 . . . b6 8 b4 a5 White can't play 9 a3 axb4 but has 9 Na4, threatening Nxb6.) 8 Bd3 0-0 9 0-0 b6 10 Bb5! Bd7 11 Bxc6 Bxc6 12 b4 Ne4 13 Bb2 a5 14 a3 Bf6 15 Qc2 (White's queenside is secure and his loss of the two bishops doesn't mean much since Black's queen bishop is bad.) bxc5 16 bxc5 Rb8 17 Rfb1+ h6 18 Bc1 Qc7 19 Be3! Nxc3 20 Qxc3 a4 21 Qd2! (White threatens to take control of the open file with Bf4.) Rxb1+ 22 Rxb1 Rb8 23 Rb4 Rxb4 24 Qxb4 e5 (Without this break White could win by maneuvering his knight to c3 to threaten Nb5-d6 or Nxa4.) 25 dxe5 Bxe5 26 Bd4! f6 27 Bxe5 fxe5 28 Qb6! Qxb6 29 cxb6 e4 30 Nd4 (good knight means good night) Bb7 31 Ne6 Ba6 32 Nc5 Bc8 33 Kf1 Kf8 34 Ke2 Ke7 35 b7 Bxb7 36 Nxb7 Resigns.

(2) Here . . . e5 is inferior to piece attack on d4. Keres–Marovic, Tallinn 1975: 1 e4 Nf6 2 e5 Nd5 3 d4 d6 4 Nf3 Bg4 5 Be2 e6 6 0-0 Be7 7 h3 Bh5 8 c4 Nb6 9 Nc3 0-0 10 Bf4 Nc6 11 exd6 Bxd6 12 Bxd6 cxd6 13 b3 d5! 14 c5 Nc8 15 Qd2 Bxf3 16 Bxf3 Qf6 17 Rfd1 N8e7 (Black has good piece play against the enemy d-pawn.) 18 Rac1 g6 19 Ne2 Nf5 20 Rc3 Nh4

21 a3 a5   22 Ng3 Rfd8 (22 . . . Nxf3+ 23 Rxf3 Qe7 is equal)
23 Be2! Kg7   24 Bb5 e5? (correct is 24 . . . Nf5) 25 dxe5
Nxe5 (on 25 . . . Qxe5   26 Rd3! Black has problems with his
d-pawn) 26 Qd4! Nc6   27 Qxf6+ Kxf6   28 Rcd3 Ne7
29 Ne4+ Kg7   30 Nc3 Rdc8   31 Re1 (31 Nxd5 Rxc5!)
Kf8   32 Nxd5   Rxc5   33 Nb6! Rxb5   34 Nxa8   Nc6
35 Nc7 Rc5   36 Nd5 Nf5   37 Red1 Rc2   38 Ne3 Nxe3
39 Rxe3 b5   40 Rd7 Ra2   41 Rc3 Resigns.

**(3) The e4/ . . . dxe4 break creates an ideal outpost for
Black.** Wl. Schmidt–Blatny, Haifa 1989: 1 Nf3 Nf6   2 c4
e6   3 Nc3 d5   4 d4 Nbd7   5 Bg5 Bb4   6 e3 c5   7 cxd5
exd5   8 Bd3 Qa5   9 Qc2 c4   10 Bf5 0-0   11 0-0 Re8
12 Nd2 Bxc3   13 bxc3 g6   14 Bh3 Ne4 (Black is willing
to occupy e4 with a P after the piece exchange because he gets
d5 in return) 15 Nxe4 dxe4   16 Bf4 Nb6   17 Bxc8 Raxc8
18 f3 Nd5! (Now 19 fxe4 Qxc3 gives Black a 3-1 queenside
majority) 19 Rac1 f5   20 Bh6 exf3   21 Rxf3 Re4   22 h3
Rce8   23 g4 Nxe3   24 Qd2 Qd5! (Based on 25 Rxe3 Rxe3
26 Bxe3 Qf3   27 Bf2 Re2 or 27 Re1 Qg3+   28 Kf1
Qxh3+   29 Kg1 Re4)   25 Bxe3 f4   26 Bf2? g5 and White
resigned in view of 27 . . . Re2.

(4) On . . . b6/cxb6 Black gets good piece play. Pirc–Larsen,
Amsterdam 1964: 1 Nf3 Nf6   2 g3 c5   3 c4 Nc6   4 Bg2
g6   5 b3 Bg7   6 Bb2 0-0   7 Nc3 d6   8 0-0 Bf5   9 d4
Qa5   10 e3 (Or 10 d5 Ne4) Rad8   11 Qd2 cxd4!
12 Nxd4 Nxd4   13 exd4 d5! (Now Black's mysterious 10th
move makes sense) 14 c5 b6   15 cxb6 axb6   16 Rfe1
(Note that White has problems mobilizing his queenside
pawns without giving Black good outposts at c4 and e4.) Rd7
17 Re2 Rc8   18 Na4 Qxd2   19 Rxd2 Rc6 (Black is at least

equal in the ending.) 20 f3 Bh6   21 Re2 Rdc7   22 Bf1 Bd3
23 Re5 Bxf1   24 Rxf1 e6   25 Re2 Nd7! (threat: . . . b5)
26 b4 Bg7   27 Rd2 Rc4!   28 a3 Ra7! and the pawns fall.
White resigned.

(5) Piece play with . . . Ne4 outruns White's queenside.
Keres–Konstantinopolsky, Moscow 1948: 1 e4 c6   2 d4 d5
3 exd5 cxd5   4 c4 Nf6   5 Nc3 e6   6 Nf3 Be7   7 a3 0-0
8 c5 Ne4! (Better than 8 . . . Nc6 which permits White to develop his B nicely at b5.) 9 Qc2 f5   10 Be2 Nc6   11 Bb5
(and here 11 b4 could have been met by 11 . . . Bf6   12 Be3
f4!) 11 . . . Bf6   12 Bxc6 bxc6   13 0-0 g5!   14 Ne5 Bxe5
15 dxe5 Nxc3 (15 . . . Nxc5   16 Ne2!) 16 Qxc3 f4! (Black
has a strong attack) 17 Bd2 Ba6   18 Rfe1 Rb8   19 Qd4
Bc4   20 Bc3 Qe8   21 Qd1 Rb7   22 a4 Qg6   23 Ra3 g4
24 Bd4 Rg7   25 f3 h5   26 Rc3 Rf5   27 Kh1 Rg5   28 b3
Ba6   29 Rg1 gxf3   30 Qxf3 Qe4   31 Qf2 Bd3   32 b4
Qf5   33 b5   Be4   34 bxc6   Rxg2   35 Rxg2   Rxg2
36 Qxg2 Bxg2+   37 Kxg2 Qe4+ and Black won.

STONEWALLS AND OTHER PRISONS

The Kingside Stonewall

STONEWALL FORMATIONS ARE OFTEN POPULAR WITH PLAYERS who prefer a relatively simple game with a closed center and little opening theory to master. The Kingside Stonewall above arises most often out of the Dutch Defense or Colle System. The Queenside Stonewall (pawns at c4, d3, and e4 for White versus c5, d6 and e5) usually comes from an English Opening or a Sicilian Defense.

The middlegame plans are fairly simple. Two important aspects stand out. Since the center pawns of each player are committed to squares of one color, each side has a bad bishop he wants to eliminate. In the Kingside Stonewall White tries to get rid of his pawn-bound queen bishop even if it means playing Bd2-e1-h4. Elimination of the bishop by trading it for the enemy's black-squared king bishop is the ideal method because then Black will be weak on the very squares on which White's center is strong.

The second feature of the formation is the natural outpost at the vantage point of the Stonewall (e5 in the Kingside version, d5 in the Queenside). Knights, not bishops, work best and work most in closed centers. The possibility of exchanges on the outpost squares also has a great impact on the course of the middlegame.

Consider this position:

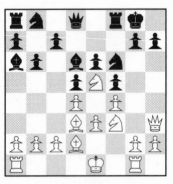

Position after 12 Rg1

It arose in Sultan Khan–Mattison, Prague 1931, after *1 d4 Nf6   2 Nf3 e6   3 e3 b6   4 Bd3 Bb7   5 Nbd2 d5   6 Ne5*

Bd6 7 f4 0-0 8 Qf3 Nfd7 9 Qh3 f5 10 Ndf3 Nf6 11 Bd2 Ba6 12 Rg1.

As soon as White established his part of the Stonewall at move seven Black began to create his own. Normally one would applaud Black's plan of exchanging off his bad queen bishop, but *12 . . . Bxd3* is a major felony of stonewall positions, giving White pawn control of his "lost" e square after *13 cxd3*.

Black has given up the privilege of occupying e4 and his position is lacking in counterplay. His collapse within a handful of moves wasn't surprising: *13 . . . Qe8 14 Ke2! Nbd7 15 Qh4 c5 16 Bc3 cxd4? 17 Bxd4 Nc5 18 g4 Bxe5 19 Nxe5 fxg4 20 Nxg4 Nxg4 21 Rxg4 g6 22 Rag1* Resigns. White's queen bishop is no longer "bad" and his threat of *23 Rxg6+* is unstoppable. Black's slow development was partly at fault, but his strategic blunder at move 12 certified defeat.

The queenside version of this is demonstrated by Albin–Janowski, Nuremberg 1896, which began *1 e4 e5 2 Nf3 Nc6 3 Bb5 Nf6 4 d3 d6 5 Bxc6+ bxc6 6 h3 Be7 7 Qe2 0-0 8 c4 Nd7 9 g4*

Position after 9 g4

The opening was an idea of Adolf Anderssen's. White locks the center and stops . . . f5 in preparation for his own kingside attack. But Black established a solid middlegame advantage in this game with 9 . . . Re8 10 Nc3 Nc5! 11 Be3 Ne6 12 Qd2 c5! 13 Ne2 c6 14 Ng3 Rb8 15 Nf5 Bf8.

Now Black has pawn control of d5 and can occupy d4 when he wants to. There was logic to Anderssen's plan. White deprived his opponent of a knight to sink into d4 when he played Bxc6+, but the concession of permitting . . . c5 and . . . c6 was too great. After 16 h4 Nd4 17 Bxd4 cxd4 18 h5 d5! the wall of stone was broken open and Black had a clear edge with 19 Kf1 dxc4 20 dxc4 f6 21 N3h4 Be6 22 b3 a5 and . . . a4.

When should you establish a Stonewall? Certainly not when you have good bishops, as the game Soloviev–Novotelnov, Moscow 1961, shows:

1 e4 e6 2 d4 d5 3 Nc3 Bb4 4 exd5 exd5 5 Bd3
Ne7 6 Qh5 Nd7 7 Bg5 Nf8! 8 Ne2 Be6 9 0-0
Qd7 10 h3 0-0-0 11 Nf4? f6 12 Nxe6 Nxe6
13 Be3 Nc6 14 a3? Bxc3 15 bxc3 g6 16 Qh4 f5

Position after 16 . . . f5

This is a partial Stonewall since the e-pawns are gone.

White's *17 f4??* is a positional horror that dooms his bishops to permanent suffocation. That it buries his queen bishop is clear, but it also hurts his king bishop by permitting Black to sink a knight permanently into e4. White should play 17 f3 followed by Qf2 and, with luck, c3-c4.

White's game deteriorated with astonishing speed: *17 . . . Rde8 18 Qf2 Na5 19 a4 Nd8! 20 Qf3 Nf7 21 Bf2 c6 22 Bh4 Re6 23 g4 Nd6 24 Kh1 Nac4 25 Rfe1 Nd2! 26 Qg2 N2e4 27 a5 fxg4 28 hxg4 h5 29 g5 Rhe8 30 a6 b5 31 Kh2 Nf5 32 Bf2 Qd6* and White resigned. He loses the first of many pawns after 33 Qf3 Nxg5.

The next diagram comes from Feuerstein–Polugaevsky, Reykjavik 1957:

1 Nf3 d5   2 b3 c5   3 e3 Nc6   4 Bb2 Nf6   5 Bb5 Bd7   6 0-0 e6   7 d4? cxd4   8 exd4 Bd6   9 a3 0-0 10 Bd3

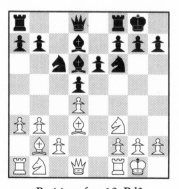

Position after 10 Bd3

White should have treated the opening like a Nimzo-Indian Defense (which it is with colors reversed) by playing 7 Bxc6+ followed by Ne5, d2-d3, and either f2-f4 or c2-c4. But 7 d4? transposes into a colors reversed version of the Orthodox Exchange formation (Chapter 7).

Black needs an active plan to combat White's toothless but solid position. He found one in *10 . . . Ne4 11 c4 f5!*, creating a partial Stonewall to support a knight on e4 and to swing a number of pieces to the vicinity of the White king.

The game proceeded: *12 b4 a5 13 b5 Ne7 14 c5 Bc7 15 Nbd2 Be8! 16 Rc1 Bh5 17 Qe1 Ng6*. To avoid . . . Nf4 White played *18 g3 Bg4 19 Kg2?* and invited *19 . . . Nf4+! 20 gxf4 Bxf4 21 Bc3 Qf6 22 Rh1 Qg6 23 Kf1 Qh6 24 Bxe4 Qh3+ 25 Kg1 fxe4 26 Qf1 exf3 27 Qxh3 Bxh3 28 Rd1 Bxd2* and White resigned.

The Kingside Stonewall

The pawn breaks in this closed structure come from c2-c4 or . . . c5 and g2-g4 or . . . g5. In a typical Dutch Defense the Stonewall is not complete because White has not played f2-f4. He can obtain good queenside play with either cxd5 or c4-c5 followed by b4-b5. The next two diagrams indicate the options.

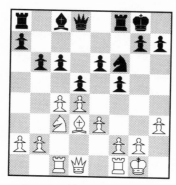

Position after 13 . . . Nxf6

This is from Ivkov–Segi, Novi Sad 1955: *1 d4 d5   2 c4 e6
3 Nc3 f5   4 Nf3 c6   5 Bf4 Nf6   6 e3 Be7   7 Bd3 0-0
8 0-0   Ne4   9 h3   Nd7   10 Ne5   Nxe5   11 Bxe5   b6
12 Rc1 Bf6   13 Bxf6 Nxf6.*

White played *14 cxd5!* and presented his opponent with a
typical dilemma. If Black recaptures with the c-pawn White
will be the first one to occupy the open file with rooks, but if
Black takes back with the e-pawn White has an excellent minority attack. This is what happened: *14 . . . exd5   15 b4!
Qd6   16 b5 cxb5? (16 . . . c5) 17 Nxb5 Qd8   18 Qc2 a6
19 Nc7 Ra7   20 Qc6 Rf7   21 Ne6 Bxe6   22 Qxe6 Rae7
23 Qxf5 Ne4   24 Rc8! Rxf5   25 Rxd8+ Rf8   26 Rxd5* and
Black resigned.

The second example also shows b4-b5 but without an exchange on d5. It comes from Pillsbury–Showalter, Nuremberg 1896: *1 d4 d5   2 c4 e6   3 Nc3 c6   4 Nf3 f5   5 Bf4 Bd6 6 e3 Nf6   7 Bd3 0-0   8 0-0 Qc7   9 g3! Ne4   10 Rc1 Bxf4   11 exf4 Qb6   12 Qe2 Nd7   13 Rfd1 Ndf6   14 Ne5 Kh8.*

Position after 14 . . . Kh8

White's opening play has been excellent since he has eliminated his bad bishop, created an e5 outpost, and retained f2-f3 to kick a Black knight out of e4. He still needs a plan, however. Pillsbury, one of the greatest planners, found one in *15 c5!*, intending to open up the b-file.

He got what he wanted after *15 . . . Qc7   16 f3 Nxc3 17 Rxc3 Bd7   18 Nxd7! Nxd7 19 b4! Rf6   20 b5.* Black's kingside attack is invisible, and White had a dominating position after *20 . . . Rg6   21 Kf2 h5   22 h4! Rf8   23 Rb3 Rf7   24 Rdb1 Qd8   25 bxc6 bxc6   26 Rb7 Qa5   27 R1b3 Rgf6   28 Qb2.*

White then rearranged his rooks with 28 ... *Kh7* *29 Be2 Nf8 30 Rb8 Ng6 31 Rc8! Rc7 32 Ra8* and *33 Ra3*. Black eventually made an unsound sacrifice on the kingside to avoid the loss that would inevitably come on the queenside.

The counterbalance to this is *Supplemental Game #1*, which shows c4-c5 working too slowly. The plusses and minuses of exchanging off the "bad" bishop can be seen in *Supplemental Games #2* and *#3*.

The other major problem of the Kingside Stonewall is how to recapture when your outpost knight is taken. The natural method is with the f-pawn—toward the center. But there are advantages to the dxe5 recapture as well—to preserve the possibility of f4-f5 or to pressure the enemy d-pawn with c2-c4 and Rad1.

A superb example of this is Rubinstein–Cohn, Karlsbad 1911, which began *1 d4 d5 2 Nf3 e6 3 c4 c6 4 e3 Nd7 5 Nc3 f5 6 Ne5 Ngf6 7 f4 Bd6 8 Be2 0-0 9 0-0 Ne4 10 Nxe4 fxe4 11 Bd2 Nxe5 12 dxe5!*.

Position after 12 dxe5!

Why should White, with a naturally freer game, exchange off rooks quickly with 12 fxe5? White keeps material on the board and now makes good use of his bad queen bishop. Black should keep his own black-squared bishop on a versatile square such as e7. But after *12 . . . Bc5? 13 b4 Bb6 14 Qc2 Bd7 15 a4 Rc8 16 a5 Bc7 17 Bc3 Qh4 18 Bd4 a6 19 Qb3 Bd8 20 Bc5* White has actually made his bad bishop work more than Black's good bishop.

In the remaining moves Black could do little about White's easy buildup on the kingside: *20 . . . Rf7 21 Rf2 Be7 22 g3 Qh6 23 Bd6! g6 24 c5 Qf8 25 Raf1 Qg7 26 Bg4 Rcf8 27 Qd1 Qh6 28 Kh1 Kh8 29 Rg1 Rg8 30 Qf1 Rgf8 31 h4! Bxd6 32 cxd6 g5* (desperation) *33 fxg5 Rxf2 34 Qxf2 Qxh4+ 35 gxh4 Rxf2 36 Rd1 Kg7 37 Kg1* Resigns.

The Queenside Stonewall

Why should the queenside version of the Stonewall be any different in theme from the kingside version? The board has been shifted one file to the left, it seems. But with the center blocked the size of the wings counts. Now there are two queenside files and three kingside files—a key reversal from the Kingside Stonewall.

This means that there is more room for a break on White's right. He or Black can achieve a forceful f2-f4 or . . . f5 with greater effect than the g2-g4 or . . . g5 break in the kingside formation. Similarly, there is less room to exploit once the queenside is opened. After b4/ . . . b6 White has less going for him whether he plays bxc5 or b4-b5 followed by a4-a5xb6.

A good comparison of this changing wing strategy is Torre–Radulov, Leningrad 1973:

1 e4 c5   2 Nf3 d6   3 Bb5+ Bd7   4 Bxd7+ Qxd7
5 c4 e5   6 Nc3 g6   7 d3 Bg7   8 a3 Nc6   9 Rb1 Nge7
10 b4 0-0   11 bxc5? dxc5   12 0-0 h6!   13 Nd5 f5
14 Qb3 b6   15 Bd2

Position after 15 Bd2

White's opening system has been popular in recent years
because it avoids the complex Sicilian positions and insures a
small positional advantage if White can play d2-d4 (a Maroczy
Bind transposition).

In the first stage, moves 8–11, White played sloppily. He
should have tried 8 0-0 Nc6   9 Nd5 Nge7?   10 Bg5! to
trade off his bishop for a more powerful knight. The exchange
at c5 was also premature and should have been delayed until
Nd5 had been played. He should have kept the b3 square vacant for a knight to support a4-a5.

Black correctly turned to the neglected kingside, the larger
wing: *15 . . . g5   16 Bc3 fxe4   17 dxe4 Rxf3!?   18 gxf3 Ng6*.
The sacrifice was promising, but Black could have obtained an

equally good attack without risk by playing 17 . . . Ng6. This interesting game was well defended by White for several moves: *19 Ba1! Nh4 20 Kh1 Qh3 21 Rg1 Nxf3 22 Rg2 Rf8 23 Qa4 Ncd4*; but after White failed to take off the knight on d4 Black won with ease: *24 Qxa7? Ne2! 25 Qxb6 Nh4 26 Rbg1 Qf3! 27 Qe6+ Kh7 28 Qg4 Nxg1 29 Kxg1 Rb8! 30 Nc3 Qxc3!* White resigns.

When both players have played Nd5/Nd4 the fluctuations in the center can create surprising dynamism. A remarkable example of this is Bobotsov–Gligoric, Belgrade 1961:

**1 c4 g6   2 Nc3 Bg7   3 g3 c5   4 Bg2 Nc6   5 e4 d6
6 Nge2 f5   7 d3 Nf6   8 0-0 0-0   9 Rb1 e5   10 Nd5
fxe4   11 dxe4 Nxd5   12 cxd5? Nd4   13 Nxd4 exd4!**

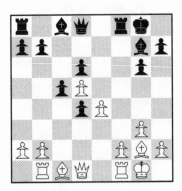

Position after 13 . . . exd4!

The knight captures have created two-pawn majorities on the opposing wings. Which counts more? The answer is Black's, since he can easily advance his queenside while

White's mating attack with kingside pawns can be blocked. After 13 . . . cxd4 the game would probably dry up into a draw.

The game continued *14 Bf4 b5 15 Qd2 a5 16 Bh6.* White's idea of exchanging bishops is somewhat feeble, but what could he do after 14 f4?

Black took the initiative with *16 . . . Bxh6 17 Qxh6 c4 18 Rbe1 b4 19 e5 c3! 20 bxc3 bxc3 21 e6 Qe7.* Black's pawns cannot be blackaded for long: *22 Re4 d3 23 Rc4 c2 24 Qd2 Ba6 25 Rc6 Bb5! 26 Rb6 Rab8 27 Rxb8 Rxb8 28 Be4 Qf6! 29 Re1 (29 Bxd3 Qd4) Qd4 30 e7 Qb4!* White resigns.

Supplemental Games

(1) A slow moving b2-b4-b5 break in the kingside Stonewall can be crushed on the opposite wing. Andric–Ivkov, Sarajevo 1952: 1 d4 e6 2 c4 f5 3 Nf3 Nf6 4 g3 d5 5 Bg2 c6 6 0-0 Bd6 7 b3 Qe7 (immediately stopping White's positional threat to exchange off his bad bishop with 8 Ba3) 8 Bb2 0-0 9 Nbd2! Bd7 10 Ne5 Be8 11 Ndf3 Bh5 12 Nd3 Nbd7 13 Nfe5 Rad8 14 Qc2 Kh8 15 e3 g5 16 c5 Bc7 17 b4 Ng4! 18 Nxd7 Qxd7 (Although White has used his knights well, Black has obtained a promising game by exchanges and by maneuvering his queen bishop.) 19 Bc1 Nf6 20 a4 a6 21 Ne5? (White needs 21 Rb1 to continue his queenside attack before Black breaks on the opposite wing with . . . e5 or . . . f4.) 21 . . . Qg7 22 Ra3 Nd7! 23 Nxd7 Rxd7 24 f4 (This stops . . . e5 and . . . f4 but loses neatly to a third line-opening idea.) 24 . . . gxf4 25 gxf4 Rg8 26 Kh1 Qg4 27 Ra2 Rdg7 28 Qd3? Qxg2+! 29 Rxg2 Rxg2 30 e4 Be2 White resigns.

(2) How the exchange of bad bishops can be good, . . .
Tarasov–Matsukevich, U.S.S.R. 1956: 1 d4 f5   2 c4 e6
3 g3 Nf6   4 Bg2 Be7   5 Nf3 0-0   6 0-0 d5   7 b3 c6
8 Ba3! Nbd7   9 Qc1 Ne4   10 Bxe7 Qxe7   11 Na3 b6
12 Nc2 Bb7   13 Qa3 Qf7? (Black's structure is geared for attack, but the endgame is preferable to the passive middlegame
he is now led into.) 14 cxd5 cxd5   15 Nce1! a5?   16 Nd3
Rfc8   17 Nfe5 Nxe5   18 Nxe5 Qe8   19 Rfc1 (With the
open file evenly contested White is still superior because of his
minor pieces.) Qd8   20 e3 Nc3?!   21 Bf1 Rc7   22 b4 axb4
23 Qb3 Ba6   24 Qxb4 Nxa2? (on 24 . . . Qc8 White plays
Rc2 and Rac1) 25 Qxb6 Nxc1   26 Rxc1 Bc4 (26 . . . Rxc1
27 Qxe6+) 27 Qxe6+ Kf8   28 Qxf5+ Kg8   29 Qe6+ Kf8
30 Nxc4 Re7   31 Qf5+ Rf7   32 Qxh7 Resigns.

(3) . . . and how it can be bad. Bozic–Nikolac, Sombor 1951:
1 d4 d5   2 Nf3 e6   3 c4 c6   4 e3 f5   5 Bd3 Nf6   6 0-0
Bd6   7 b3 0-0   8 Ba3 Ne4   9 Bxd6 Qxd6   10 Ne5?
(This is premature because the knight cannot be supported for
long on e5. White could have maintained the outpost if his
bishop were still on the board.) 10 . . . Nd7   11 Nxd7 Bxd7
12 f3? Nf6   13 Qc2 (Only 13 f4 would have saved the game.
White has kept e4 clean but pays the price of too many weakening pawn moves.) 13 . . . f4!   14 c5 Qc7   15 exf4 Qxf4
16 Qf2 e5!   17 dxe5 Qxe5   18 Nd2 Ng4!   19 fxg4 Rxf2
White resigns.

**(4) An example of a typical mistake—trading off the good
bishop on the premise of making an attack**. Kevitz–
Santasiere, New York 1957: 1 Nf3 Nf6   2 c4 b6   3 d3 g6
4 e4 d6   5 Nc3 Bg7   6 g3 (6 d4 looks more promising)

0-0   7 Bg2   Bb7   8 0-0   c5   9 h3   Nc6   10 Be3   e5!?
11 Qd2 Nd4   12 Bh6?? Nh5! (Black has the first chance to
take kingside action with . . . f5. On 13 Nxd4 cxd4! Black uses
his kingside pawns for attack.) 13 g4? (Not only is this a hor-
rible positional move—making his surviving bishop a lifetime
prisoner—but it loses a pawn to a clever combination.) Bxh6!
14 Qxh6   Nxf3+!   15 Bxf3   Nf4   16 Rad1   Qg5!
17 Qxg5 Nxh3+   18 Kg2 Nxg5   19 Be2 Ne6 and Black
won the endgame.

(5) Another queenside-vs.-kingside majority battle. Freiman–
Belavyenets, Kiev, 1938: 1 e4 c5   2 Nf3 d6   3 c4 e5!
(Black is at least equal since he can advance his f-pawn
quickly. White can't.) 4 Nc3 Nc6   5 h3 g6   6 d3 Bg7
7 Nd5 f6   8 Be3 Nh6   9 Qd2 Nf7   10 Be2 Be6 (or 10 . . .
f5 with a good game) 11 h4 h5   12 Bd1!? (White brings his
bad bishops to the queenside where it can enter the action at
a4. His play is extremely ambitious considering his 11th
move.) 12 . . . a6   13 Ba4 Rb8   14 b4 b5!   15 Bb3 Bxd5
(White has a very good position after 15 . . . bxc4   16 Bxc4
Nxb4   17 Nxb4 Bxc4   18 Nc6 or 16 . . . cxb4   17 Bb6)
16 exd5 (on 16 cxd5 White has no counterplay against . . . f5)
Nd4   17 Bxd4 cxd4 (Black could have recaptured with the
e-pawn in order to seize the e-file and the h6-c1 diagonal)
18 a4 Bh6   19 Qe2 0-0   20 0-0 f5!   21 axb5 (White has
long-term trumps after 21 cxb5 axb5   22 a5 but no middlegame plan) axb5   22 c5 Re8   23 g3 Qf6!   24 Rfd1?
(This only appears to stop the Black pawns from advancing.
Mandatory was 24 Bc2.) e4!   25 dxe4 d3!   26 Qa2 (or
26 Qxd3 fxe4) fxe4 White resigns. White's queenside progress
is hardly comforting when being mated after . . . e3.

THE CLOSED
SICILIAN-ENGLISH

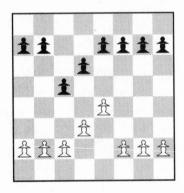

WHEN NO PAWNS ARE EXCHANGED IN THE EARLY STAGES OF AN English Opening or Sicilian Defense we have one of the most sophisticated structures. Each side concentrates on a wing attack as in a chain or stonewall. But the center can be opened—a fact that must be taken into account before a player dislocates his pieces in expectation of a wing breakthrough.

This is one of the hardest formations to evaluate. Black has good pressure on black squares, especially d4. White has prospects of a mating attack or of a thrust in the center with c2-c3 and d3-d4. It is true that after 1 e4 c5 most opening books frown on 2 Nc3, which leads to the Closed Sicilian formation. But the same books suggest that after 1 c4 e5 2 Nc3 Black's best chance for fighting play may lie in 2 . . . Nc6.

In its pure form (e2-e4 versus . . . c7-c5 as in the above diagram), the wing attacks can proceed with surprising speed, as in Blatny–Taimanov, Decin 1975:

1 e4 c5   2 Nc3 Nc6   3 g3 g6   4 Bg2 Bg7   5 d3 d6
6 f4 Rb8   7 a4? Nf6   8 Nf3 0-0   9 0-0 a6   10 Nh4
Bg4   11 Qd2 Bd7   12 Ne2 b5!   13 axb5 axb5   14 h3
Qb6

Position after 14 . . . Qb6

White has allowed his queen and minor pieces to be confused and has permitted Black to open a file on the side of the board White would like to forget about. White began his own pawn storm, *15 f5 b4!   16 g4*, and learned there was another tempest brewing on the board: *16 . . . c4+   17 Kh1 b3!*.

Black has two heavy pieces and his king bishop bearing down on b2. White could have kept the position partially closed with 17 d4 Ne8 18 c3 Na5 and 19 . . . Nb3, but Black would still be able to penetrate. White must avoid 18 dxc4 Ne5! 19 cxb3 Qxb3 because then his c-pawn, b-pawn, and e-pawn are all weak.

White tried one last idea, *18 g5 Ne8 19 Nf4* to occupy d5 with a knight, but the queenside storm broke with *19 . . . c3!! 20 bxc3 b2* and White lost a piece. (The best he could have done was 19 c3 cxd3 20 Qxd3 Ne5 21 Qd1 with only a poor, not lost, game.)

The wing attack on the kingside is no less violent. During the last century the closed variations of the Sicilian were preferred by White for many years because Black's defenses against mate were ill understood. Case in point is Tchigorin–Clemenz, St. Petersburg 1880:

**1 e4 c5   2 Nc3 Nc6   3 g3 Nf6   4 Bg2 e6   5 d3 Be7
6 f4 d6?   7 Nge2 0-0   8 0-0 Qc7   9 b3 a6   10 a4
e5?**

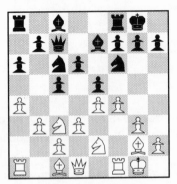

Position after 10 . . . e5?

Black has made a mess of the opening. He could have fi-anchettoed his king bishop and remained uncommitted in the center (no move of his e-pawn); or he could have played 5 ... d5 or 6 ... d5, not fearing e4-e5 because then Black would have good chances with ... d4 and bringing a knight to d5.

Black's last move may restrain the scope of White's king bishop, but it gives the enemy a virtually unimpeded kingside storm: *11 f5 Bd7   12 Kh1 Nd4   13 Bg5 Nxe2?   14 Qxe2 Bc6   15 g4! b5   16 Bd2.*

Position after 16 Bd2

Black's queenside storm has been contained while White's kingside pawns are rolling. Black has no chance for . . . d5 (e.g., 16 . . . b5   17 Nd1 d5   18 g5). Black's *pawn* play has denied him *counter*play: *16 . . . b5   17 Nd1 Nd7   18 g5 f6?* (18 . . . Rfd8 was better) *19 g6! h6   20 Qh5 Nb6   21 Ne3 Ra7   22 Ng4 Bd8   23 Rf3 Be8   24 Rg3.* Black resigned—a re-markable act in a blocked position—because a sacrifice on h6 will win (24 . . . Nc8   25 Bxh6).

In the previous examples we see that White's f4-f5 and Black's . . . b5 in the Closed Sicilian (colors reversed in the

Closed English) are basic themes. The counterideas take on great importance because of the strength of these themes.

White's Counterideas in the English

The simplest way to take the sting out of White's f4-f5 is to play . . . f5 before the enemy f-pawn gets to the fifth rank. A fine illustration of the tension created is Keene–Perkins, Bognor Regis 1967, with colors reversed:

1 Nf3 g6   2 c4 Bg7   3 g3 Nf6   4 Bg2 0-0   5 Nc3 d6   6 0-0 e5   7 d3 Nbd7   8 Rb1 Nh5   9 b4 h6 10 Nd2 f5   11 Bb2 Nhf6   12 Qc2 Re8   13 e3! Nf8 14 Rbe1 Kh7   15 Nd5

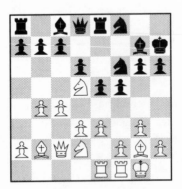

Position after 15 Nd5

White's play seems mysterious but there is a method in it. After b2-b4 was achieved he turned his attention to the center with Nd2, Bb2, e2-e3, and Rbe1. If Black plays . . . f4 White can open the center and occupy e4 with a knight. The move Nd5 is a common idea of White's in the Closed English. If Black captures the knight White will pressure c7 by recapturing with his c-pawn.

Black played 15 . . . Ne6, and White set the enemy e-pawn up as a target with 16 f4!. After 16 . . . exf4 17 exf4 Nxd5 Black equalizes by using d4. But 16 . . . exf4 17 gxf4! leaves White safe on the kingside and with terrific pawn control in the center. He could then follow up with Bc3 and Qb2 .

Black played 16 . . . c6, just the move White was waiting for. On 17 Nxf6+ Bxf6 18 c5! the Black center is ruined and White will occupy excellent squares after 18 . . . exf4 19 Bxf6 Qxf6 20 gxf4 d5 21 Nf3 followed by Ne5 and b4-b5. Notice that b4-b5 has much greater effect after . . . c6 than it would have, for example, at move 10.

Black disintegrated on cue: 18 . . . dxc5 19 fxe5 Be7 20 bxc5 Nxc5 21 d4 Na6 22 Qb3 Bf8 23 e4! (conquest of the center) Bg7 24 exf5 gxf5 (24 . . . Bxf5 25 Ne4) 25 Bc3 Qe7 26 Qb1! Be6 (26 . . . Kh8 eventually loses the f-pawn to Nf3-h4 and Bh3) 27 g4 Qa3 28 Nb3 Resigns.

See also *Supplemental Game #1*, in which White plays f2-f4 in coordination with d2-d4, and *Supplemental Game #2*, in which he does the latter without the former.

Another reaction to f2-f4 or . . . f7-f5 is to exchange your e-pawn off for the enemy f-pawn. This poses a problem. If the opponent recaptures on f4/f5 with a piece, he gives you an outpost. If he recaptures with his g-pawn, you can fix his pawns with your f-pawn or attack in the center with your d-pawn.

Position after 8 . . . exf4!

This position occurred in Bilek–Evans, Lugano 1968, after
*1 e4 c5   2 Nc3 Nc6   3 g3 g6   4 Bg2 Bg7   5 d3 d6   6 f4
e5!   7 Nh3 Nge7   8 0-0 exf4!*.

The timing has to be exact here since the routine move, 8
. . . 0-0, is punished by 9 f5! gxf5 (otherwise 10 g4 maintains
the storm) 10 exf5 Bxf5 (10 . . . Nxf5   11 Qh5   and
12 Be4) 11 Rxf5! Nxf5   12 Be4 Nfd4   13 Qh5 with a
strong attack.

After 8 . . . exf4! White has three recaptures to consider.
The most solid plan is Bxf4 and Qd2. The most committal is
9 gxf4 although after 9 . . . f5! Black has a promising game.
Bilek played 9 *Nxf4 0-0   10 Nfd5*, a logical but not particularly forceful plan. Black need not play . . . f5 now and can protect his kingside easily: *10 . . . Nxd5   11 Nxd5 Be6   12 Nf4
Bd7   13 c3 b5!   14 a3 a5   15 Be3 Ne5* (to meet 16 d4
with 16 . . . Nc4) *16 h3 a4   17 Qd2 Bc6   18 Rf2 Rb8
19 Raf1 Qd7*.

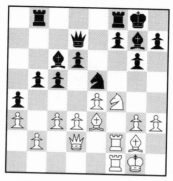

Position after 19 . . . Qd7

In this position White has a lot of armor arrayed on the king's wing but nothing to aim at. At d5 White's outpost knight was all-seeing but lacked destructive power. With . . . b4 by Black and a few slips by White the game ended: *20 Qd1 Qb7 21 Bc1? b4 22 axb4? cxb4 23 c4 b3! 24 Kh2 Qa6 25 Re1 Rb7 26 Be3 a3! 27 Qe2 Nxc4! 28 dxc4 Bxb2 29 Qd3 Be5 30 Bd4 b2 31 Ne6* (else . . . a2 wins) *a2! 32 Bxe5 b1(Q) 33 Qxd6 Re8! 34 Nc7 Rxc7 35 Bc3 Qxe1 36 Bxe1 a1(Q) 37 Qxc7 Qb7* and White resigned.

Black's Counterideas in the English

What Black can do goes beyond attacking the kingside and waiting for a mistake. He has a few queenside chances and can make waves in the center.

Since White's prime advantage in the Closed English is his white-square pressure, a Black counterattack on those squares, especially a fight for d5, can be dangerous to the first player. One game that reminds us of this Filep–Osnos, Debrecen 1969:

> 1 c4 e5 2 Nc3 Nc6 3 g3 f5 4 Bg2 g6 5 d3 Bg7
> 6 Bd2 d6 7 Rb1 a5 8 a3 Nf6 9 b4 axb4 10 axb4
> 0-0 11 Qc1 Ne7! 12 Nh3

Position after 12 Nh3

White's last move leaves open the possibility of f2-f4. Black can complete his development but will that make him happy? Not without a constructive plan. He makes room for his pieces with *12 . . . c6! 13 0-0 d5.*

After this Black has a fine center and need not trouble himself about 14 cxd5 cxd5 15 Nb5 Nc6 or 15 . . . Bd7. White's king bishop bites on d5 granite and his queen knight lacks the excellent central outpost. He could play 14 Bh6 but there is little to attack to follow. On the queenside, 14 b5 d4 isn't productive. So he tried *14 c5*, perhaps intending Na4-b6 at some point, and obtained a bad game after *14 . . . d4! 15 Nd1 Nfd5*.

Black's seizure of what is normally White's favorite center square (d5) led White into speculative play: *16 e4? dxe3 17 fxe3 Nc7 18 Nb2 h6! 19 Nf2 Be6 20 Nc4 Nb5 21 Kh1 Kh7 22 Nb6 Ra2 23 Ra1 Rxa1 24 Qxa1 f4! 25 exf4 exf4 26 Qe1 fxg3 27 hxg3 Nf5! 28 Qxe6 Nbd4 29 Qe1 Nxg3+ 30 Kh2 Qh4+* White resigns.

A second way of battling for d5 is to answer Nd5 with . . . Nxd5 and . . . c6. This may give Black a pawn majority in the center or a weak pawn. Both situations occurred in Bilek–Smyslov, Polanica Zdroj 1968:

1 g3 e5   2 c4 d6   3 Bg2 Nc6   4 Nc3 g6   5 e3 Bg7
6 Nge2 Nge7   7 d3 0-0   8 Nd5

Position after 8 Nd5

Here 8 . . . Nxd5!? 9 cxd5 Ne7 presents White with a
d5 crisis. He should try to maintain control of the square with
10 Nc3 c6 11 0-0 cxd5 12 Nxd5 Be6 13 Qb3, al-
though 11 . . . Bd7 11 Qb3 Rb8 gives Black a reasonable
game.

White chose 10 0-0 c6 11 dxc6? and fell into a bad game
as he isolated Black's c-pawn: 11 . . . bxc6 12 d4? Ba6
13 Re1 Qb6! 14 dxe5 dxe5.

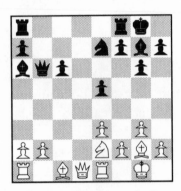

Position after 14 . . . dxe5

Black has a weak pawn on c6, but his play on the open files
against an underdeveloped opponent makes all the difference.
After 15 Qc2 Rfd8 16 Bd2 Bd3 17 Qc1 Nd5 18 Nc3
Nb4 19 Na4 Qb5 20 Bxb4 Qxb4 21 Nc3 e4! White
has only defensive chores left to perform. He failed to perform
them adequately: 22 Rd1 Rab8 23 Rd2 c5 24 Qe1 Bxc3!
25 bxc3 Qa5 (25 . . . Qxc3 26 Bxe4!) 26 Rc1 c4! 27 Qd1
Rd5 28 Qg4 Rdb5 29 Qf4 Qa3 30 Rdd1 Re8 31 Bh3

*Rb2   32 Bd7   Re7   33 Bg4   Qc5   34 Qf6   Qe5   35 Qa6
Kg7   36 a4 Rc7!   37 a5 Rb5   38 Ra1 Rbc5* and White resigned because of 39 . . . R5c6 trapping his queen.

The Nimzo-Botvinnik Formation

A close relative of what we've just examined is a structure in
which White has pawns at c4 and e4 while his opponent has
a pawn at *either* e5 or c5. Nimzovich was the first master to ex-
press enjoyment at having the two pawns in the center. It appeared to be another of his prejudices for what Tarrasch called
"ugly moves."

It is "ugly" to concede d4 to enemy pieces. But when
Botvinnik began to play the structure with e2-e4 and c2-c4 it
gained the stamp of approval. Against the Closed Sicilian
(1 e4 c5   2 Nc3 Nc6   3 g3 g6   4 Bg2 Bg7   5 d3 d6
6 Nge2) Botvinnik introduced 6 . . . e5! as a method of obtaining solid center play. His game with Smyslov in the 1954
world championship match continued 7 Nd5 Nge7   8 c3
(8 Nec3!) Nxd5!   9 exd5 Ne7   10 0-0 0-0   11 f4 Bd7
12 h3 Qc7   13 Be3 Rae8   14 Qd2 Nf5   15 Bf2 h5
16 Rae1 Qd8   17 Kh2 Bh6   18 h4 Qf6! and Black already
had a winning game.

The c2-c4 + e2-e4 vs. . . c7-c5 version of this formation is
equally challenging, as this opening shows:

1 c4 Nf6   2 Nc3 g6   3 g3 Bg7   4 Bg2 0-0   5 e4 d6
6 Nge2

Position after 6 Nge2

Black has played the basic moves of a King's Indian Defense and now must make a decision about the center. He can forget about . . . c6 and . . . d5: White simply outguns him on the d5 square. The choice is between . . . e5 and . . . c5. The former has great strength if Black can scare up a kingside attack quickly with . . . f5, but here his f-pawn is blocked and it will take time to play . . . Nh5 and . . . f5. After 6 . . . *e5* 7 0-0 *Nc6* 8 *d3* Black should continue with 8 . . . Ne8 in order to meet 9 f4 with 9 . . . f5.

A good example of what may happen when f4-f5 is permitted is D. Byrne–Myagmasuren, Varna 1962:

8 . . . a6   9 f4 Rb8   10 h3 b5   11 f5! b4   12 Nb1 Nd4   13 g4 Nd7   14 Nd2 c5   15 Nf3

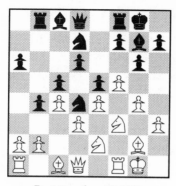

Position after 15 Nf3

Black's queenside has stalled and he makes the transition into a Queenside Stonewall. Remember that in the queenside version there are more files capable of being opened on the kingside. This means that a kingside storm is more likely to succeed than a queenside storm.

The rest of the game bore this simple evaluation out: *15 . . . Nxf3+ 16 Rxf3 Qh4 17 Be3 Bh6 18 Bf2!* (preserving the good bishop) *Qe7 19 h4 gxf5 20 Rxf5! Bg7 21 Ng3! Nf6 22 g5 Ne8 23 Be3! f6 24 Qe2 Bxf5 25 exf5 Nc7 26 Qh5 Rfd8 27 g6 Bf8 28 Ne4 Rd7 29 Rf1 Ne8 30 Ng5! fxg5 31 hxg5 Qg7 32 Bd5+ Kh8 33 Be4 Be7 34 Qh4! Nf6 35 gxf6 Bxf6 36 Qh5 Qe7 37 Rf3 Rf8 38 Rh3 a5 39 Bh6 Rfd8 40 Bd5 Rg8 41 Bxg8 Kxg8 42 gxh7+ Kh8 43 Rg3 Qf7 44 Rg8+ Resigns.* A brilliant strategic plan carried out by the late American master.

Going back to the position after 6 Nge2, it seems clear that 6 . . . c5! is a more optimistic and also more secure method of handling the center. On 7 d4 Black may avoid an inferior form of the Maroczy Bind (7 . . . cxd4) by playing 7 . . . Nc6! (threatening 8 . . . cxd4 8 Nxd4 Nxe4!).

After 7 d3 Nc6 8 0-0 Ne8! Black begins one of the most familiar maneuvers of the Nimzo-Botvinnik formation: by moving his king knight Black prepares to bring this piece to d4 and to meet f2-f4 with . . . f5. Black can always kick a White knight off d5 with . . . e6, but White cannot return the compliment. Also, f6 is not weak (no . . . e5) so he does not fear f4-f5 and g4-g5.

If White decides that f2-f4 goes nowhere he will turn to b2-b4: 9 a3 Nc7 10 Rb1 Ne6 11 b4 Ned4.

Position after 11 . . . Ned4

This is a typical position, and when it occurred in a 1957 game between two Soviet masters (Stolyar–Nezhmetdinov) White simplified the situation in the belief that his advantage in space would be clearer with fewer minor pieces. A more hopeful idea might be 12 Nf4 or 12 b5. After *12 Nxd4 Nxd4 13 Ne2 b6 14 Nxd4 Bxd4 15 Bb2 Bxb2 16 Rxb2 Bb7 17 f4 e6* we have the bare skeleton of the structure.

Black holds the balance here because 18 d4, the attempt to exploit an edge in overall terrain, may lead to a counterattack against White's c-pawn following 18 . . . Qc7. In the game cited, White tried a kingside attack with *18 f5 exf5 19 exf5 Bxg2 20 Rxg2* and discovered to his surprise that he was overextended.

Black is the first to penetrate by occupying a vital central square: *20 . . . Qf6! 21 Rgf2 Qd4!*. One more slip, *22 Kg2 Rae8 23 Rf4 Qe3 24 R1f2 Re5 25 Qf1?*, and Black forced the win: *25 . . . g5 26 R4f3 Qd4 27 h4 Rfe8 28 Qc1* (else . . . Re1) *Re3! 29 hxg5 Rxd3 30 Qh1 Rxf3 31 Rxf3 Qd2+ 32 Kh3 Qxg5 33 Qd1 Qh5+ 34 Kg2 Re3! 35 bxc5 Rxa3* White resigns.

The lesson here is twofold: it is usually better to meet c2-c4/d2-d3/e2-e4 with . . . c5 than with . . . e5; and the knight maneuver to occupy d4, either in the above example or in *Supplemental Game #3*, is a key to accurate defense.

Supplemental Games

(1) **A combination of the restraining f2-f4 and the liquidating d3-d4 in the Closed English.** Szabo–Damjanovic, Beverwijk 1966: 1 c4 e5 2 Nc3 Nc6 3 g3 g6 4 Bg2 Bg7 5 e3 d6 6 Nge2 Nge7 7 d3 0-0 8 0-0 h6 9 Rb1 g5 10 b4 Ng6 11 b5 Nce7 12 Qb3 Kh8 13 a4 Rb8 14 Nd5 f5 15 f4! (White has a slight advantage, which he increases steadily after this move. A double exchange of pawns on f4 will only weaken Black's f-pawn and kingside.) 15 . . . Be6 16 Nxe7 Qxe7 17 Qc2 Qd7 18 d4! (Now on

18 . . . e4 White can play d4-d5 and Nd4 or prepare for c4-c5.)
gxf4   19 exf4 exd4   20 Bb2 c6   21 bxc6 bxc6   22 Bxd4
(White's game is strategically won) c5   23 Bxg7+ Qxg7
24 Rfd1! Qe7   25 a5! Rxb1   26 Rxb1 Bc8   27 Kf2 Ba6
28 Qd3 Qf6   29 Bb7! Bxb7   30 Rxb7 Re8   31 Rxa7 Re6
32 a6 Ne7   33 Rc7 Kg7   34 a7 Resigns.

(2) A case of d3-d4 without the restraining f2-f4.
Goldin–Murei, Moscow 1966: 1 c4 e5   2 Nc3 Nc6   3 g3
g6   4 Bg2 Bg7   5 e3 Nge7   6 Nge2 0-0   7 0-0   d6
8 b3 Be6   9 Nd5 f5   10 Nxe7+ Qxe7   11 d4 f4! (This is
one of the most potent thrusts in Closed English. On 12 gxf4
Black plays 12 . . . exd4   13 Nxd4 Nxd4 or 13 Bxc6 d3! with
a better pawn structure for Black) 12 d5 Bg4 (Also good is
12 . . . f3   13 Bxf3 Rxf3   14 dxc6 bxc6!   15 Nd4 Bg4.
Black's use of the . . . f3 threat and the long dark diagonal is
often dangerous after . . . f4.) 13 f3 e4!   14 fxg4 f3
15 Rb1 (safer is 15 dxc6! Bxa1   16 cxb7) fxg2   16 Rxf8+
Rxf8   17 Kxg2 Ne5   18 Nf4 g5   19 Ne6 Rf3   20 Nxg7?
(20 Nd4 Qf7!   21 Nxf3 exf3+   22 Kg1 f2+   23 Kg2
Qg6! should also lose) 20 . . . Nxg4   21 Ne6 Qf6   22 Kg1
Rxg3+! White resigns.

**(3) A clever exploitation of the d5 hole in the Nimzo-
Botvinnik.** Schoneberg–Minic, Berlin 1968: 1 e4 c5
2 Nc3 d6   3 Nge2 e5!? (This stops d2-d4 once and for
all but pays the usual price.) 4 Nd5 Nc6   5 Nec3! a6   6 a4
g6   7 Bc4   Bg7   8 d3 Be6   9 0-0 Rb8?   10 f4! (The
use of d5 and the f2-f4 break work well here since Black
has not castled and cannot cope with weaknesses on both
e5 and f6.) 10 . . . exf4   11 Bxf4 Ne5   12 Qd2 h6   13 Kh1
Ne7?   14 Bxe5!   Bxe5   15 Nf6+   Bxf6   16 Bxe6   fxe6

17 Rxf6 Kd7 18 Raf1 (the rest is a rout) Qb6 19 Qf4
Rbe8 (or 19 . . . Qxb2 20 Qg4!) 20 Qg4 Nc6 21 Rxe6!
Rxe6 22 Rf7+ Kc8 (22 . . . Ne7 23 Rxe7+! Kxe7
24 Nd5+) 23 Qxe6+ Kb8 24 Qxd6+ Ka8 25 b3 Qb4
26 Qf6 Rb8 27 Nd5 Qd2 28 h3 Nd4? 29 Qb6 Resigns.

**(4) A case of c2-c4 plus e2-e4 vs . . . e5 in which both sides
advance their f-pawns.** Uhlmann–Kholmov, Moscow, 1960:
1 c4 e5 2 Nc3 d6 3 g3 Nc6 4 Bg2 g6 5 e4 Bg7
6 Nge2 Nge7 7 d3 0-0 8 0-0 Be6 9 a3? (If White
doesn't want to play f2-f4 he should prepare b2-b4 with the
more aggressive 9 Rb1. He may want to play a2-a4-a5 later
on, after b2-b4-b5.) 9 . . . Qd7 10 Nd5 f5 11 Bd2 (On
11 b4 Black plays 11 . . . f4!. Then White might try 12 gxf4!
exf4 13 Bxf4 Bxa1 14 Qxa1.) 11 . . . Rf7! 12 Rb1
Raf8 13 f3! (This is the proper defensive arrangement.
White doesn't fear 13 . . . fxe4 14 dxe4 Bh3 because Black
will have improved White's pawn structure and exchanged
off his bad bishop in the process.) 13 . . . h6 14 b4 g5
15 b5 Nd8 16 f4?? (This prevents . . . f4 but opens up the
kingside at a most inopportune time. Seven moves ago the
kingside forces of the two players were roughly equal. The
balance is gone. A more thematic method of play was
16 Nxe7+ followed by Nc3-d5 or 16 Nec3 immediately; e.g.
16 Nec3 f4 17 Nxe7+ Qxe7 18 g4 h5 19 h3.) 16
. . . gxf4 17 gxf4 Ng6! 18 fxe5 Nxe5 19 Ndf4 fxe4
20 Bxe4 c6 21 bxc6 bxc6 22 Kh1 Bh3! 23 Rf2 d5!
24 cxd5 cxd5 25 Bxd5 Qxd5+!! 26 Nxd5 Rxf2
27 Bf4 Nf3 and White resigned in view of mate. He would
also have been lost on 23 Rg1 Bg4! or 23 Bg2 Bxg2+ 24
Kxg2 Nxd3!.

"Enough, there are still problems to be solved; the whole truth in chess is not by any means known yet—fortunately."
—Emanuel Lasker

INDEX

ABOUT THE AUTHOR

ANDREW SOLTIS is an International Grandmaster, a former U.S. Open Champion, and the author of more than seventy books. He writes an award-winning column for *Chess Life* magazine.